CHAPTER 1: INTRODUCTION TO GRAPHQL FEDERATION

In the evolving landscape of data management and application architecture, GraphQL Federation has emerged as a pivotal approach for scaling GraphQL across distributed services. This chapter aims to provide a comprehensive introduction to GraphQL Federation, outlining its necessity, fundamental principles, and distinguishing features compared to traditional monolithic GraphQL schemas.

GraphQL Federation addresses a critical challenge faced by organizations adopting GraphQL: scaling GraphQL to handle complex, distributed data environments. In traditional GraphQL implementations, a single, monolithic schema is used to access and manage data from various sources. While this approach can be effective in simpler scenarios, it often encounters limitations as applications grow and the need for integration across multiple services becomes more pronounced. A monolithic schema can become unwieldy, difficult to manage, and less flexible, leading to potential performance bottlenecks and challenges in maintaining a cohesive data model.

Federation, on the other hand, offers a more modular and

scalable solution. It allows for the creation of a unified GraphQL schema that seamlessly integrates data from multiple services, each with its own schema. This approach enables teams to develop and manage individual services independently, while still providing a cohesive and integrated experience for the end-users. Federation achieves this by defining a set of common principles and mechanisms that allow different GraphQL services to work together effectively.

At its core, GraphQL Federation introduces the concept of a "gateway" that serves as the entry point for GraphQL queries. This gateway coordinates requests, delegates them to the appropriate services, and then aggregates the results into a single, unified response. The gateway does not handle business logic or data storage directly but rather orchestrates the interaction between various federated services. Each service in a federated architecture can define its own schema, including types and resolvers, and expose these through a GraphQL endpoint. The federation layer then combines these individual schemas into a single schema, allowing clients to interact with the aggregated data as if it were coming from a single source.

One of the key benefits of GraphQL Federation is its ability to promote modularity and separation of concerns. By enabling teams to build and deploy services independently, federation reduces the complexity associated with managing a large, monolithic schema. Each team can focus on their specific domain, develop their GraphQL schema, and evolve it independently of other services. This modular approach also facilitates better scalability, as teams can scale individual services based on their specific needs rather than scaling a monolithic schema.

Another advantage of federation is its support for incremental adoption. Organizations can gradually transition from a monolithic GraphQL schema to a federated architecture, enabling a smoother migration process. This gradual approach allows for the integration of existing services with new federated ones, without requiring a complete overhaul of the existing system.

In addition to these benefits, GraphQL Federation also introduces several challenges that need to be addressed. One of the primary challenges is ensuring consistency and compatibility between the different schemas and services. Since each service can define its own schema, it is essential to establish conventions and best practices for schema design and integration to avoid conflicts and ensure a coherent overall schema. The federation layer must also handle issues related to performance and optimization, as aggregating and resolving data from multiple services can introduce latency and complexity.

Despite these challenges, the adoption of GraphQL Federation has been growing rapidly as organizations seek to build more scalable and flexible GraphQL architectures. By enabling the integration of multiple services into a unified schema, federation provides a powerful solution for managing complex data environments and meeting the demands of modern applications.

In conclusion, GraphQL Federation represents a significant advancement in the evolution of GraphQL technology, offering a scalable and modular approach to managing distributed data. By understanding the core principles of federation, including the role of the gateway, the modular nature of services, and the challenges associated with schema integration, you will be well-equipped to leverage this approach in building scalable and flexible GraphQL architectures. This foundational understanding sets the stage for exploring the more detailed aspects of federation in subsequent chapters, including implementation strategies, best practices, and real-world use cases.

GraphQL Federation not only streamlines the integration of multiple services but also enhances the flexibility and scalability of GraphQL applications. To understand the benefits fully, it is essential to delve into the core principles that underpin GraphQL Federation.

The first principle is schema composition. In a federated GraphQL architecture, each service maintains its schema and provides a subset of the overall application's data. These individual schemas are then composed into a single, unified schema by the federation layer. This composition is achieved through a process called schema stitching, where types and fields defined in different services are merged into a single coherent schema. This unified schema allows clients to query across multiple services with a single request, providing a seamless experience as if all data were sourced from a single GraphQL endpoint.

Another fundamental principle is service delegation. In a federated setup, the GraphQL gateway, or the federation layer, delegates queries to the appropriate service based on the requested fields. Each service is responsible for resolving the data it manages, thus isolating the data management responsibilities and enabling each team to focus on their specific domain. The federation layer aggregates these responses, handling the orchestration and combining results into a single response that is returned to the client. This delegation ensures that each service remains focused on its core functionality while the gateway manages the complexity of querying across services.

The principle of extensibility is also crucial in a federated architecture. Federation allows for the incremental evolution of schemas and services without requiring a complete overhaul of the existing system. New services can be added, and existing services can be updated or deprecated without disrupting the overall architecture. This flexibility is particularly valuable in dynamic environments where business requirements and technologies frequently change.

Moreover, decentralized development is a significant advantage of GraphQL Federation. Teams can independently develop, deploy, and manage their services, allowing for more agile and efficient development processes. Each team can focus on their specific domain, use their preferred technologies, and iterate on their schemas without being constrained by a monolithic schema. This decentralization promotes better scalability and reduces the risk of introducing errors or bottlenecks that can arise from a single, centralized schema management.

The concept of cross-service querying is another essential aspect of federation. Traditional monolithic schemas often face challenges when dealing with complex queries that span multiple data sources. Federation solves this problem by allowing clients to perform queries that span across different services. The federation layer takes care of querying each relevant service and aggregating the results, simplifying the process for clients and providing a more unified view of the data.

However, implementing GraphQL Federation does come with its own set of challenges. One such challenge is schema design and coordination. While federation promotes modularity, it also requires careful planning and coordination between teams to ensure that schemas are designed in a way that facilitates smooth integration. Teams need to agree on common types, fields, and how they interact with other services to avoid conflicts and ensure consistency across the federated schema.

Performance considerations are also critical when working with federation. Since the gateway orchestrates queries across multiple services, it must handle potentially complex interactions and aggregations efficiently. Optimizing the performance of the federation layer and ensuring that services are designed to handle their responsibilities effectively is crucial for maintaining a responsive and scalable system.

Despite these challenges, the advantages of GraphQL Federation make it a compelling choice for modern, distributed architectures. By embracing the principles of schema composition, service delegation, extensibility, decentralized development, and cross-service querying, organizations can build more scalable, flexible, and efficient GraphQL systems. As we progress through this chapter, we will further explore the practical implementations and use cases of GraphQL Federation, offering insights into how these principles are applied in real-world scenarios to achieve successful outcomes.

GraphQL Federation's capability to handle cross-service querying is transformative for modern data architectures. Unlike traditional monolithic schemas, where all data is tightly coupled within a single schema, federation facilitates a more flexible and distributed approach. This capability allows queries to span multiple services seamlessly, reflecting the distributed nature of modern applications.

In a federated architecture, queries can reach into various services as if they were querying a single database, thus simplifying client-side queries. For instance, if a client needs data about a user and their recent orders, in a federated system, a single query can fetch user details from one service and order history from another. The federation layer orchestrates these queries, invoking the respective services and combining their responses into a cohesive result. This process hides the complexity of multiple underlying services from the client, delivering a unified and simplified interface.

Additionally, federation promotes schema versioning and management. Unlike a monolithic approach where schema changes can have widespread and disruptive effects, federated schemas allow for more granular control. Each service can evolve its schema independently, and the federation layer ensures backward compatibility by managing schema versions. This flexibility is particularly valuable in large, evolving systems where different services may need to adapt to changing requirements or technologies at different rates.

The approach also introduces performance optimizations. Federated systems can leverage caching mechanisms at both the service and gateway levels. By caching frequently requested data or query results, the system can reduce load times and improve response times for end users. For example, if a certain user profile or product detail is requested frequently, the federation layer or individual services can cache this data to minimize redundant processing and database queries.

Security and access control in a federated architecture is another key consideration. Each service in a federation can implement its own security policies and access controls, tailored to its specific needs and data sensitivity. The federation layer consolidates these controls, ensuring that security policies are enforced consistently across all services. This approach allows for more granular and flexible security configurations, as opposed to a monolithic schema where security controls might be more rigid and difficult to adjust.

Furthermore, federation supports evolutionary development and experimentation. In a federated system, teams can experiment with new features or modifications in their services without impacting the rest of the system. This capability encourages innovation and iterative improvements, as changes can be rolled out incrementally and tested in isolation before being integrated into the broader system. This experimental flexibility accelerates development cycles and supports more agile methodologies.

To successfully implement GraphQL Federation, organizations must consider several best practices. One of these is establishing clear service boundaries. Effective federation requires well-defined boundaries between services to avoid overlap and ensure clear responsibilities. Services should encapsulate specific domains or functionalities and expose well-defined APIs that the federation layer can integrate.

Another best practice involves schema design. While federation allows for distributed schemas, maintaining a cohesive and consistent schema design is crucial. Each service should adhere to shared design principles and conventions to ensure that the unified schema remains intuitive and easy to use. Additionally, documentation of the federated schema and the individual service schemas is essential for maintaining clarity and usability.

Testing and monitoring are also critical components of a successful federation strategy. Continuous integration and deployment pipelines should include tests that verify the correctness of the federated schema and the interactions between services. Monitoring tools can track query performance, service health, and error rates, providing insights into the system's overall performance and helping to identify and address issues proactively.

In summary, GraphQL Federation represents a significant advancement in scaling GraphQL to meet the demands of modern, distributed applications. By leveraging federation, organizations can achieve a more flexible, scalable, and manageable architecture, where services operate independently yet integrate seamlessly. The principles of schema composition, service delegation, extensibility, decentralized development, and cross-service querying collectively enable a powerful and efficient system. As technology continues to evolve, GraphQL Federation will remain a crucial strategy for building robust, scalable, and agile data architectures.

CHAPTER 2: CORE CONCEPTS OF GRAPHQL FEDERATION

GraphQL Federation represents a paradigm shift in how GraphQL APIs are constructed and managed, facilitating a modular approach to schema design. At the heart of this architecture are several core concepts that enable the seamless integration of multiple GraphQL services into a single, cohesive API. This chapter explores these fundamental concepts—subgraphs, gateways, and schema stitching—providing a comprehensive understanding of how they work together to create a unified API from disparate GraphQL services.

To begin with, the concept of subgraphs is central to GraphQL Federation. A subgraph, also known as a federated service, represents an individual GraphQL service that handles a specific part of the overall schema. Each subgraph is responsible for a distinct domain of data and operations. For example, in an e-commerce application, there might be separate subgraphs for user management, product catalog, and order processing. These subgraphs define their schemas and resolvers, encapsulating the logic and data related to their domain.

Each subgraph adheres to the GraphQL specification, allowing it to provide queries, mutations, and subscriptions relevant to its domain. However, the key innovation of GraphQL Federation is how these individual subgraphs interact. The schema of each subgraph is extended with federated directives that specify how it relates to other subgraphs. For instance, a subgraph managing user data might include directives indicating how to link user profiles to their orders, which are managed by a different subgraph.

The gateway is another crucial component of GraphQL Federation. It acts as a central hub that federates the schemas from multiple subgraphs into a single schema that is exposed to the client. The gateway aggregates the schemas of all federated services, resolving the interdependencies and stitching them together to create a unified schema. It handles the complexities of querying multiple services by forwarding requests to the appropriate subgraphs and consolidating the responses.

The gateway is responsible for query planning and execution. When a client sends a query, the gateway parses it, determines which subgraphs need to be queried, and constructs a plan to retrieve the necessary data. This process ensures that queries are efficiently executed, with minimal round-trips to the various services involved. By managing this orchestration layer, the gateway abstracts the underlying complexity of the federated services, presenting a simplified API to the client.

Schema stitching is a concept that plays a critical role in the federation architecture. It involves combining multiple GraphQL schemas into a single schema that reflects the complete set of available data and operations. In GraphQL Federation, schema stitching is handled by the gateway, which merges the schemas of all subgraphs into a unified schema. This unified schema incorporates all types, queries, and mutations defined by the individual subgraphs, while also resolving references between them.

The process of schema stitching ensures that the federated schema maintains consistency and integrity. It involves mapping fields and types from different schemas, resolving conflicts, and ensuring that the relationships between types from different subgraphs are correctly represented. For example, if a user type defined in the user management subgraph references orders from the order processing subgraph, schema stitching ensures that this reference is properly integrated into the unified schema.

An essential aspect of schema stitching is type extension. In a federated architecture, types defined in one subgraph can be extended by other subgraphs. This capability allows for the modularization of schema development, where different services can contribute to and extend the base types defined elsewhere. For instance, the user type defined in the user management subgraph might be extended by the order processing subgraph to include additional fields related to user order history.

Understanding these core concepts—subgraphs, gateways, and schema stitching—provides a foundation for working with GraphQL Federation. By leveraging these components, organizations can build scalable and modular GraphQL architectures that facilitate the integration of multiple services while maintaining a unified API for clients. The flexibility and power of GraphQL Federation enable the development of complex, distributed systems with the simplicity and ease of use that GraphQL provides.

In the architecture of GraphQL Federation, schema stitching plays a pivotal role in unifying disparate GraphQL schemas into a coherent whole. Schema stitching involves the process of combining the schemas from various subgraphs to form a single, federated schema that clients interact with. This concept is fundamental in addressing the complexity that arises from having multiple services each with their own schema.

The stitching process begins with each subgraph defining its schema independently. These schemas are enriched with federated directives that specify how they connect with other schemas. For instance, a subgraph might use the `@key` directive to indicate that it can be used to reference a particular entity, such as a user or product, across other subgraphs. This creates a linkage between services, allowing for the integration of data and operations that span multiple subgraphs.

Once the individual schemas are defined and enriched with federated directives, the schema stitching mechanism is employed to merge these schemas into a single, unified schema. This process involves resolving potential conflicts between schemas, such as overlapping type definitions or conflicting field names. The stitching engine intelligently combines the schemas, ensuring that the resulting federated schema accurately represents the complete API surface.

The resulting federated schema exposes a unified API to clients, providing a seamless experience despite the underlying complexity of multiple services. Clients can query across different domains of data and perform operations as if they were interacting with a single GraphQL service. The federation framework handles the intricacies of routing and aggregating data, allowing clients to benefit from a unified view of the system without needing to be aware of the underlying service boundaries.

A critical aspect of GraphQL Federation is how it handles service composition. Service composition involves aggregating the various subgraphs into a cohesive schema that maintains the integrity of the overall data model. This includes managing relationships between different types and fields defined across subgraphs. The composition process ensures that the federated schema correctly reflects the relationships and interactions between data entities, enabling complex queries that span multiple subgraphs.

For example, consider a scenario where a subgraph for user management defines a `User` type, and another subgraph for orders defines an `Order` type that references the `User`. The schema stitching process must ensure that the `User` type from the user management subgraph and the `Order` type from the order subgraph are correctly composed. This involves resolving references and ensuring that queries for `Order` data correctly include user information from the appropriate subgraph.

Another important consideration in schema stitching is schema evolution. As services evolve, their schemas may change, requiring updates to the federated schema. Federation frameworks support schema evolution by allowing incremental updates to subgraphs without disrupting the overall system. This ensures that the federated schema remains consistent with the latest changes while minimizing the impact on clients.

In practice, the implementation of GraphQL Federation often involves using tools and libraries designed to facilitate schema stitching and composition. These tools provide functionality for defining subgraphs, managing federated directives, and composing schemas. They also offer capabilities for querying, caching, and optimizing performance across federated services.

The integration of GraphQL Federation into an organization's architecture can significantly enhance its ability to scale and manage complex APIs. By breaking down the monolithic API into modular subgraphs, organizations can achieve greater flexibility and agility in their API development. Each subgraph can be developed, deployed, and maintained independently, allowing for more efficient and focused development processes.

Moreover, GraphQL Federation supports the evolution of APIs over time. As new services are added or existing services are updated, the federated schema can be adjusted to reflect these changes. This approach aligns with modern architectural practices, such as microservices and modular development, providing a robust foundation for building scalable and maintainable GraphQL APIs.

In conclusion, the core concepts of GraphQL Federation—subgraphs, gateways, and schema stitching—form the backbone of a scalable and flexible API architecture. By understanding these components and how they work together, you can leverage GraphQL Federation to build a unified API that integrates multiple services seamlessly. This approach not only simplifies the client experience but also enhances the scalability and maintainability of your API ecosystem.

The concept of subgraphs is central to understanding GraphQL Federation. Subgraphs are essentially modular components of a larger federated schema, each representing a distinct domain of the data model. They operate as independent GraphQL services with their own schemas but are designed to integrate seamlessly into the federation framework.

Each subgraph typically represents a specific business capability or domain, such as user management, product catalog, or order processing. By dividing the data model into subgraphs, organizations can manage and develop different parts of their system independently, allowing for more granular control and flexibility. This modular approach helps in scaling the system, as each subgraph can be developed, deployed, and scaled individually based on its specific requirements.

The role of the gateway is to act as the entry point for client queries in a federated GraphQL architecture. It is responsible for coordinating the requests across the various subgraphs and aggregating the responses into a unified result. When a client sends a query, the gateway parses it and determines which subgraphs need to be queried to fulfill the request. It then sends requests to the appropriate subgraphs, collects the responses, and merges them into a single response before sending it back to the client.

The gateway handles the orchestration of queries by leveraging the federated schema, which includes information about how different subgraphs are connected and how data should be fetched from each subgraph. This orchestration is crucial for ensuring that queries are resolved efficiently and accurately, especially in scenarios where a query spans multiple subgraphs.

The process of integrating and managing subgraphs within a federated schema is often facilitated by the use of federated directives. These directives provide a way to annotate the schema with information about how different types and fields are related across subgraphs. For example, the `@key` directive is used to specify a unique identifier for an entity that can be referenced across subgraphs. Similarly, the `@extends` directive allows a type to be extended with additional fields in another subgraph, while the `@external` directive indicates that a field is defined in another subgraph.

The integration of these directives enables the gateway to resolve queries that involve entities and fields from multiple subgraphs. It allows the gateway to understand how to fetch data from the appropriate subgraphs and how to stitch the responses together. This capability is fundamental for delivering a seamless and coherent API experience to clients.

GraphQL Federation also introduces the concept of federation resolvers, which are responsible for handling the resolution of fields that are defined across different subgraphs. Federation resolvers are implemented in each subgraph and handle the logic for fetching and returning data for specific fields. When a query requires data from multiple subgraphs, the gateway utilizes these resolvers to gather the necessary data and compose it into a unified response.

The flexibility and scalability offered by GraphQL Federation are particularly advantageous for organizations with complex data models and distributed systems. By allowing different teams to develop and maintain their own subgraphs, federation facilitates a more agile development process. Teams can work independently on their respective subgraphs, without the need for extensive coordination with other teams. This modular approach also simplifies the process of adding new features or modifying existing ones, as changes can be made to individual subgraphs without impacting the entire system.

Furthermore, the use of federation helps to mitigate the challenges associated with monolithic GraphQL schemas. In a monolithic schema, all types and fields are defined in a single schema file, which can become unwieldy and difficult to manage as the system grows. Federation addresses this issue by distributing the schema across multiple subgraphs, each managed independently. This division of responsibility leads to a more manageable and maintainable system.

As organizations continue to embrace microservices and distributed architectures, the role of GraphQL Federation will become increasingly important. Its ability to unify multiple GraphQL services into a single, cohesive API makes it a powerful tool for modern, scalable applications. By leveraging the core concepts of subgraphs, gateways, schema stitching, and federated directives, organizations can build flexible and efficient GraphQL architectures that meet the demands of today's dynamic business environments.

CHAPTER 3: SETTING UP YOUR FIRST FEDERATED SCHEMA

To embark on the journey of setting up a federated schema, it is essential to first establish a clear understanding of the foundational steps involved in creating and integrating multiple GraphQL services. Federation allows for a scalable and modular approach to GraphQL schemas, and this chapter will provide a step-by-step guide to setting up your first federated schema. This will involve creating individual GraphQL services, defining their schemas, and configuring them for integration using federation principles.

The initial step in creating a federated schema is to define the individual GraphQL services. Each service, or subgraph, should be designed to represent a specific domain or business capability. For example, in an e-commerce application, you might have separate services for user management, product catalog, and order processing. Each service will have its own GraphQL schema, which outlines the types, queries, and mutations relevant to its domain.

Begin by creating the GraphQL schema for each service. This involves defining the types and fields that each service will expose. In a GraphQL schema, types are the core building blocks, and they define the structure of the data that can be queried or mutated. For instance, a `User` type might include fields such as `id`, `name`, and `email`, while a `Product` type might include `id`, `name`, `price`, and `description`.

Once you have defined the schemas for each service, the next step is to configure these schemas for federation. Federation is built on the concept of extending and integrating schemas across multiple services. To facilitate this, you will need to use GraphQL Federation-specific directives. These directives are part of the GraphQL specification that enable services to share and extend their schemas with other services.

The most commonly used directives in federation are `@key`, `@extends`, `@external`, and `@provides`. The `@key` directive is used to define a unique identifier for a type that can be referenced across different services. For instance, if your `User` type has an `id` field that is unique, you would annotate it with `@key(fields: "id")` to indicate that it can be used as a reference by other services.

The `@extends` directive allows a type defined in one service to be extended with additional fields in another service. This is useful when you want to add more details to a type that is already defined elsewhere. For example, if your `User` type is defined in a user management service, you might extend it in an order processing service to include additional fields related to orders.

The `@external` directive indicates that a field is defined in another service and is used to reference it. This directive is necessary when a field is needed by a service but is not defined within its own schema. For example, if the `Product` type is defined in a product catalog service, and another service needs to query `Product` details, the field would be marked as `@external`.

The `@provides` directive is used to indicate that a service provides a specific field or data that other services can consume. This helps in ensuring that the data required by other services is available and can be resolved efficiently.

After defining and annotating the schemas with the appropriate directives, the next step is to integrate these services using a federated gateway. The gateway acts as the central point of access for the federated schema, coordinating requests between the different services and aggregating their responses.

To set up the gateway, you will need to use a federated GraphQL server implementation, such as Apollo Server, which supports federation out of the box. You will configure the gateway to use the schemas from the individual services and manage the interactions between them. The gateway will also handle the orchestration of queries, ensuring that the data is fetched from the correct services and combined into a single response.

Once the gateway is configured, you can deploy the individual services and the gateway. Ensure that each service is accessible and that the gateway can successfully communicate with them. The deployment process typically involves setting up the necessary infrastructure, such as containers or cloud services, and ensuring that the services are properly registered with the gateway.

Testing is a crucial step in verifying that the federated schema is working as expected. You should test various queries and mutations to ensure that they are correctly resolved across the different services. This involves sending queries to the gateway and checking that the responses include data from the appropriate services.

By the end of this chapter, you will have a working federated schema composed of multiple GraphQL services, integrated and managed by a federated gateway. This setup will provide a scalable and modular approach to managing GraphQL schemas, allowing for efficient development and deployment of complex applications.

To effectively set up your first federated schema, integrating your individual GraphQL services involves several key configurations and tools that ensure a seamless connection between them. The primary goal is to enable these services to operate cohesively, presenting a unified API to clients while maintaining modularity and independence within each service.

Having defined the schemas and used federation-specific directives, the next step is to implement a gateway service. The gateway is a central component that acts as the entry point for client requests and aggregates responses from the various federated services. This service orchestrates the communication between the client and the subgraphs, combining their schemas into a single, cohesive GraphQL schema.

To set up a gateway, you will typically use a federation-compatible GraphQL server library, such as Apollo Server. Apollo Server is widely used for its robust support of federation and its comprehensive toolset for building and managing GraphQL APIs. The gateway will utilize this server to manage schema stitching and query resolution, providing a unified interface for clients.

The configuration of the gateway involves specifying the subgraphs it will interact with. This is done by providing the gateway with a list of endpoints where each federated service is available. The gateway then fetches the schemas from these services, merges them, and sets up the necessary resolvers to handle the queries. In an Apollo Server setup, this configuration is typically handled in the server setup code, where you define the list of subgraphs and their URLs.

Once the gateway is configured, you must ensure that it can handle query routing efficiently. This involves setting up the appropriate resolvers to delegate queries to the correct subgraph. The gateway uses the `@key` directive to determine how to fetch and combine data across different services. For example, if a client queries for user data and order details, the gateway will utilize the `@key` directive to fetch the user information from the user service and the order details from the order service, then merge these results into a single response.

Testing the federated schema is crucial to ensure that all services are correctly integrated and that queries return the expected results. Begin by running queries against the gateway to verify that data from multiple services is correctly aggregated. Utilize tools like GraphiQL or Apollo Studio to interact with the unified API, testing various queries and mutations to validate that the federated schema behaves as expected. Pay particular attention to cross-service queries, ensuring that references and extensions between services are functioning correctly.

Another critical aspect of setting up a federated schema is managing schema evolution and versioning. As your services evolve, it is important to handle changes in a way that does not disrupt the overall federated schema. Implementing a versioning strategy and adhering to backward compatibility practices will help ensure that updates to individual services do not adversely affect the entire system. Utilize schema validation tools to test changes before deploying them to production, and maintain clear documentation to track schema changes across services.

Effective monitoring and debugging of a federated schema are also essential. Set up logging and monitoring tools to track the performance of your gateway and subgraphs. These tools can provide insights into query execution times, error rates, and service health, allowing you to quickly identify and address issues. Implementing tracing and error handling mechanisms will help ensure that any problems are promptly detected and resolved.

In conclusion, setting up a basic federated schema involves defining individual GraphQL services with their respective schemas, configuring a gateway to aggregate and route queries, and thoroughly testing the integration. By following these steps and utilizing the appropriate tools, you will establish a scalable and modular GraphQL architecture that leverages the power of federation. This approach not only enhances the flexibility and maintainability of your API but also provides a unified interface for clients to interact with. With a solid foundation in place, you can further explore advanced federation concepts and continue to refine your GraphQL services as your application evolves.

Once the basic setup of your federated schema is complete, it is essential to address issues related to schema evolution and maintenance. As your application grows and evolves, your federated schema may require updates or expansions. Managing these changes effectively is crucial to ensure that the integration remains robust and reliable.

Schema evolution in a federated architecture typically involves updating individual subgraph schemas and then propagating these changes through the gateway. Each subgraph service can be developed and deployed independently, but the integration requires careful coordination. When a subgraph schema is updated, it is important to validate that these changes do not introduce breaking changes or conflicts with other subgraphs. Using versioning strategies for your subgraph schemas can help manage these changes, allowing you to evolve your schemas without disrupting existing functionality.

To facilitate smooth updates, implement automated testing and deployment pipelines. These pipelines should include steps to test individual subgraphs as well as their integration through the gateway. Automated tests can simulate queries and mutations to verify that the federated schema operates correctly and returns expected results. This practice ensures that updates to one part of your schema do not inadvertently affect other parts, maintaining overall system integrity.

Another important consideration is performance optimization. As your federated schema grows, the complexity of queries and the number of interactions between subgraphs may impact performance. Monitoring and optimizing query performance is crucial to ensure that your federated service remains responsive. Tools such as Apollo Studio provide insights into query performance, allowing you to identify bottlenecks and optimize your schema or resolver logic. Caching strategies can also be employed to improve response times, particularly for frequently accessed data.

In addition to performance, security is a critical aspect of managing a federated schema. Ensure that each subgraph service enforces proper authentication and authorization mechanisms. The gateway should act as a central point for authentication, validating client requests and passing relevant authentication tokens to the subgraphs. Implementing a consistent security strategy across all services helps protect sensitive data and prevent unauthorized access.

Documentation is another key element in maintaining a federated schema. Comprehensive documentation for each subgraph, including schema definitions and usage patterns, facilitates easier development and integration. Additionally, documenting the federated schema at the gateway level helps teams understand the overall API structure and interactions between subgraphs. This documentation serves as a valuable resource for developers working with the federated schema and helps streamline onboarding and troubleshooting processes.

Finally, fostering collaboration between teams responsible for different subgraphs is essential for the success of a federated architecture. Regular communication and coordination between teams ensure that schema changes are managed effectively and that the integration between subgraphs remains seamless. Establishing clear guidelines and processes for schema development, testing, and deployment helps maintain consistency and quality across the federated system.

In summary, setting up your first federated schema involves creating individual GraphQL services, defining their schemas, and integrating them through a gateway. This process requires careful configuration, testing, and ongoing maintenance to ensure a unified and efficient API. As you advance, focusing on schema evolution, performance optimization, security, documentation, and team collaboration will help you manage and scale your federated architecture effectively. With these practices in place, you'll be well-equipped to leverage the full potential of GraphQL federation in your applications.

CHAPTER 4: UNDERSTANDING THE FEDERATED SCHEMA LANGUAGE

In the realm of GraphQL Federation, the Federated Schema Language (FSDL) plays a crucial role in defining how services interact and combine to form a cohesive API. This chapter delves into FSDL, providing a detailed exploration of its syntax, capabilities, and how it builds upon the traditional GraphQL Schema Definition Language (SDL). By the end of this chapter, you will have a comprehensive understanding of how to utilize FSDL to define and manage federated schemas effectively.

The Federated Schema Language extends the traditional GraphQL SDL by introducing additional constructs designed to handle the complexities of distributed systems. While SDL is fundamental for defining schemas within a single GraphQL service, FSDL introduces new elements that address the requirements of federated architectures, such as the need to unify multiple services into a single graph.

At its core, FSDL retains the basic structure of SDL, which includes defining types, queries, mutations, and subscriptions. However, it introduces specific directives and annotations to facilitate federation. One of the primary directives is `@key`, which designates a field or combination of fields as the primary key for a type within the federated schema. This directive is essential for establishing unique identifiers across different subgraphs, ensuring that types can be consistently referenced and resolved in the unified API.

In addition to the `@key` directive, FSDL employs the `@extends` directive to indicate that a type defined in one subgraph is being extended in another. This allows for schema composition where types can be augmented with additional fields or functionality. The `@extends` directive is used in conjunction with the `@provides` directive to specify that a particular field is provided by a subgraph, enabling it to fulfill queries for extended fields defined in other subgraphs.

Another critical aspect of FSDL is the `@requires` directive, which is used to indicate that a field requires additional fields from the same or other subgraphs to resolve. This directive helps in managing dependencies between fields and ensures that all necessary data is available for the resolution of a particular query. By explicitly defining these requirements, FSDL supports efficient query planning and execution across federated services.

Defining a federated schema involves more than just applying directives. It requires a clear understanding of how different subgraphs interact and how their schemas are combined. To create an effective federated schema, start by identifying the core entities and types that will be shared across your services. Each subgraph should focus on a specific domain or functionality while exposing types that can be referenced by other subgraphs. Use the `@key` directive to mark the primary keys of these types, ensuring they are accessible and resolvable throughout the federation.

When extending types, consider the impact on both the original type and the extended schema. The `@extends` directive should be used judiciously to avoid creating overly complex or interdependent schemas. Clear and well-defined boundaries between subgraphs help maintain the modularity and maintainability of the overall schema. Ensure that each subgraph only extends types it directly interacts with, and that it provides fields that are meaningful and necessary for the federated graph.

Combining federated schemas requires a careful orchestration of schema stitching and merging. In practice, this involves configuring the gateway to aggregate the schemas of all participating subgraphs into a single schema that can be queried by clients. The gateway uses the directives specified in FSDL to resolve and unify the types and fields across different services. It is essential to validate the combined schema to ensure that all types, queries, and mutations are correctly integrated and that the resulting graph functions as intended.

In summary, the Federated Schema Language introduces powerful extensions to the traditional GraphQL SDL, enabling the definition and management of federated schemas. By utilizing directives such as `@key`, `@extends`, `@provides`, and `@requires`, you can effectively manage the complexity of distributed systems and ensure seamless integration across multiple subgraphs. Understanding and applying these concepts will empower you to build scalable and maintainable federated architectures, making GraphQL Federation a robust solution for modern API development.

The Federated Schema Language (FSDL) is a powerful extension of the traditional GraphQL Schema Definition Language (SDL) designed to handle the complexities of federated systems. Understanding how FSDL builds upon SDL is key to effectively implementing and managing federated schemas.

A fundamental concept in FSDL is the use of the `@key` directive, which plays a critical role in defining how entities are uniquely identified across different subgraphs. In traditional GraphQL SDL, types are defined with their fields and types, but there is no concept of a global identifier that spans multiple services. The `@key` directive in FSDL addresses this by allowing you to specify one or more fields as the key for a type. This key is crucial for ensuring that each instance of the type can be uniquely identified and accessed across the federated schema.

For example, in a federated architecture where you have a `User` type defined in one subgraph and extended in another, the `@key` directive ensures that the `User` type has a globally unique identifier. This allows different subgraphs to reference the same `User` entity without ambiguity. When you define a `User` type, you would use `@key` to designate a field like `id` as the unique identifier. Other subgraphs can then extend the `User` type by adding fields or resolving queries based on this identifier.

In addition to `@key`, FSDL introduces the `@extends` directive, which enables schema composition by allowing types to be extended across different subgraphs. The `@extends` directive is used in a subgraph to indicate that a type is an extension of a type defined in another subgraph. This is particularly useful for adding additional fields or functionality to types without modifying their original definitions.

Alongside `@extends`, the `@provides` directive specifies that a field in a subgraph provides data required by another field in an extended type. This directive is instrumental in managing how data is shared and resolved across subgraphs. For instance, if a `User` type in one subgraph includes basic information like `id` and `name`, another subgraph could extend this `User` type to include additional fields such as `profilePicture` or `email`, using `@provides` to indicate that these fields are fulfilled by the extending subgraph.

Another essential directive in FSDL is `@requires`. This directive is used to specify that a field in a federated type requires additional fields to resolve its value. This is important for ensuring that all necessary data is available and correctly resolved. The `@requires` directive helps in managing dependencies between fields, ensuring that queries are executed efficiently and that all required data is retrieved.

Defining federated schemas involves not only applying these directives but also understanding how to compose and integrate schemas from multiple sources. Each subgraph must be designed to include types and fields that can be referenced and extended by other subgraphs. This requires careful planning to ensure that types are defined with clear keys and that fields are available as needed.

When integrating schemas using FSDL, it is also important to consider the schema stitching process. Schema stitching involves combining multiple GraphQL schemas into a single schema that clients can query. While FSDL facilitates this by defining how types and fields interact across subgraphs, schema stitching also requires practical considerations such as managing conflicts and ensuring that the combined schema remains consistent and functional.

In summary, the Federated Schema Language extends traditional GraphQL SDL by introducing new directives and constructs to support federation. The `@key`, `@extends`, `@provides`, and `@requires` directives are central to defining how types and fields interact across different subgraphs. Understanding and applying these directives effectively is crucial for creating a unified federated schema that leverages the strengths of distributed services while maintaining coherence and integrity. Through careful definition and integration of schemas, FSDL enables the creation of scalable and flexible GraphQL APIs that can efficiently handle complex data requirements across multiple services.

The Federated Schema Language (FSDL) enhances GraphQL's traditional Schema Definition Language (SDL) by addressing the challenges inherent in a federated architecture. It provides mechanisms for types and fields to be shared and extended across multiple services, ensuring cohesive data interaction and seamless integration.

One significant aspect of FSDL is its ability to manage entity relationships across subgraphs. The `@key` directive enables the definition of unique identifiers that are crucial for resolving entities in a distributed system. When using `@key`, the specified field or fields become globally accessible identifiers for the type, allowing different services to reference and resolve these entities consistently. This capability is essential for maintaining data integrity and coherence in a federated environment, where types may be split across various services.

The `@extends` directive is another cornerstone of FSDL, facilitating the extension of existing types across different services. This directive allows a type defined in one subgraph to be augmented with additional fields or functionality in another subgraph. For example, if a service defines a `Product` type with basic attributes like `id` and `name`, another service can extend this `Product` type to include details like `price` and `reviews` using the `@extends` directive. This extension capability is crucial for enabling modular development and maintaining a flexible schema architecture.

In conjunction with `@extends`, the `@provides` directive is used to indicate that a particular field in one subgraph provides data required by fields in another subgraph. This directive is instrumental in defining how different services contribute to the overall schema. For instance, if one subgraph defines a `User` type with a `name` field and another subgraph extends this type to include a `profilePicture`, the `@provides` directive ensures that the `profilePicture` field is fulfilled by the first subgraph's `User` type. This clear delineation of data responsibility helps in managing dependencies and ensuring that fields are correctly resolved across the federated schema.

Moreover, FSDL extends SDL by introducing mechanisms for managing schema composition and merging. The `@link` directive is used to link subgraph schemas together, specifying how different schemas should be combined into a unified API. This linking process is crucial for creating a seamless experience for clients consuming the federated API, as it ensures that queries can traverse multiple subgraphs transparently.

The use of `@link` allows for a structured approach to schema composition. For example, if you have a `Product` type defined in one service and a `Review` type defined in another, you can use `@link` to establish relationships between these types. This linkage enables clients to query for products and their reviews in a single request, despite the underlying data being distributed across multiple services.

Understanding how to use these directives effectively is vital for designing and implementing a robust federated schema. Each directive serves a specific purpose in managing type extensions, data resolution, and schema composition. Mastery of these concepts will allow you to build scalable, modular, and efficient federated APIs that meet the demands of modern applications.

The Federated Schema Language, while extending SDL, retains the core principles of GraphQL schema design. It emphasizes the need for clear type definitions and well-structured schemas, while providing additional tools for handling the complexities of a distributed system. By leveraging FSDL, you can create a federated schema that integrates multiple services into a cohesive and efficient API, enhancing both the development and user experience.

As you progress with implementing federated schemas, you'll find that understanding and applying these FSDL constructs will significantly improve your ability to manage distributed data and service interactions. This foundational knowledge will pave the way for more advanced topics in GraphQL Federation, enabling you to address the challenges of scaling and integrating complex data systems.

CHAPTER 5: IMPLEMENTING FEDERATION IN A MICROSERVICES ARCHITECTURE

Federation offers a robust solution for managing complex systems in a microservices architecture, where different services are responsible for distinct parts of the overall application. Implementing GraphQL Federation in such environments requires careful consideration of service boundaries, schema design, and inter-service communication. This chapter will explore these facets in detail, providing a comprehensive guide on how to leverage federation to enhance the scalability and maintainability of microservices architectures.

A fundamental aspect of implementing federation in a microservices environment is defining clear service boundaries. Each microservice should encapsulate a specific domain or functionality, thus allowing it to manage its own data and schema independently. This segregation helps in maintaining modularity and ensures that services can evolve independently without impacting others. When designing a federated schema, it is crucial to identify these boundaries and ensure that the types and fields exposed by each service are well-defined and relevant to their domain.

The schema design process in a federated microservices architecture involves creating individual schemas for each service that are then integrated into a unified schema. Each service's schema should adhere to the principles of federation, such as defining types with the `@key` directive for entity resolution and using the `@extends` directive to enable schema extension across services. For example, a `User` service might define the core attributes of a user, while an `Order` service can extend the `User` type to include information about orders associated with that user. This design approach ensures that services remain loosely coupled yet can collaborate seamlessly.

When integrating federated services, schema stitching plays a critical role. Schema stitching involves combining multiple GraphQL schemas into a single schema that clients can interact with. This process typically involves a gateway service that aggregates the individual schemas and provides a unified API. The gateway service is responsible for handling incoming queries, delegating them to the appropriate subservices, and composing the results into a single response. Proper configuration of the gateway is essential to ensure efficient query resolution and minimize latency in inter-service communication.

Managing inter-service communication is another crucial consideration in a federated microservices architecture. Services need to communicate effectively to resolve queries that span multiple services. This communication can be achieved through various methods, such as direct service-to-service calls or using message brokers for asynchronous communication. Implementing a robust communication strategy is vital to maintain performance and ensure that data is accurately resolved and aggregated across services.

Additionally, handling errors and timeouts in communication is critical to avoid cascading failures and ensure the reliability of the federated system.

Best practices for implementing federation in microservices include establishing clear API contracts between services, using versioning to manage schema changes, and employing comprehensive monitoring and logging. Clear API contracts define the expected inputs and outputs for each service, facilitating smooth integration and reducing the risk of compatibility issues. Schema versioning allows services to evolve independently while maintaining backward compatibility, thus ensuring a smooth transition during upgrades. Monitoring and logging provide visibility into the system's performance and help diagnose issues that may arise during inter-service communication or query resolution.

Security considerations are also paramount when implementing federation. Ensuring that data access is properly controlled and that services only expose necessary information is crucial for protecting sensitive data. Implementing authentication and authorization mechanisms at both the service and gateway levels helps in securing the federated API and preventing unauthorized access. Additionally, securing inter-service communication channels and implementing encryption for data in transit can further enhance the security of the federated architecture.

In summary, implementing federation in a microservices architecture involves designing clear service boundaries, integrating schemas effectively through schema stitching, and managing inter-service communication. By adhering to best practices and addressing key considerations such as API contracts, versioning, monitoring, and security, organizations can build scalable and maintainable systems that leverage the benefits of GraphQL Federation. This approach not only enhances the flexibility of the architecture but also provides a unified and coherent API experience for clients.

When implementing federation in a microservices architecture, one of the foremost challenges is managing the interaction between services. Each service operates independently and may have its own data store, which can complicate the process of aggregating and resolving data across services. Therefore, effective communication strategies are essential for ensuring that data from different services can be seamlessly integrated.

One method for facilitating this communication is through the use of REST or gRPC APIs between services. RESTful APIs can provide a straightforward means for services to request data from one another, while gRPC, with its support for efficient binary serialization and built-in support for streaming, can offer performance benefits in high-throughput scenarios. Both approaches require careful consideration of error handling, security, and versioning to ensure that services can interact reliably.

Another approach is to leverage a message broker, such as Apache Kafka or RabbitMQ, to facilitate asynchronous communication between services. This method can be particularly useful in scenarios where services need to react to changes in other services' data. By publishing events to a message broker, services can decouple their interactions and maintain responsiveness even when the underlying services experience delays or failures.

In addition to managing communication, it's also crucial to address the issue of service discovery. In a dynamic microservices environment, services may scale up or down, and their network locations may change. Implementing a service discovery mechanism helps ensure that the gateway can locate and communicate with the appropriate instances of each service. This can be achieved through service registries such as Consul or Eureka, which keep track of available services and their current locations.

To ensure effective operation of federated services, it is important to implement comprehensive monitoring and logging. This involves tracking the performance and health of individual services, as well as the interactions between them. Monitoring tools can provide valuable insights into system behavior, identify bottlenecks, and help diagnose issues that arise in the federated architecture. Centralized logging solutions can aggregate logs from different services, facilitating easier troubleshooting and analysis.

Testing federated services is another crucial aspect of implementation. Given the complexity of interactions between services, it is essential to develop a robust testing strategy. Unit testing for individual services ensures that each service operates correctly in isolation. Integration testing, on the other hand, verifies that services interact as expected when combined. End-to-end testing of the entire federated system is also important to ensure that the integrated services deliver the expected functionality and performance.

Security considerations are paramount in a federated microservices architecture. Each service needs to enforce appropriate security measures to protect its data and functionality. This includes implementing authentication and authorization mechanisms to ensure that only authorized clients and services can access sensitive information. Additionally, data encryption both in transit and at rest helps safeguard against unauthorized access and breaches.

Managing schema evolution is another important aspect of working with federated schemas. As services evolve, their schemas may change, which can impact other services that depend on them. Implementing a strategy for schema versioning and deprecation helps mitigate these issues. This approach allows services to evolve independently while maintaining compatibility with existing consumers. By following best practices for schema evolution, such as maintaining backward compatibility and providing clear migration paths, you can ensure that changes are introduced smoothly and with minimal disruption.

In summary, implementing federation in a microservices architecture requires a multifaceted approach that addresses service boundaries, schema design, inter-service communication, and security. By carefully considering these aspects and applying best practices, you can create a robust federated system that supports scalable and maintainable architectures. This ensures that services can collaborate effectively while maintaining their independence, ultimately delivering a unified and cohesive experience for clients and users.

When implementing federation within a microservices architecture, one must also consider how to handle schema evolution and versioning. As services evolve independently, maintaining compatibility between the federated schemas becomes critical. One common approach to manage schema evolution is to use backward-compatible changes. This means adding new fields or types in a way that does not disrupt existing queries or mutations. By ensuring that changes to the schema are additive rather than breaking, services can be updated without affecting the overall federated system.

Additionally, versioning strategies can help manage changes in services that might necessitate breaking changes. Implementing versioned endpoints or adopting a versioning strategy within the federated schema itself allows for controlled and gradual migration. For example, a new version of a service can be deployed alongside the existing version, giving consumers time to transition to the new API while maintaining compatibility with older clients.

In federated architectures, managing authentication and

authorization across services is another vital consideration. Each microservice may have its own security requirements and mechanisms, which can complicate the process of enforcing consistent security policies. Implementing a centralized authentication service can help streamline this process. For instance, a single sign-on (SSO) solution or an identity provider can handle user authentication and pass secure tokens to individual services. These tokens can then be validated by each service to ensure that requests meet the necessary authorization criteria.

Another critical aspect is handling the consistency of data across services. In a federated system, data is often distributed across multiple services, which can lead to challenges in maintaining consistency. Techniques such as eventual consistency or distributed transactions can help address these challenges. Eventual consistency ensures that all services will eventually have the same data state, even if there are temporary discrepancies. Distributed transactions involve coordinating updates across multiple services to ensure that all changes are applied consistently, though they can be complex and require careful design to avoid pitfalls.

To further streamline the development and management of federated services, adopting automation tools and practices can be highly beneficial. Continuous integration and continuous deployment (CI/CD) pipelines can automate the process of building, testing, and deploying services, ensuring that changes are propagated smoothly across the federated system. Infrastructure as code (IaC) tools can also assist in managing the deployment and configuration of services, providing a repeatable and scalable approach to infrastructure management.

Additionally, using GraphQL-specific tools can enhance the management of federated services. Tools like Apollo Federation or GraphQL Mesh offer capabilities for creating and managing federated schemas, including features for schema composition, query planning, and resolving data from multiple services. These tools help simplify the process of integrating services and can provide valuable insights into the performance and health of the federated system.

In conclusion, implementing federation in a microservices architecture involves addressing several key challenges, including managing service communication, ensuring schema compatibility, handling authentication and authorization, and maintaining data consistency. By employing best practices in service design, communication strategies, and schema management, and leveraging automation tools, organizations can effectively implement and manage a federated system that is robust, scalable, and adaptable to evolving business needs. As you proceed with building your federated architecture, keep in mind the principles of modularity, flexibility, and resilience to ensure a successful and sustainable implementation.

CHAPTER 6: ADVANCED FEDERATION PATTERNS AND TECHNIQUES

Having established the foundational concepts of GraphQL federation, this chapter ventures into more complex patterns and techniques that enhance the flexibility and capability of federated systems. Advanced federation patterns can significantly improve the scalability, maintainability, and functionality of federated GraphQL schemas, addressing sophisticated use cases and complex inter-service relationships.

One critical area of advanced federation is the use of custom directives. In GraphQL, directives are a powerful feature that allow developers to attach metadata to schemas and operations, which can then be used to alter their behavior at runtime. Federation introduces the possibility of creating custom directives that cater specifically to the needs of a federated system. These directives can be employed to handle a variety of tasks, such as injecting metadata into federated services, controlling access to specific fields or types, or even modifying query behavior based on service-specific logic. For example, a custom directive might be used to enforce security policies or to dynamically resolve fields based on the service providing them, thus allowing for a more granular and flexible approach to schema management.

Another advanced technique in federation is enhanced schema stitching. Schema stitching, the process of merging multiple GraphQL schemas into a single unified schema, is fundamental to federation. However, as schemas become more complex, the need for sophisticated stitching techniques becomes apparent. Advanced schema stitching involves not only merging schemas but also resolving conflicts and optimizing queries. Techniques such as aliasing, fragment merging, and custom resolvers can help manage schema overlaps and ensure that queries are efficiently executed across services. For instance, aliasing can be used to handle naming conflicts when integrating schemas from different sources, while custom resolvers can manage complex data retrieval scenarios that span multiple services.

Managing complex relationships between services is another area that benefits from advanced federation techniques. In a federated architecture, services often need to interact with each other in complex ways, such as sharing data or invoking operations across service boundaries. One approach to handling these complex relationships is through the use of inter-service communication patterns, such as asynchronous messaging or event-driven architectures. By employing these patterns, services can communicate and coordinate their operations without tightly coupling to each other. For example, an event-driven approach allows services to publish and subscribe to events, enabling them to react to changes in other services' data or state without direct dependencies.

Additionally, implementing resolvers that span multiple services requires careful consideration of performance and consistency. For instance, a resolver that needs to aggregate data from several services should be designed to handle partial failures gracefully and to avoid introducing significant latency. Techniques such as caching, batching, and parallel data fetching can be employed to improve the performance and reliability of such resolvers. Caching can reduce the number of redundant queries sent to services, batching can group multiple requests into a single operation, and parallel fetching can enable simultaneous data retrieval from multiple sources.

Another advanced federation pattern involves the use of distributed tracing and monitoring tools to gain insights into the performance and behavior of federated systems. Distributed tracing allows developers to track the flow of requests across multiple services, providing visibility into potential bottlenecks or issues. Monitoring tools can help track metrics such as response times, error rates, and service dependencies, enabling proactive management of the federated system. Implementing distributed tracing and monitoring can be crucial for maintaining the health and performance of a complex federated architecture, ensuring that issues are detected and addressed promptly.

Furthermore, handling schema evolution and versioning becomes more intricate as federated systems grow. Advanced patterns for schema evolution involve strategies such as schema deprecation, gradual migration, and versioned interfaces. Schema deprecation allows developers to mark fields or types as obsolete while still maintaining backward compatibility, providing a transition period for clients to adapt to new schemas. Gradual migration involves incrementally introducing new schema versions and features, allowing for a smoother transition and minimizing disruption. Versioned interfaces enable the coexistence of multiple schema versions, allowing clients to select the appropriate version for their needs.

As federated schemas become more complex, ensuring consistent and coherent documentation is also crucial. Advanced documentation techniques, such as auto-generating schema documentation from the federated schema and providing interactive documentation interfaces, can help developers understand and navigate the federated system. Tools that integrate with federated GraphQL systems can generate comprehensive documentation that reflects the combined schema, including details about the relationships between services, the capabilities of each service, and how to use the unified API effectively.

Through these advanced patterns and techniques, organizations can enhance their federated GraphQL systems, addressing complex use cases and ensuring that their architecture remains robust, scalable, and maintainable. By leveraging custom directives, sophisticated schema stitching, effective inter-service communication, and advanced monitoring, developers can tackle the challenges of modern federated architectures and drive the successful implementation of GraphQL federation in their systems.

Emily was momentarily paralyzed by Lucas's confession. The words hung in the air between them, laden with the weight of unspoken emotions and unresolved tensions. Her heart raced, caught in the crossfire of her internal conflict. She had always known Lucas as her dependable friend, a source of encouragement and comfort. His revelation, however, turned that familiarity into something unfamiliar, and the boundaries of their relationship seemed to blur into an uncharted territory.

Lucas's eyes, usually so calm and steady, were now brimming with vulnerability. He looked at Emily with an earnestness that left no room for misinterpretation. He had laid bare his feelings, the protective friend now transformed into someone openly seeking something more profound. The intensity of his confession seemed to cast a spotlight on the very feelings Emily had been trying to ignore.

The atmosphere in the rehearsal space was thick with tension. Tyler's absence, a blessing and a curse, allowed the space to become a crucible for Emily's decision. Her mind raced through the past weeks, replaying every interaction with Lucas and Tyler. Lucas's protective nature, his encouragement to audition, and his growing presence in her life all started to coalesce into something more significant. Yet, Tyler's charm and attention had also been hard to ignore, complicating her feelings further.

Emily took a deep breath, attempting to regain her composure. The silence stretched, and she could see Lucas's hopeful gaze wavering as the seconds passed. It was clear that his confession had taken a toll on him, his bravado replaced by a quiet desperation.

"I... I don't know what to say," Emily finally managed, her voice trembling slightly. "I never realized you felt this way."

Lucas nodded, his expression a mixture of relief and apprehension. "I didn't want to make things awkward between us. I just couldn't keep it in any longer. I care about you, Emily, and it's been hard to watch Tyler getting so close to you. I just needed you to know how I feel."

Emily's mind swirled with conflicting emotions. The idea of losing Lucas as a friend was terrifying, but the thought of exploring a deeper relationship with him was equally daunting. She had always valued their friendship, and the potential for romantic involvement was both exciting and intimidating.

As she struggled to find the right words, Lucas's gaze fell to the floor, his shoulders slumping slightly. The vulnerability he displayed only made Emily's internal struggle more pronounced. She knew that whatever her response, it would forever alter the dynamics of their relationship.

"I value our friendship so much," Emily began slowly, her voice steadying. "And I've been thinking about everything that's happened lately. Tyler's been pushing me, and I've been confused about what I want. I don't want to hurt you, Lucas, but I also need to figure out what's right for me."

Lucas looked up, his eyes searching hers for some sign of hope. "I understand if you need time to think. I just wanted you to know where I stand."

The sincerity in his voice was palpable, and Emily could see how much courage it had taken for him to express his feelings. She realized that her own feelings were still unclear, a jumble of emotions she needed to untangle before making any decisions. The space between them felt charged, as if every word, every gesture, held the potential to shift their relationship in a new direction.

"I appreciate you being honest with me," Emily said softly. "And I promise I'll take the time I need to sort through my feelings. But right now, I need to focus on the play and everything that's going on."

Lucas nodded, a mixture of understanding and disappointment crossing his face. "Of course. I'll be here, whatever you decide."

The rehearsal resumed, but the atmosphere had irrevocably changed. The playful banter and lighthearted moments that once defined their interactions were now replaced by an undercurrent of unspoken words and suppressed emotions. Emily threw herself into her role with renewed intensity, trying to channel her confusion and anxiety into her performance. The lines and cues that had once seemed mundane now took on a new significance, each one a way to escape her swirling thoughts.

Lucas, for his part, remained professional during rehearsals. His interactions with Emily were marked by a respectful distance, though the occasional glance or subtle gesture betrayed the emotional turmoil he was experiencing. The chemistry between them, both on and off stage, was undeniable, adding a layer of complexity to their performances that neither could ignore.

As the days passed, Emily found herself increasingly drawn into the play's narrative, her personal struggles weaving into the fabric of her character. The intensity of the rehearsals became a double-edged sword, providing an outlet for her emotions while also magnifying the strain between her and Lucas.

The opening night of the play loomed closer, and with it came the culmination of the tension and unresolved feelings. Emily knew that whatever decision she made about her relationship with Lucas would be influenced by the outcome of the play. As she prepared to step into the spotlight, she couldn't shake the feeling that the resolution to her personal conflict was as imminent as the curtain rising on the stage.

Emily took a deep breath, attempting to navigate the turbulent waters of her emotions. The prospect of opening up to Lucas in a way that transcended their long-standing friendship was daunting. Yet, the sincerity in Lucas's eyes and the weight of his confession urged her to confront her own feelings. She had to consider whether she could envision their relationship evolving beyond friendship, or if maintaining their current bond was more prudent.

"I need some time to think," Emily said softly, her gaze falling to the floor as she spoke. "This is a lot to process, and I want to be fair to both you and myself."

Lucas's shoulders sagged slightly, but he managed a nod of understanding. "Of course. Take all the time you need. I didn't mean to rush you into anything."

With that, Lucas turned and walked away, his footsteps echoing in the empty rehearsal space. Emily watched him leave, her heart aching with a mixture of sympathy and confusion. She was left alone, grappling with the realization that her feelings for Lucas were more complex than she had previously acknowledged. Yet, she also knew that the attention she was receiving from Tyler had complicated her emotions further, making her decision even more challenging.

As the days passed and the play's opening night approached, Emily tried to focus on her performance, but her thoughts kept drifting back to Lucas and Tyler. Each interaction with Tyler seemed to highlight the growing divide between them, and his persistent advances were starting to wear on her nerves. She was increasingly uncomfortable with his behavior but was unsure how to address it without escalating the situation further.

Meanwhile, Lucas remained a constant source of support. His encouragement and understanding were a comfort, and as the rehearsals continued, Emily found herself leaning on him more than ever. Their shared experiences and moments of laughter helped to ease the tension between them, but the underlying issue remained unresolved.

One evening, as Emily sat alone in the empty theater, she heard the familiar sound of footsteps approaching. It was Lucas. He had come to check on her, sensing perhaps that she needed a friend.

"Hey," he said softly, taking a seat beside her. "Mind if I join you for a bit?"

Emily looked at him, her expression a mixture of gratitude

and uncertainty. "I'd actually like that," she replied. "I've been thinking a lot lately and could use some company."

Lucas smiled gently, his presence a comforting balm to her troubled mind. They sat in silence for a while, the soft hum of the theater's ventilation system their only company. Emily could feel the weight of her decision pressing on her, but Lucas's calm demeanor provided a sense of clarity she had been missing.

Finally, Emily broke the silence. "Lucas, I've been thinking about what you said. It's not easy for me to sort out my feelings, especially with everything that's been happening."

Lucas turned to face her, his eyes full of understanding. "I know it's a lot to take in. I just want you to know that whatever you decide, I value our friendship above all else. I don't want to put you in a position where you feel pressured."

Emily nodded, her heart swelling with appreciation for his consideration. "That means a lot to me. I've realized that my feelings for you are stronger than I thought, but I'm still not sure what the right path is."

Lucas reached out, gently squeezing her hand. "Whatever you decide, we'll figure it out together. I just want you to be happy."

As the days continued to blend together, Emily felt a growing sense of resolve. She began to understand that her feelings for Lucas were genuine and that their friendship had the potential to evolve into something deeper, but she needed to approach this transition thoughtfully.

The night of the play arrived, and the excitement was palpable. Backstage was a whirlwind of activity as cast members prepared for their performances. Emily and Lucas exchanged encouraging glances, their bond evident in the ease of their interactions. Despite the pressure of their roles, they found solace in their shared commitment to the play and to each other.

As they took the stage, Emily felt a renewed sense of confidence. The performance went off without a hitch, the audience's applause a testament to their hard work. The final curtain call was met with cheers, and Emily, amidst the chaos, found herself reflecting on the journey she had undertaken.

Backstage, amidst the congratulatory chaos, Emily and Lucas found a quiet corner to talk. The play had been a success, but the most significant achievement for Emily was coming to terms with her feelings.

"Lucas," Emily began, her voice steady, "I've thought a lot about what you said. I want to be honest with you. I have feelings for you, too. But I think we need to take things slowly and see where this leads us. I don't want to rush anything."

Lucas's face lit up with a warm smile, his eyes reflecting the relief and happiness he felt. "I'm glad to hear that. We'll take it one step at a time, together."

As they stood there, surrounded by the remnants of the evening's performance, Emily felt a sense of peace. She knew that navigating this new phase of their relationship would require patience and understanding, but she was ready to embrace the possibilities. The future was uncertain, but with Lucas by her side, she felt confident that they could face whatever came their way.

CHAPTER 7: MANAGING FEDERATION IN LARGE TEAMS

Scaling federation often involves navigating the complexities that arise when multiple contributors are involved in managing and evolving schemas. As teams grow, so do the challenges associated with maintaining a coherent and efficient federated architecture. This chapter explores best practices for managing federated schemas in a team environment, focusing on versioning strategies, documentation, and coordination to ensure seamless collaboration across large teams.

When multiple team members contribute to a federated schema, version control becomes essential. Implementing a robust versioning strategy allows teams to track changes, manage updates, and ensure compatibility between different schema versions. One effective approach is to adopt semantic versioning, which uses a versioning scheme composed of major, minor, and patch numbers. Major versions signify breaking changes that are not backward-compatible, minor versions indicate new features or improvements that are backward-compatible, and patch versions are used for backward-compatible bug fixes.

Semantic versioning provides a clear and consistent method for communicating changes and their impact on the schema. This practice not only helps in maintaining compatibility but also facilitates easier troubleshooting and rollback if issues arise. To implement semantic versioning, teams should establish a clear process for version increments and ensure that all contributors adhere to this process when making schema changes.

Documentation is another critical aspect of managing federation in large teams. Comprehensive and up-to-date documentation serves as a reference for all team members, providing clarity on schema design, usage guidelines, and change histories. It is important to document not only the schema itself but also the rationale behind design decisions, the relationships between different schema components, and any specific guidelines for extending or modifying the schema.

Good documentation practices involve maintaining an accessible and organized repository of information. Tools such as schema definition language (SDL) comments, markdown files, and documentation generators can be employed to create and maintain detailed schema documentation. Additionally, incorporating examples and use cases into the documentation can help team members understand the practical applications of the schema and facilitate more effective development and troubleshooting.

Effective coordination among team members is essential for managing federated schemas in a large team environment. This includes establishing clear communication channels, defining roles and responsibilities, and implementing processes for reviewing and approving changes. Regular meetings and collaboration tools can help keep everyone aligned and ensure that updates are communicated promptly.

One useful practice is to set up a schema review process, where changes to the schema are reviewed by a designated group of stakeholders before being merged into the main codebase. This review process helps ensure that changes are thoroughly vetted, adhere to established guidelines, and do not introduce unintended issues. Additionally, it provides an opportunity for team members to discuss and address any potential conflicts or inconsistencies in the schema.

In a federated architecture, where different teams or individuals may be responsible for distinct parts of the schema, it is crucial to establish clear boundaries and interfaces between different schema components. This involves defining how different parts of the schema interact, managing dependencies, and ensuring that changes in one part of the schema do not negatively impact other parts. Clear interface definitions and well-defined protocols for interaction can help prevent issues and facilitate smoother integration.

To maintain coherence across multiple contributors, it is also important to enforce consistent coding and design standards. Establishing guidelines for schema design, naming conventions, and code formatting can help ensure that contributions from different team members are consistent and compatible. Implementing automated linting and validation tools can assist in maintaining these standards and catching potential issues early in the development process.

Managing federation in large teams also requires a proactive approach to addressing potential conflicts and resolving issues. This involves establishing procedures for handling merge conflicts, coordinating schema updates, and addressing any discrepancies that may arise. Regularly reviewing and refactoring the schema can help identify and address potential issues before they escalate.

In summary, managing federated schemas in large teams involves a combination of strategic versioning, thorough documentation, effective coordination, and adherence to design standards. By implementing these best practices, teams can navigate the complexities of federation and maintain a coherent and efficient schema, even as they scale and evolve.

schema are reviewed and approved by peers before being integrated into the main codebase. This review process helps catch potential issues early, ensures adherence to established guidelines, and maintains consistency across the schema. It also fosters a culture of collaboration and knowledge sharing among team members, which is crucial for managing complex federated schemas.

In addition to formal review processes, establishing clear guidelines for schema contributions is essential. These guidelines should cover aspects such as coding standards, naming conventions, and best practices for extending or modifying schemas. By setting these standards, teams can ensure that contributions are uniform and compatible with the overall schema architecture. Clear guidelines also help new team members get up to speed quickly and contribute effectively.

Another key aspect of managing federated schemas in large teams is handling schema evolution. As the system evolves, the schema must adapt to new requirements and changes in the underlying data models. A well-defined strategy for managing schema changes is crucial to avoid disruptions and ensure smooth transitions. This involves planning for schema migrations, versioning strategies, and backward compatibility.

When introducing changes to the schema, it is important to consider how these changes will impact existing services and consumers of the schema. Planning for backward compatibility involves ensuring that new schema versions do not break existing functionality. Techniques such as deprecating old fields or providing alternative solutions can help ease the transition for services relying on the previous schema version.

Effective schema evolution also involves maintaining a clear change log that documents the history of changes and the reasons behind them. This log serves as a reference for team members and stakeholders, providing transparency and facilitating understanding of how the schema has evolved over time. It can also help in troubleshooting issues and ensuring that changes align with the overall goals of the federated architecture.

Another crucial element of managing federation in large teams is establishing strong communication channels. Regular and structured communication helps coordinate efforts, align objectives, and address any challenges that arise. This can be achieved through regular team meetings, status updates, and collaborative platforms that facilitate information sharing and discussion.

In addition to communication, leveraging automation tools can significantly enhance the management of federated schemas. Tools such as automated testing frameworks, continuous integration pipelines, and deployment automation can streamline processes and reduce the likelihood of errors. Automated testing ensures that changes to the schema do not introduce regressions or issues, while continuous integration and deployment tools facilitate the seamless integration and delivery of schema updates.

Ultimately, successful management of federated schemas in large teams requires a combination of well-defined processes, clear documentation, effective communication, and the right tools. By implementing these practices, teams can navigate the complexities of scaling federation, maintain a coherent schema, and ensure that their federated architecture remains robust and adaptable to changing requirements.

integration and updates. By incorporating these tools into the development workflow, teams can ensure that schema changes are rigorously tested and integrated with minimal manual intervention, thus reducing the risk of errors and enhancing overall efficiency.

Maintaining schema consistency across multiple contributors also requires effective conflict resolution strategies. In large teams, conflicts may arise when multiple members work on overlapping parts of the schema or introduce competing changes. To address these issues, it is essential to establish clear protocols for resolving conflicts. This often involves collaborative discussions, where contributors negotiate and agree on the best course of action for integrating their changes. Utilizing version control systems with robust merge capabilities can facilitate this process, allowing for the effective management of concurrent changes.

Additionally, adopting a modular approach to schema design can help manage complexity and improve maintainability. By breaking down the schema into smaller, more manageable components or modules, teams can work on different parts of the schema independently while maintaining a clear overall structure. This modular approach not only enhances collaboration but also simplifies testing and deployment, as changes to individual modules can be isolated and evaluated before being integrated into the main schema.

To further enhance schema management, it is beneficial to establish a governance framework that defines roles and responsibilities for schema management. This framework should outline who is responsible for different aspects of the schema, such as design, review, and maintenance. Clear governance ensures accountability and helps prevent overlaps or gaps in responsibilities, contributing to a more organized and efficient schema management process.

In addition to governance, fostering a culture of continuous learning and improvement is crucial for managing federated schemas effectively. Encouraging team members to stay updated on best practices, emerging tools, and evolving methodologies can contribute to the overall success of the schema management process. This can be achieved through regular training sessions, workshops, and knowledge-sharing initiatives.

Finally, establishing metrics and performance indicators can provide valuable insights into the effectiveness of the schema management process. Metrics such as the frequency of schema changes, the time taken to resolve conflicts, and the number of issues reported can help assess the efficiency and effectiveness of the management practices in place. By regularly reviewing these metrics, teams can identify areas for improvement and make data-driven decisions to enhance their schema management strategies.

In summary, managing federated schemas in large teams requires a multifaceted approach that encompasses versioning strategies, documentation, coordination, and conflict resolution. By implementing best practices such as semantic versioning, comprehensive documentation, regular schema reviews, and modular design, teams can maintain a coherent and efficient schema architecture. Leveraging automation tools and establishing clear governance frameworks further enhance the management process, while fostering a culture of continuous learning and using performance metrics ensure ongoing improvement. Through these practices, teams can navigate the complexities of federation and achieve successful collaboration across multiple contributors.

CHAPTER 8: PERFORMANCE OPTIMIZATION FOR FEDERATED GRAPHQL

Performance is a critical factor in federated GraphQL architectures, where efficiency directly impacts user experience and system scalability. This chapter will delve into the various techniques and strategies essential for optimizing the performance of federated schemas. By focusing on query optimization, caching strategies, and monitoring, you will learn how to enhance the efficiency of your federated services and ensure they perform optimally under load.

In a federated GraphQL system, where multiple services collaborate to fulfill queries, performance optimization begins with efficient query design. One of the primary considerations is query optimization, which involves refining how queries are structured and executed to minimize response times and resource consumption. Effective query optimization requires a deep understanding of the underlying data models and how queries interact with these models.

One common approach to optimizing queries is through batching and deduplication. Batching involves grouping multiple requests into a single query, which reduces the number of round-trips between the client and server. This can significantly improve performance, especially in scenarios where multiple related pieces of data are requested. Deduplication, on the other hand, addresses redundant queries by ensuring that the same request is not processed multiple times. By combining these techniques, you can reduce unnecessary load on your federated services and improve overall efficiency.

Another important aspect of query optimization is the use of efficient data fetching strategies. Techniques such as data loader libraries can help manage and optimize the process of fetching data from various services. Data loaders are designed to batch and cache requests, reducing the number of redundant calls and improving response times. By incorporating data loaders into your federated GraphQL setup, you can enhance the efficiency of data retrieval and processing.

Caching strategies play a crucial role in optimizing performance in federated GraphQL systems. Caching involves storing frequently accessed data temporarily to reduce the need for repeated data retrieval. Implementing caching can significantly reduce response times and alleviate the load on backend services. There are several levels at which caching can be applied, including client-side caching, server-side caching, and intermediate caching layers.

Client-side caching allows the client to store and reuse data from previous queries. This can reduce the frequency of network requests and improve the responsiveness of the application. Server-side caching, on the other hand, involves storing query results on the server to avoid redundant data fetching. Intermediate caching layers, such as reverse proxies or dedicated caching servers, can also be used to cache responses and further optimize performance.

Effective cache management is essential to ensure that cached data remains up-to-date and relevant. Implementing cache invalidation strategies, such as time-based expiration or event-based invalidation, can help maintain the accuracy of cached data. Additionally, monitoring cache performance and hit rates can provide insights into the effectiveness of your caching strategies and help identify opportunities for further optimization.

Monitoring and performance analysis are crucial for maintaining and enhancing the performance of federated GraphQL services. By continuously monitoring the system, you can identify bottlenecks, track performance metrics, and diagnose issues before they impact users. Key performance indicators (KPIs) such as response times, error rates, and throughput can provide valuable insights into the health and efficiency of your federated services.

Implementing monitoring tools and dashboards can help visualize performance data and facilitate real-time analysis. Tools such as application performance management (APM) solutions, log aggregators, and metrics collectors can provide comprehensive visibility into system performance and help identify areas for improvement. Regular performance reviews and analyses should be conducted to ensure that the system remains responsive and scalable under varying load conditions.

In summary, optimizing performance in federated GraphQL architectures involves a combination of query optimization, caching strategies, and monitoring. By implementing techniques such as batching, deduplication, efficient data fetching, and effective caching, you can enhance the efficiency of your federated services and ensure optimal performance. Continuous monitoring and performance analysis will provide valuable insights and help maintain a high level of performance as your system scales and evolves.

Intermediate caching layers, such as those provided by edge servers or API gateways, can further enhance performance by caching data closer to the client. This reduces latency and minimizes the need for repeated queries to backend services. By strategically placing these caches, you can improve the overall response time of your federated GraphQL system and reduce the load on your core services.

While caching is a powerful tool for performance optimization, it must be carefully managed to avoid potential pitfalls such as stale or inconsistent data. Implementing cache invalidation strategies is essential to ensure that cached data remains up-to-date and consistent with the source of truth. Techniques for cache invalidation include setting expiration times for cached entries, using cache busting mechanisms, and employing real-time data synchronization methods. Properly managing cache lifecycles helps maintain the integrity of the data while maximizing the benefits of caching.

In addition to query optimization and caching, effective performance monitoring is critical for maintaining optimal performance in federated GraphQL systems. Monitoring involves tracking various metrics and performance indicators to identify potential issues and areas for improvement. Key metrics to monitor include query response times, request rates, error rates, and resource utilization.

Tools for monitoring federated GraphQL systems typically provide insights into the performance of individual services, as well as the overall system. These tools can generate detailed reports and visualizations, helping teams identify bottlenecks and diagnose performance issues. By regularly analyzing monitoring data, teams can make informed decisions about where to focus their optimization efforts and ensure that their federated services continue to perform efficiently.

Another important aspect of performance optimization is load testing. Load testing involves simulating various levels of traffic to evaluate how the system performs under different conditions. By conducting load tests, you can assess the system's capacity, identify performance bottlenecks, and determine how well it handles peak loads. This proactive approach helps ensure that your federated GraphQL system can handle real-world traffic and maintain performance under high demand.

Load testing should be an integral part of the development and deployment process. By incorporating load tests into your continuous integration and deployment pipelines, you can identify potential performance issues early in the development cycle. This allows for timely adjustments and improvements, reducing the likelihood of performance problems in production environments.

Furthermore, optimizing the performance of federated GraphQL systems requires a comprehensive approach that encompasses both backend and frontend considerations. On the backend, optimizing the performance of individual services and their interactions is crucial. This includes efficient data retrieval, processing, and handling of service requests. On the frontend, optimizing how queries are sent and responses are processed can also impact overall performance.

For backend optimization, consider implementing techniques such as query optimization within individual services, optimizing database queries, and leveraging indexing to speed up data retrieval. Additionally, efficient service orchestration and load balancing can help distribute the load evenly across services and improve system performance.

On the frontend, optimizing how queries are constructed and minimizing the amount of data transferred can enhance performance. Techniques such as query batching, minimizing data payloads, and optimizing client-side processing can contribute to a more responsive user experience.

In summary, optimizing performance in federated GraphQL architectures involves a multifaceted approach that includes query optimization, effective caching strategies, and comprehensive monitoring. By implementing these techniques and strategies, you can ensure that your federated services perform efficiently under load, providing a responsive and reliable experience for users. Regular monitoring, load testing, and performance tuning are essential for maintaining optimal performance and addressing any issues that arise as the system scales and evolves.

on the backend, optimizing database queries and ensuring efficient data access patterns are essential. Indexing frequently queried fields, optimizing SQL queries, and employing database partitioning techniques can improve response times and reduce the load on your data sources. In addition, utilizing asynchronous processing and background tasks for non-critical operations can free up resources for handling real-time queries more efficiently.

On the frontend, ensuring efficient data fetching and rendering practices is equally important. Avoiding excessive or redundant queries by employing client-side query optimization techniques can reduce the overall load on the federated GraphQL services. Leveraging tools and libraries that support efficient data management and state handling, such as React Query or Apollo Client, can enhance the performance of client applications. Implementing techniques like lazy loading and pagination can also improve the user experience by loading data incrementally and only when necessary.

Another consideration for performance optimization is the design and architecture of the federated schema itself. Schema design should prioritize efficient data access patterns and minimize unnecessary data fetching. Implementing schema stitching and federated query planning effectively can help optimize how data is retrieved and aggregated from different services. By carefully designing the schema to align with the needs of the application and the capabilities of the backend services, you can reduce the complexity and improve the performance of the federated GraphQL system.

In addition to these technical measures, fostering a culture of performance awareness within the development team is crucial. Encouraging team members to consider performance implications when designing and implementing features can lead to more optimized solutions. Regularly reviewing performance metrics, conducting performance audits, and sharing insights and best practices across the team can help maintain a focus on performance throughout the development lifecycle.

Lastly, staying informed about advancements in GraphQL technology and best practices is vital for ongoing performance optimization. The field of GraphQL is continuously evolving, with new tools, techniques, and standards emerging regularly. By keeping abreast of these developments and incorporating relevant advancements into your performance optimization strategies, you can ensure that your federated GraphQL system remains efficient and scalable in the face of changing demands and technologies.

In summary, optimizing performance in federated GraphQL architectures requires a multifaceted approach that encompasses query optimization, caching strategies, performance monitoring, and effective schema design. By implementing these strategies and maintaining a focus on performance at every stage of development, you can ensure that your federated services operate efficiently and effectively under load, delivering a seamless and responsive experience to users.

CHAPTER 9: SECURITY CONSIDERATIONS FOR FEDERATED GRAPHQL

Security is paramount when dealing with distributed systems, and federated GraphQL architectures are no exception. In a federated GraphQL setup, where multiple services collaborate to provide a unified API, ensuring robust security measures is crucial to protect sensitive data and maintain the integrity of the system. This chapter explores security considerations specific to federated GraphQL, focusing on authentication, authorization, and data protection. We will discuss strategies to secure your federated services and safeguard against potential vulnerabilities.

Authentication is the process of verifying the identity of users or systems accessing your federated GraphQL services. In a federated environment, authentication must be managed consistently across all services to ensure that only legitimate users can access the system. One common approach to authentication in federated GraphQL systems is to use token-based authentication, such as JSON Web Tokens (JWT). Tokens are issued by an authentication service and included in requests to prove the identity of the user. Each service within the federation can validate the token to ensure that it is legitimate and has not expired.

When implementing token-based authentication, it is essential to handle token issuance and validation securely. Tokens should be signed and encrypted to prevent tampering and ensure confidentiality. Additionally, token expiration should be managed to limit the window of opportunity for unauthorized access. Implementing token refresh mechanisms can provide a balance between security and user convenience, allowing users to maintain their session without exposing the system to undue risk.

Authorization, on the other hand, involves determining what actions or resources authenticated users are permitted to access. In a federated GraphQL system, authorization must be enforced consistently across all services. This requires a unified approach to defining and managing user roles and permissions. One effective method for handling authorization is to implement a centralized authorization service that maintains and enforces access control policies. This service can be queried by each federated service to determine whether a user has the appropriate permissions for a given operation.

To implement fine-grained authorization, it is important to design access control policies that align with the specific requirements of your application. This may involve defining roles and permissions at various levels, such as individual fields or types within the GraphQL schema. By incorporating these policies into your federated schema, you can ensure that users have appropriate access based on their roles and the context of their requests.

Data protection is another critical aspect of securing federated GraphQL systems. Protecting sensitive data involves implementing measures to safeguard data both in transit and at rest. For data in transit, it is essential to use secure communication channels, such as HTTPS, to encrypt data as it is transmitted between clients and services. This prevents unauthorized parties from intercepting or tampering with the data during transmission.

For data at rest, encryption should be applied to protect sensitive information stored within databases or other storage systems. Employing strong encryption algorithms and managing encryption keys securely are fundamental practices for ensuring data confidentiality. Additionally, access to encrypted data should be restricted to authorized personnel or systems, and regular audits should be conducted to verify compliance with security policies.

Implementing logging and monitoring is also crucial for detecting and responding to security incidents. By maintaining comprehensive logs of access and operations, you can monitor for unusual or unauthorized activities that may indicate a security breach. Real-time monitoring tools can alert you to potential threats, allowing for prompt investigation and remediation. Ensuring that logs are protected and stored securely is essential to prevent tampering or unauthorized access.

Another important consideration is securing the federation layer itself. In a federated GraphQL architecture, the gateway or federation service acts as a central point of interaction between clients and the underlying services. Securing this layer involves implementing measures such as rate limiting, input validation, and protection against common web vulnerabilities like cross-site scripting (XSS) and SQL injection. By securing the federation layer, you can mitigate risks that may arise from malicious requests or attacks targeting the central coordination point of your system.

In addition to these technical measures, fostering a security-aware culture within your development team is vital. Regular security training, awareness programs, and adherence to security best practices can help ensure that all team members are vigilant about potential threats and follow secure coding practices. Conducting regular security assessments and penetration testing can also help identify vulnerabilities and assess the effectiveness of your security measures.

In conclusion, securing federated GraphQL systems involves a comprehensive approach that encompasses authentication, authorization, data protection, and monitoring. By implementing robust security measures and maintaining a focus on security best practices, you can safeguard your federated services and protect sensitive data from potential threats. This proactive approach not only enhances the security of your system but also ensures the trust and confidence of your users and stakeholders.

Data protection is a critical aspect of securing federated GraphQL services, as it involves safeguarding sensitive information from unauthorized access and ensuring data integrity. In a federated system, where data is distributed across multiple services, implementing comprehensive data protection strategies is essential to prevent data breaches and ensure compliance with regulatory requirements.

One key measure for data protection is encryption. Encrypting data at rest and in transit ensures that sensitive information is secure, even if unauthorized access occurs. For data in transit, using Transport Layer Security (TLS) encrypts the communication between clients and servers, protecting against eavesdropping and man-in-the-middle attacks. For data at rest, employing encryption mechanisms provided by database systems or file storage solutions can help protect data from unauthorized access, even if physical security measures are breached.

Another important consideration is implementing input

validation and sanitization to protect against injection attacks, such as SQL injection or GraphQL-specific attacks. Input validation involves ensuring that data received from clients is checked for correctness and validity before it is processed or stored. This includes validating data types, lengths, and formats, as well as rejecting any unexpected or malicious inputs. Sanitization involves cleaning or escaping data to remove any potentially harmful content before it is included in queries or responses. By incorporating robust input validation and sanitization practices, you can reduce the risk of attacks that exploit vulnerabilities in your federated services.

Moreover, implementing proper error handling is essential to prevent information leakage that could assist attackers in exploiting vulnerabilities. Error messages should be generic and not disclose sensitive information about the underlying system or data. Detailed error logs should be kept secure and only accessible to authorized personnel to aid in troubleshooting and ensuring that any issues are addressed promptly without exposing system internals to potential attackers.

Additionally, ensuring proper access controls at the service level is crucial for protecting sensitive data within a federated architecture. Each service within the federation should enforce its own security measures to restrict access to sensitive data based on user roles and permissions. This involves defining and applying security policies at the service level, including ensuring that only authorized services can access or modify data. Implementing role-based access control (RBAC) or attribute-based access control (ABAC) can help manage permissions effectively and ensure that each service adheres to consistent security practices.

Regular security audits and vulnerability assessments are also essential to maintaining the security of your federated

GraphQL system. Conducting periodic security reviews helps identify and address potential weaknesses or vulnerabilities in the system. These audits should include assessing the security of authentication and authorization mechanisms, reviewing data protection practices, and evaluating the overall resilience of the system against common attack vectors. By staying proactive and addressing security issues as they arise, you can minimize the risk of security breaches and ensure that your federated services remain secure over time.

Finally, promoting a security-aware culture within your development team is crucial for maintaining a strong security posture. Encouraging team members to stay informed about security best practices, participate in security training, and adopt a security-first mindset can help ensure that security considerations are integrated into every aspect of the development lifecycle. By fostering an environment where security is a priority, you can enhance the overall security of your federated GraphQL system and better protect sensitive data against evolving threats.

services. Regular security audits involve systematically reviewing your federated architecture for potential vulnerabilities and compliance with security best practices. These audits can help identify weaknesses, assess the effectiveness of existing security measures, and ensure that security policies are being followed. Vulnerability assessments involve testing your system against known threats and security flaws to discover potential risks before they can be exploited.

Another critical aspect of securing federated GraphQL systems is managing secrets and sensitive configurations. Secret management involves securely storing and accessing credentials, API keys, and other sensitive information required by your services. Using secret management solutions, such as environment variables, secret vaults, or encrypted configuration files, can help ensure that sensitive data is protected and only accessible to authorized components. It is also important to rotate secrets regularly and audit access to prevent unauthorized usage.

Implementing logging and monitoring practices is vital for maintaining security in a federated environment. Effective logging involves capturing detailed records of access, changes, and other significant events within your services. These logs are invaluable for detecting suspicious activity, diagnosing security incidents, and providing forensic evidence in the event of a breach. Monitoring systems should be configured to alert administrators to potential security threats, unusual patterns of behavior, or system anomalies. By actively monitoring and analyzing these logs, you can promptly respond to security incidents and mitigate potential risks.

Security considerations for federated GraphQL also extend to managing dependencies and third-party integrations. External libraries, tools, and services can introduce vulnerabilities if not properly vetted and maintained. Regularly updating dependencies to address security patches and vulnerabilities is crucial for maintaining a secure environment. Additionally, thoroughly evaluating third-party integrations for security risks and ensuring they comply with your security policies can prevent potential exploits from affecting your federated services.

Furthermore, ensuring that security practices are integrated into the development lifecycle is essential for long-term security. Implementing security practices during the design, development, and deployment phases of your federated services helps identify and address security concerns early in the process. This includes conducting threat modeling, performing security reviews, and incorporating security testing into your continuous integration and delivery pipelines. By embedding security into your development practices, you can create a more resilient and secure federated GraphQL system.

Lastly, fostering a security-aware culture within your development team is crucial for maintaining robust security practices. Regular training and awareness programs can help team members understand security risks, best practices, and their roles in protecting the federated architecture. Encouraging a proactive approach to security and promoting a culture of vigilance can enhance the overall security posture of your federated GraphQL system.

In conclusion, securing federated GraphQL systems involves a comprehensive approach that encompasses authentication, authorization, data protection, and effective management of secrets, logging, and monitoring. By implementing robust security measures, conducting regular audits, and integrating security practices into the development lifecycle, you can safeguard your federated services against potential threats and ensure the protection of sensitive data. Through continuous vigilance and a commitment to security best practices, you can maintain a secure and resilient federated GraphQL architecture.

CHAPTER 10: ERROR HANDLING AND DEBUGGING IN FEDERATED GRAPHQL

Error handling and debugging in federated GraphQL environments present unique challenges due to the distributed nature of the system. With multiple services contributing to a single GraphQL schema, identifying and resolving issues can become more complex compared to monolithic architectures. This chapter provides strategies for effectively managing errors and debugging issues within federated GraphQL systems, focusing on techniques for logging, tracing, and debugging to ensure robust error management.

One of the primary strategies for handling errors in a federated GraphQL environment is implementing comprehensive logging practices. Effective logging involves capturing detailed and relevant information about the system's operations, including errors, warnings, and other significant events. In a federated setup, each service should have its own logging mechanism to record events that occur within that service. This ensures that when issues arise, logs from all relevant services can be reviewed to diagnose and resolve problems.

To enhance the effectiveness of logging, it is important to establish a consistent logging format and include contextual information that can aid in troubleshooting. This may include timestamps, service identifiers, request identifiers, and detailed error messages. By maintaining a standardized logging format, logs from different services can be more easily correlated, and issues can be tracked across the federated system.

In addition to logging, implementing distributed tracing is a valuable technique for debugging federated GraphQL systems. Distributed tracing involves tracking the flow of requests as they traverse through various services in the federation. This provides visibility into how requests are handled, where delays or errors occur, and how different services interact with each other. By using tracing tools, such as OpenTelemetry or Jaeger, you can capture and visualize traces that show the path of a request through the federated system, allowing for more effective identification of bottlenecks and issues.

To facilitate distributed tracing, it is essential to instrument your federated services to generate trace data. This typically involves integrating tracing libraries or agents into your services and configuring them to capture relevant data about incoming and outgoing requests. The collected trace data can then be analyzed to understand the performance and behavior of the system, providing insights into areas that may require optimization or troubleshooting.

Another critical aspect of debugging in federated GraphQL environments is implementing error handling mechanisms within each service. Proper error handling involves catching and managing exceptions or errors that occur during the processing of requests. Each service should be designed to handle errors gracefully, providing informative error messages and ensuring that the system remains operational even in the presence of errors.

When designing error handling mechanisms, it is important to consider how errors are propagated between services. In a federated system, errors may need to be communicated back to the client in a structured manner. GraphQL provides a standardized approach for reporting errors through its response format, which includes an `errors` field that can be used to convey details about the error encountered. By leveraging this approach, you can ensure that clients receive meaningful error information and can handle errors appropriately on their end.

Furthermore, implementing health checks and monitoring can help proactively identify and address issues before they impact the system. Health checks involve regularly assessing the status of your federated services to ensure they are functioning correctly. Monitoring tools can track metrics such as response times, error rates, and resource utilization, providing visibility into the overall health of the system. By setting up alerts based on these metrics, you can quickly respond to anomalies or performance degradation and take corrective action as needed.

To effectively manage and resolve issues in a federated GraphQL environment, it is also important to have a well-defined incident response process. This process should outline the steps to be taken when an error or issue is detected, including how to investigate, diagnose, and resolve the problem. Having a clear incident response plan ensures that issues are addressed in a systematic and efficient manner, minimizing the impact on the system and users.

In summary, error handling and debugging in federated GraphQL systems require a multifaceted approach that includes effective logging, distributed tracing, robust error handling, and proactive monitoring. By implementing these strategies, you can enhance the ability to identify and resolve issues within a federated environment, ensuring that your GraphQL services remain reliable and performant.

process of requests. Each service should be designed to handle errors gracefully, providing informative error messages and maintaining the integrity of the system even when issues occur. Proper error handling involves categorizing errors based on their severity and impact, and implementing appropriate responses for each category. For example, client errors such as invalid queries should result in informative error messages that guide users on how to correct their requests, while server errors should trigger alerts for further investigation and remediation.

Implementing structured error responses is also essential in a federated GraphQL environment. A structured error response provides a consistent format for error messages, making it easier for clients to interpret and handle errors. This may involve including error codes, descriptions, and additional context that can assist in troubleshooting. By standardizing error responses, you can simplify error handling for clients and improve the overall user experience.

In addition to logging, tracing, and structured error handling, proactive monitoring is crucial for effective error management in federated GraphQL systems. Monitoring involves continuously tracking the performance and health of your services to detect issues before they escalate. This includes setting up alerts for unusual patterns, such as increased error rates or slow response times, that may indicate underlying problems.

Monitoring tools can provide real-time insights into the status of your federated services, helping you to identify and address issues quickly. Integrating monitoring tools with your logging and tracing systems can enhance visibility into the overall health of your federated GraphQL environment. This integration allows for more comprehensive analysis and quicker identification of root causes when issues arise.

Another important aspect of error handling and debugging is the use of automated testing and validation. Automated tests, including unit tests, integration tests, and end-to-end tests, can help ensure that your federated services are functioning as expected and can detect issues early in the development process. Incorporating automated tests into your continuous integration and deployment pipelines can help catch errors before they reach production, reducing the risk of downtime and improving overall system reliability.

In addition to automated tests, implementing validation mechanisms within your federated services can help catch and address issues related to data integrity and schema compliance. Validating input data, query structures, and responses against predefined schemas or rules can help prevent errors and ensure that your services adhere to expected standards.

Effective collaboration and communication among development teams also play a critical role in managing errors in federated GraphQL systems. In a federated environment, multiple teams are often responsible for different services, and coordinating efforts to resolve issues requires clear communication and collaboration. Establishing processes for sharing information about errors, incidents, and resolutions can help ensure that teams work together effectively to address and resolve issues.

Finally, learning from past incidents and continuously improving your error handling and debugging practices is essential for maintaining a robust federated GraphQL environment. Conducting post-incident reviews and retrospectives can provide valuable insights into the causes of errors and the effectiveness of your response strategies. By analyzing past incidents and incorporating lessons learned into your error management practices, you can enhance the resilience and reliability of your federated GraphQL system.

In summary, effective error handling and debugging in federated GraphQL environments involve a multifaceted approach that includes comprehensive logging, distributed tracing, structured error responses, proactive monitoring, automated testing, and collaborative communication. By implementing these strategies and continuously improving your practices, you can ensure robust error management and maintain the overall health and reliability of your federated GraphQL services.

a federated GraphQL environment, where multiple teams might be responsible for different services, establishing clear communication channels and protocols is essential. When issues arise, it is crucial to have mechanisms in place for effective collaboration and knowledge sharing among teams. This can involve setting up regular meetings or communication platforms where teams can discuss ongoing issues, share insights, and coordinate on resolutions. Implementing a shared documentation system that includes known issues, troubleshooting steps, and best practices can also facilitate smoother coordination and faster resolution of problems.

Another important aspect of managing errors in a federated system is handling versioning and backward compatibility. As federated services evolve, changes to the schema or service implementations can introduce potential issues. It is important to adopt versioning strategies that allow for smooth transitions and minimize disruptions. For example, adopting semantic versioning practices can help manage changes in a way that communicates the nature and impact of updates. Additionally, maintaining backward compatibility ensures that existing clients continue to function correctly even as services are updated.

When implementing versioning, it is beneficial to incorporate strategies such as deprecation warnings and phased rollouts. Deprecation warnings inform clients of upcoming changes and provide them with time to adapt. Phased rollouts allow for gradual deployment of changes, enabling teams to monitor the impact and address issues incrementally before a full-scale rollout.

Debugging in a federated GraphQL environment also requires careful consideration of schema design and query composition. Complex queries that span multiple services can introduce additional challenges when troubleshooting. Analyzing the schema and understanding the relationships between different services can provide valuable context for debugging. Tools that visualize schema dependencies and query execution paths can assist in identifying potential issues and optimizing query performance.

Integrating a robust debugging environment into your development workflow can further enhance your ability to manage errors. This might involve using development tools that support real-time debugging, such as GraphQL IDEs that provide query execution previews and error highlighting. Additionally, implementing local testing environments that simulate the federated setup can allow developers to test and debug their services in isolation before deploying changes to production.

As federated GraphQL systems scale and evolve, it is crucial to continuously refine and adapt your error handling and debugging strategies. Regularly reviewing and updating your practices based on lessons learned from previous incidents and ongoing performance metrics can help improve the robustness and resilience of your system. Staying informed about emerging tools and techniques in the GraphQL ecosystem can also provide new opportunities for enhancing error management and debugging capabilities.

In summary, effective error handling and debugging in federated GraphQL environments involve a combination of comprehensive logging, distributed tracing, structured error responses, proactive monitoring, automated testing, and collaborative communication. By implementing these strategies and continuously refining your approach, you can manage errors more effectively, ensuring the reliability and stability of your federated services.

CHAPTER 11: INTEGRATING FEDERATED GRAPHQL WITH EXISTING SYSTEMS

Integrating federated GraphQL with existing systems is a common challenge for many organizations. As businesses evolve and technology stacks become more complex, it is often necessary to bridge the gap between new federated architectures and legacy systems, REST APIs, and databases. This chapter provides a comprehensive guide to integrating federated GraphQL schemas with various existing systems, offering strategies and techniques for achieving seamless connectivity and interoperability.

Legacy systems, which may include older databases, services, or applications, often present unique integration challenges. These systems may not be designed to work with modern GraphQL APIs or may lack the flexibility required for real-time data access. To integrate legacy systems with federated GraphQL, one effective approach is to use a layer of abstraction that interfaces between the legacy system and the GraphQL federation.

One common method is to create an adapter or connector that

translates between the legacy system's data format and the GraphQL schema. This adapter serves as a bridge, translating GraphQL queries into the appropriate requests for the legacy system and converting the legacy system's responses into the format expected by GraphQL. By encapsulating the legacy system's interactions within this adapter, you can maintain a clean separation between the legacy system and the federated GraphQL environment, facilitating integration without requiring extensive modifications to the legacy system itself.

In cases where the legacy system provides a REST API, integrating it with a federated GraphQL setup can be approached by creating a GraphQL resolver that acts as a proxy to the REST API. This resolver handles GraphQL queries and invokes the appropriate REST API endpoints to retrieve data. The response from the REST API is then mapped to the GraphQL schema format and returned to the client. This approach allows you to leverage the existing REST API while providing a unified GraphQL interface for clients.

When integrating with REST APIs, it is important to consider aspects such as authentication, rate limiting, and error handling. The GraphQL resolver should manage these concerns by implementing mechanisms to handle authentication tokens, respecting rate limits imposed by the REST API, and translating REST API errors into appropriate GraphQL error responses. This ensures that the integration is robust and maintains the reliability and security of the overall system.

In addition to legacy systems and REST APIs, integrating federated GraphQL with databases is another crucial aspect of connecting disparate systems. When integrating with databases, particularly those that use SQL or NoSQL formats, you need to map database queries and operations to GraphQL queries and mutations. This often involves implementing data loaders or query builders that efficiently fetch and aggregate data from the database to fulfill GraphQL requests.

For relational databases, creating GraphQL resolvers that translate GraphQL queries into SQL queries is a common approach. This may involve constructing SQL queries dynamically based on the GraphQL request and handling any necessary joins or aggregations to return the desired data. For NoSQL databases, such as MongoDB, the process involves mapping GraphQL queries to database queries, taking into account the specific data structures and querying capabilities of the NoSQL database.

When working with databases, performance optimization is key. Techniques such as query batching, caching, and indexing can significantly improve the efficiency of data retrieval operations. Query batching allows for combining multiple database queries into a single request, reducing the number of round-trips between the application and the database. Caching frequently accessed data can minimize the need for repeated database queries, while indexing can improve query performance by optimizing data retrieval operations.

To ensure successful integration, it is also important to conduct thorough testing and validation. Testing should cover a range of scenarios, including edge cases and error conditions, to verify that the integration performs correctly and handles various inputs gracefully. Validation involves ensuring that the integrated system meets the functional and performance requirements of the federated GraphQL setup and that data consistency and accuracy are maintained.

Ultimately, integrating federated GraphQL with existing systems requires a thoughtful approach that considers the specific characteristics and constraints of each system. By employing strategies such as creating adapters, using GraphQL resolvers, mapping queries, and optimizing performance, you can effectively connect disparate systems and create a cohesive and efficient federated GraphQL environment.

databases, which often requires translating between different data models and query languages. In a federated GraphQL setup, each service may be backed by its own database, and integrating these databases into a cohesive GraphQL schema involves careful planning and execution.

One approach to integrating databases with federated GraphQL is to use data loaders or batch loaders to optimize data retrieval and reduce the number of database queries. Data loaders aggregate and batch requests to the database, minimizing the number of round-trips and improving performance. This technique is especially useful when dealing with complex queries that involve multiple related entities, as it can significantly reduce the overhead associated with fetching data from the database.

When integrating with relational databases, it is important to map the database schema to the GraphQL schema effectively. This often involves defining GraphQL types that correspond to database tables or views and implementing resolvers that translate GraphQL queries into SQL queries. By creating resolvers that handle data fetching and transformation, you can ensure that GraphQL queries are executed efficiently and return the appropriate results.

For non-relational databases, such as document stores or key-value stores, the integration process may involve different considerations. Non-relational databases often use flexible data models, and integrating them with GraphQL requires defining GraphQL types and resolvers that align with the database's data structure. This may involve using aggregation pipelines or custom queries to retrieve and format data according to the GraphQL schema.

Another important aspect of integrating federated GraphQL with databases is managing schema changes and ensuring compatibility. As your federated GraphQL schema evolves, it is crucial to ensure that changes to the schema do not disrupt the underlying database or existing integrations. Implementing versioning strategies for your GraphQL schema and coordinating schema updates with database changes can help maintain compatibility and avoid breaking changes.

In addition to integrating with databases, it is essential to address security considerations when connecting federated GraphQL with existing systems. Ensuring that data access and interactions are secure involves implementing proper authentication and authorization mechanisms, as well as securing data in transit and at rest. For example, when integrating with external REST APIs or databases, you should use secure connections (e.g., HTTPS) and validate input data to prevent security vulnerabilities.

Handling data consistency and synchronization is another critical aspect of integration. In a federated GraphQL environment, data may be distributed across multiple services and databases, leading to potential issues with data consistency. Implementing strategies for data synchronization and consistency, such as using event-driven architectures or distributed caches, can help ensure that data remains accurate and up-to-date across the system.

Testing and validating integrations are crucial to ensuring that the federated GraphQL setup functions as expected. Comprehensive testing involves verifying that the integration points between GraphQL services, legacy systems, REST APIs, and databases work correctly and handle edge cases effectively. This includes testing for data integrity, performance, and error handling to ensure that the system performs reliably under various conditions.

To support ongoing maintenance and troubleshooting, it is beneficial to implement monitoring and logging for integrated systems. Monitoring tools can provide visibility into the performance and health of the integration points, while logging can capture detailed information about interactions and errors. This information can be used to diagnose issues, optimize performance, and ensure that the integrated system operates smoothly.

As you work to integrate federated GraphQL with existing systems, it is important to adopt a modular and scalable approach. Designing integration components in a modular fashion allows for easier maintenance and updates, while scalability ensures that the system can handle growing data volumes and increasing demands. By focusing on modular design and scalability, you can build a robust and flexible integration that supports the evolving needs of your organization.

synchronized across these services, which can present challenges in maintaining data integrity and consistency. Implementing strategies to manage data synchronization and consistency is vital for ensuring that the federated GraphQL setup operates smoothly and reliably.

One approach to managing data consistency is to implement mechanisms for data synchronization between different services and systems. This might involve using background synchronization processes or event-driven architectures to propagate changes across services. For example, when data is updated in one service, you can use events or notifications to trigger updates in other services that rely on that data. This helps keep the data consistent across the federated GraphQL environment and ensures that clients receive accurate and up-to-date information.

In some cases, achieving eventual consistency may be acceptable, especially in distributed systems where real-time consistency is not critical. Eventual consistency allows for temporary discrepancies between data in different services, with the assurance that the data will eventually converge to a consistent state. To manage eventual consistency, it is important to implement mechanisms for conflict resolution and data reconciliation to address any discrepancies that may arise.

In addition to synchronization, implementing robust error handling and recovery mechanisms is essential for managing integration issues. When integrating with existing systems, unexpected errors or failures can occur, and having strategies in place to handle these situations is crucial. This might involve implementing retry logic for failed requests, fallback mechanisms for handling service outages, and monitoring tools to detect and alert on issues. By preparing for and addressing potential errors, you can minimize disruptions and maintain the stability of your federated GraphQL environment.

Testing is another critical aspect of integrating federated GraphQL with existing systems. Comprehensive testing helps ensure that the integration is functioning as expected and that all components work together seamlessly. This includes testing individual services, the interactions between services, and the overall federated GraphQL schema. Automated tests, including unit tests, integration tests, and end-to-end tests, can help identify issues early in the development process and ensure that changes to the system do not introduce new problems.

Finally, documentation and communication are key to successful integration. Providing clear documentation for the federated GraphQL schema, the integration points with existing systems, and the data flow between services can help ensure that all stakeholders understand how the system operates. This documentation should include information about the GraphQL schema, any adapters or resolvers used for integration, and any specific considerations or constraints related to the existing systems.

Effective communication among development teams is also important for coordinating integration efforts and addressing any issues that arise. Regular meetings, status updates, and collaborative problem-solving can help ensure that integration efforts are aligned and that any challenges are addressed in a timely manner.

In summary, integrating federated GraphQL with existing systems involves addressing a range of challenges, from connecting legacy systems and REST APIs to managing databases and ensuring data consistency. By implementing strategies for abstraction, error handling, synchronization, and testing, and by maintaining clear documentation and communication, you can successfully integrate federated GraphQL with your existing technology stack and provide a unified and efficient API for your organization.

CHAPTER 12: FEDERATED GRAPHQL AND REAL-TIME DATA

Real-time data requirements are increasingly becoming a central aspect of modern applications, driving the need for sophisticated handling of real-time interactions within federated GraphQL environments. This chapter delves into the challenges and strategies associated with integrating real-time capabilities into a federated GraphQL setup. We will explore the implementation of subscriptions, the management of real-time updates, and the use of event-driven architectures to ensure that your federated services can effectively handle real-time data.

At the core of handling real-time data in GraphQL is the concept of subscriptions. Subscriptions allow clients to receive real-time updates from the server based on specific events or changes in the data. This is particularly useful in applications where data needs to be updated dynamically, such as live feeds, chat applications, or collaborative tools. In a federated GraphQL environment, implementing subscriptions requires careful consideration of how these real-time updates are managed across multiple services and how they integrate with the overall federated schema.

To implement subscriptions in a federated GraphQL setup, you need to first define the subscription types in your GraphQL schema. Subscriptions are similar to queries but are designed to handle streaming data. They specify the types of events clients are interested in and how the server should push updates when these events occur. Each federated service that participates in real-time updates must support the subscription types defined in the schema and implement the logic to handle these subscriptions.

Integrating subscriptions into a federated architecture often involves using a pub/sub (publish/subscribe) system or message broker. This system facilitates communication between different services and ensures that updates are distributed efficiently. When an event occurs in one service that affects data in another service, the pub/sub system can propagate this event to all relevant services, which in turn can push the updates to clients through GraphQL subscriptions. Tools like Redis Pub/Sub, Apache Kafka, or RabbitMQ are commonly used for this purpose.

Managing real-time updates in a federated GraphQL environment also requires addressing the challenges of data consistency and synchronization. Since multiple services may be involved, ensuring that updates are propagated accurately and in a timely manner can be complex. Implementing mechanisms for data reconciliation and conflict resolution is crucial for maintaining the integrity of the real-time data. This may involve using versioning, timestamps, or conflict detection algorithms to handle scenarios where multiple updates occur simultaneously.

Event-driven architectures are another key component in integrating real-time data with federated GraphQL. In an event-driven architecture, services react to events or changes in the system rather than polling for updates. This approach aligns well with the requirements of real-time data handling, as it enables services to respond to changes as they occur. By leveraging events to trigger updates and notifications, you can achieve a more responsive and efficient real-time data flow.

For instance, when integrating real-time data from a legacy system or external service, you might use an event-driven approach to listen for changes or updates in the external system. These changes can be captured and propagated through the federated GraphQL setup, ensuring that clients receive up-to-date information without having to continually query for new data.

In addition to technical implementation, it is important to consider the scalability and performance of real-time data handling in a federated environment. Real-time updates can introduce additional load on the system, particularly as the number of active subscriptions and events increases. To address these challenges, you may need to implement optimization strategies such as load balancing, horizontal scaling, and caching of subscription data.

Monitoring and debugging are also critical aspects of managing real-time data in a federated GraphQL setup. Real-time systems can be more challenging to debug due to the asynchronous nature of data updates and the potential for race conditions or timing issues. Implementing comprehensive logging and monitoring solutions can help track the flow of real-time data, identify performance bottlenecks, and diagnose issues. Tools that provide real-time metrics and insights into subscription performance can be valuable in maintaining the reliability and efficiency of the system.

Overall, integrating real-time data into a federated GraphQL environment requires a careful balance of schema design, event management, and system optimization. By leveraging subscriptions, event-driven architectures, and robust data handling techniques, you can build a federated GraphQL setup that meets the demands of real-time data while maintaining scalability and performance.

One of the significant challenges of integrating real-time data within a federated GraphQL setup is ensuring that all relevant services and components can handle and propagate updates efficiently. The complexity increases when dealing with multiple services that each have their own data sources and update mechanisms. Therefore, careful planning is required to ensure that these services can work together seamlessly in real-time scenarios.

A common approach to addressing these challenges is to employ an event-driven architecture. In this model, services communicate through events rather than direct calls. When a service generates an event, such as a data change or user action, it publishes this event to a central message broker or event stream. Other services that are interested in these events can then subscribe to the stream and react accordingly. This architecture decouples the services, allowing them to scale independently and react to changes in real-time.

Implementing an event-driven architecture within a federated GraphQL environment often involves choosing the right technology stack. Popular choices for event streaming and message brokering include Apache Kafka, RabbitMQ, and AWS SNS/SQS. These technologies provide robust mechanisms for publishing and subscribing to events, ensuring reliable delivery and processing of real-time data. Integrating these technologies with GraphQL subscriptions involves creating resolvers that handle incoming events and push updates to clients.

In practice, this means setting up a system where your federated services can both publish and subscribe to events through the message broker. For instance, when a service updates its data, it publishes an event to the broker. Other services that depend on this data can subscribe to the relevant events and update their state or notify clients as needed. This approach not only ensures that all services remain synchronized but also supports scalability and flexibility as new services or data sources are added.

Another important aspect of integrating real-time data is handling client subscriptions. Clients need a mechanism to subscribe to specific data changes and receive updates when these changes occur. GraphQL subscriptions provide this mechanism by allowing clients to specify their interests and receive real-time updates via a persistent connection, such as WebSockets. The server then pushes updates to the clients whenever relevant events are detected.

To support subscriptions effectively, federated GraphQL setups typically utilize WebSocket connections. WebSockets enable bidirectional communication between clients and servers, allowing for real-time data exchange. In a federated environment, each service that supports subscriptions must manage its WebSocket connections and integrate with the overall schema to push updates to clients. This requires careful coordination to ensure that updates from various services are combined and delivered appropriately.

One consideration when using WebSockets for subscriptions is managing connection lifecycle and scalability. Each client subscription requires an open connection, which can put a strain on server resources if not managed properly. Strategies for managing WebSocket connections include connection pooling, load balancing, and efficient resource management. It is also essential to implement mechanisms for reconnecting and resubscribing clients in case of connection failures.

In addition to handling subscriptions, another aspect of integrating real-time data is ensuring data consistency and accuracy across services. Real-time updates can introduce challenges related to data consistency, especially when multiple services are involved. For example, if one service updates its data and sends a real-time notification, other services must process this update and ensure that their own data remains consistent.

To manage data consistency, federated GraphQL setups often employ strategies such as event versioning, timestamps, and conflict resolution mechanisms. Versioning allows services to track changes and manage updates based on the version of the data they have. Timestamps can help determine the most recent changes and resolve conflicts when multiple updates occur simultaneously. Implementing robust conflict resolution strategies ensures that data remains accurate and consistent across the federated environment.

Finally, it is crucial to consider security implications when dealing with real-time data. Subscriptions and real-time updates can expose additional attack vectors, such as unauthorized access to sensitive data or denial-of-service attacks. Implementing security measures such as authentication, authorization, and data encryption is essential to protect the integrity and confidentiality of real-time data.

Authentication ensures that only authorized clients can access real-time updates, while authorization controls what data clients can access based on their permissions. Data encryption protects data in transit, preventing unauthorized interception or tampering. By incorporating these security measures, you can ensure that your federated GraphQL setup remains secure while providing real-time capabilities.

In conclusion, integrating real-time data into a federated GraphQL environment involves addressing a range of challenges, from managing subscriptions and event-driven architectures to ensuring data consistency and security. By employing the right technologies and strategies, you can create a robust system that supports real-time interactions and delivers timely updates to clients.

The integration of real-time capabilities within a federated GraphQL environment also necessitates careful attention to resource management and performance optimization. Real-time data handling can impose significant demands on system resources, including memory, CPU, and network bandwidth. Therefore, it is crucial to implement strategies that manage these resources effectively to ensure that the system remains responsive and scalable.

One approach to managing resources in a federated setup is to implement rate limiting and throttling mechanisms for real-time updates. Rate limiting helps control the frequency of events and updates sent to clients, preventing overwhelming the system with too many simultaneous requests. Throttling can be used to manage the rate at which updates are processed and distributed, ensuring that the system can handle bursts of activity without degradation in performance.

Caching is another important technique to enhance performance and reduce the load on federated services. By caching the results of frequently accessed queries or subscription updates, you can minimize the need for repeated processing and data retrieval. This can be particularly beneficial in scenarios where multiple clients subscribe to the same data or where updates are frequent. Implementing a caching layer that stores the latest state of data can help alleviate the pressure on backend services and improve overall responsiveness.

Moreover, effective monitoring and logging are essential for maintaining the health of a real-time federated GraphQL environment. Implementing robust monitoring solutions allows you to track the performance of real-time data streams, identify bottlenecks, and diagnose issues promptly. Logs can provide valuable insights into the operation of subscriptions, the frequency of events, and any errors that occur. By analyzing these logs and metrics, you can make informed decisions about optimizing your real-time data handling processes and ensuring that your system remains reliable.

Another consideration in managing real-time data is ensuring data security and integrity. Real-time systems often involve the transmission of sensitive information, which requires safeguarding against unauthorized access and data breaches. Implementing encryption for data in transit and at rest, as well as using secure authentication and authorization mechanisms, is crucial for protecting the data and maintaining user privacy.

In addition to these practices, it is important to plan for scalability when integrating real-time data. As the volume of real-time data and the number of clients increase, the system must be capable of handling additional load without performance degradation. Horizontal scaling, where additional instances of services or infrastructure are added, can help distribute the load and maintain responsiveness. Load balancing and auto-scaling techniques can also be employed to dynamically adjust the resources based on current demand.

In summary, integrating real-time data into a federated GraphQL setup involves several key considerations. Implementing subscriptions and using event-driven architectures can provide the necessary mechanisms for real-time updates. Managing resource consumption through rate limiting, caching, and performance monitoring helps ensure that the system remains responsive and scalable. Securing real-time data and planning for scalability are also crucial for maintaining a robust and reliable federated GraphQL environment. By addressing these challenges and adopting best practices, you can effectively incorporate real-time capabilities into your federated services and deliver a dynamic and engaging user experience.

CHAPTER 13: TESTING FEDERATED GRAPHQL SERVICES

Testing is a fundamental aspect of developing and maintaining high-quality federated GraphQL services. Given the complexity of federated architectures, which involve multiple interconnected services, ensuring the reliability and correctness of the overall system requires a robust and comprehensive testing strategy. This chapter will explore various testing strategies tailored to federated GraphQL environments, including unit testing, integration testing, and end-to-end testing. We will also discuss relevant tools and practices to ensure the effectiveness of your testing efforts.

Unit testing is the foundation of any testing strategy and focuses on verifying the functionality of individual components in isolation. In the context of federated GraphQL services, unit tests are used to validate the behavior of resolver functions, schema definitions, and other core logic within a single service. The goal of unit testing is to ensure that each component performs as expected under different conditions and to identify any issues early in the development process.

When implementing unit tests for federated GraphQL services, it is crucial to mock external dependencies, such as databases or other services, to isolate the component under test. This allows you to verify the functionality of the component without interference from external systems. Tools like Jest and Mocha are commonly used for unit testing in JavaScript/TypeScript environments, providing support for mocking and asserting behavior. By writing comprehensive unit tests, you can catch issues related to data processing, error handling, and business logic before they affect other parts of the system.

Integration testing builds on unit testing by verifying the interactions between different components or services. In a federated GraphQL setup, integration tests are designed to ensure that the interactions between federated services work as intended. This includes testing how services communicate through the federated schema, how data is passed between services, and how changes in one service affect others.

Integration tests often involve setting up a test environment that mimics the real federated architecture, including all relevant services and data sources. This can be achieved through the use of containerization technologies such as Docker, which allow you to spin up isolated environments for testing purposes. During integration tests, you should verify that queries and mutations perform correctly across service boundaries, that data is correctly aggregated from different services, and that error handling mechanisms are functioning as expected.

End-to-end testing takes a broader approach by validating the entire system from the perspective of the end user. This type of testing simulates real-world scenarios and interactions with the federated GraphQL services to ensure that the system meets user requirements and performs reliably under various conditions. End-to-end tests focus on testing the complete workflow, including user interactions, data retrieval, and response handling.

For federated GraphQL services, end-to-end testing involves

executing queries and mutations through the GraphQL API and verifying that the responses are accurate and meet the expected outcomes. Tools like Cypress and Selenium can be employed for end-to-end testing, allowing you to automate interactions with the GraphQL endpoint and validate the overall system behavior. These tests are essential for ensuring that the integrated services work together seamlessly and that the system provides a positive user experience.

In addition to these primary testing strategies, there are several practices and tools that can further enhance the testing of federated GraphQL services. For instance, contract testing is a valuable approach for verifying that the interactions between services adhere to agreed-upon contracts or schemas. Contract testing tools, such as Pact, allow you to define and enforce expectations for service interactions, helping to prevent issues arising from mismatched expectations.

Monitoring and observability also play a crucial role in testing federated systems. By implementing monitoring tools and logging mechanisms, you can gain insights into the performance and behavior of your federated services in real-time. This allows you to detect issues, analyze failures, and make data-driven decisions to improve system reliability.

Furthermore, incorporating continuous integration and continuous deployment (CI/CD) practices can significantly improve the efficiency of your testing process. By automating the execution of unit tests, integration tests, and end-to-end tests as part of your CI/CD pipeline, you can ensure that each code change is validated thoroughly before being deployed to production. This approach helps maintain high-quality standards and reduces the risk of introducing defects into the live system.

Testing federated GraphQL services involves a combination

of unit, integration, and end-to-end testing approaches, each addressing different aspects of system reliability and correctness. By leveraging appropriate tools, practices, and automation techniques, you can ensure that your federated services perform as expected and deliver a robust and reliable experience to users.

End-to-end testing takes a comprehensive approach by validating the entire federated GraphQL system from the perspective of an end user or client application. This type of testing ensures that the complete workflow of the system functions as expected, encompassing all services, their interactions, and the final integration of data presented to the user. The primary aim of end-to-end testing is to simulate real-world scenarios and ensure that the system behaves correctly under various conditions.

To conduct effective end-to-end testing in a federated GraphQL environment, it is necessary to set up a testing framework that can interact with the entire system. This often involves using testing tools that support automation and can simulate user interactions with the system. Tools like Cypress or Puppeteer are commonly employed for this purpose, as they allow you to script complex scenarios and validate the functionality of the GraphQL API through automated test cases.

When creating end-to-end tests, it is important to design scenarios that cover a broad range of use cases. These scenarios should reflect typical user interactions, such as querying data, performing mutations, and handling subscriptions. By including diverse scenarios, you ensure that the system is tested thoroughly and that any potential issues in the integration between services are identified. Additionally, end-to-end tests should verify that the system maintains data consistency and integrity across services, and that it performs efficiently under load.

A critical aspect of end-to-end testing is managing test data.

Since federated GraphQL services often interact with various data sources, ensuring that the test data is representative and consistent is crucial for reliable testing outcomes. One approach is to use test data generators or mock services to create controlled and predictable data environments. This helps ensure that the tests are reproducible and that any failures can be traced to specific issues within the system.

In addition to unit, integration, and end-to-end testing, performance testing plays a vital role in validating federated GraphQL services. Performance tests are designed to assess how well the system performs under different conditions, such as high traffic volumes or large data sets. This type of testing helps identify potential bottlenecks and performance issues that could impact the user experience.

Performance testing for federated GraphQL services often involves simulating various load conditions and measuring key performance metrics such as response times, throughput, and resource utilization. Tools like Apache JMeter or Artillery can be used to generate load and measure the system's performance. These tests should be designed to stress-test different parts of the system, including individual services, the federated gateway, and the overall data aggregation process.

Incorporating continuous integration (CI) and continuous deployment (CD) practices is also essential for maintaining the reliability of federated GraphQL services. CI/CD pipelines automate the process of running tests, building, and deploying services, ensuring that changes are validated and deployed efficiently. By integrating testing into the CI/CD pipeline, you can catch issues early in the development cycle and reduce the risk of introducing defects into the production environment.

For effective CI/CD integration, it is important to configure the pipeline to execute all relevant tests, including unit, integration, end-to-end, and performance tests. This ensures that any changes to the codebase are thoroughly validated before deployment. Additionally, setting up automated alerts and monitoring can help detect issues quickly and provide feedback to developers in real time.

Overall, testing federated GraphQL services requires a multi-faceted approach that addresses various aspects of the system, from individual components to the entire integrated architecture. By implementing a combination of unit, integration, end-to-end, and performance tests, and integrating these tests into CI/CD pipelines, you can ensure that your federated services are robust, reliable, and capable of meeting the needs of users and clients.

Performance testing for federated GraphQL services involves creating simulations that mimic real-world usage patterns to identify how the system handles high traffic volumes or complex queries. It is essential to test not only the individual services but also the interactions between them to ensure that the entire federated architecture can handle the expected load. Performance tests should measure various aspects of system behavior, including query execution times, latency, and the ability to scale horizontally as more services are added or traffic increases.

In addition to the tools mentioned, incorporating real-time monitoring during performance tests provides valuable insights into the system's behavior under load. Monitoring tools such as Grafana, Prometheus, or New Relic can be integrated to track performance metrics in real time and help identify any unexpected issues or degradation in service. Analyzing these metrics can guide optimization efforts and highlight areas where the system may need adjustment to meet performance requirements.

Another crucial component of a robust testing strategy is the implementation of continuous integration and continuous deployment (CI/CD) practices. CI/CD pipelines can automate the execution of unit, integration, and end-to-end tests whenever changes are made to the codebase. This ensures that any new code or updates are thoroughly tested before being deployed to production, reducing the risk of introducing bugs or performance issues. Tools like Jenkins, CircleCI, or GitHub Actions facilitate the automation of these testing processes, integrating them into the development workflow to ensure timely and reliable releases.

Testing strategies should also include error handling and recovery scenarios. These tests are designed to verify how the system responds to and recovers from various types of failures or unexpected situations. For federated GraphQL services, this could involve testing how the system behaves when individual services are unavailable or when data inconsistencies occur. By simulating these failure scenarios, you can ensure that your system has appropriate mechanisms for error detection, logging, and recovery.

Effective error handling and recovery mechanisms are critical in maintaining the reliability and stability of federated GraphQL services. Proper logging and monitoring are essential for identifying and diagnosing issues as they arise. Implementing centralized logging solutions, such as ELK Stack (Elasticsearch, Logstash, Kibana) or similar platforms, helps aggregate logs from various services, making it easier to track down and resolve issues. Additionally, structured logging formats and detailed error messages improve the effectiveness of debugging and troubleshooting processes.

In conclusion, testing federated GraphQL services requires a multi-faceted approach that encompasses unit testing, integration testing, end-to-end testing, and performance testing. Each type of test plays a distinct role in ensuring the reliability and quality of the system. By employing comprehensive testing strategies, leveraging automation tools, and incorporating real-time monitoring, you can identify and address issues early in the development cycle, ensuring that your federated services perform reliably and efficiently in production. Continuous improvement of testing practices and adaptation to new challenges will contribute to maintaining high standards of service quality and user satisfaction.

CHAPTER 14: FUTURE TRENDS IN GRAPHQL FEDERATION

The landscape of GraphQL Federation is poised for continued evolution as the technology adapts to emerging requirements and innovations. As we look toward the future, several key trends and potential developments are likely to shape the trajectory of federated GraphQL. This exploration not only reflects on the current advancements but also anticipates the directions that could redefine the way federated architectures are designed and implemented.

One of the most notable trends is the ongoing refinement and standardization of GraphQL specifications. As GraphQL continues to gain traction across various industries, the need for standardized practices and protocols becomes increasingly critical. The GraphQL community, including the GraphQL Foundation and other key contributors, is actively working on refining the GraphQL specification to address emerging use cases and challenges. This includes enhancements to the core GraphQL language and extensions that facilitate more complex querying and data manipulation scenarios.

Another significant development is the rise of enhanced federation capabilities. The current federation specification, while robust, has room for growth in handling more complex use cases and integration scenarios. Future iterations of federated GraphQL are expected to introduce new features that improve the handling of cross-service interactions, optimize query execution, and provide more granular control over service composition. This could include advancements in schema stitching, improved support for service versioning, and more sophisticated mechanisms for managing inter-service dependencies.

Real-time data handling is also poised to see considerable advancements. As the demand for real-time applications continues to rise, federated GraphQL systems will need to enhance their support for subscriptions and real-time data synchronization. Future developments may include more efficient protocols for real-time updates, better integration with event-driven architectures, and improved tools for managing real-time data flows across distributed systems. These enhancements will help federated systems better support applications that require instantaneous data updates and high levels of interactivity.

The integration of GraphQL with other technologies and platforms is another area of active development. As organizations seek to leverage GraphQL within broader technology stacks, there will be an increased emphasis on interoperability with various data sources, including databases, REST APIs, and microservices. Future trends may include more seamless integration strategies and tooling that simplify the connection of federated GraphQL with diverse systems. This will enable organizations to build more cohesive and flexible architectures that can adapt to changing technological landscapes.

Security remains a critical focus as federated GraphQL continues to evolve. As data privacy regulations become more stringent and cyber threats become more sophisticated, ensuring the security of federated services will be paramount. Future developments in federated GraphQL are likely to include enhanced security features, such as more robust authentication and authorization mechanisms, improved encryption protocols, and better tools for monitoring and responding to security incidents. These advancements will help organizations protect sensitive data and maintain compliance with evolving security standards.

The community-driven nature of GraphQL development means that staying informed about emerging trends and participating in discussions is crucial for developers and organizations. Engaging with the GraphQL community through conferences, forums, and contribution to open-source projects can provide valuable insights into future directions and best practices. By staying connected with the community, organizations can ensure they are aware of the latest advancements and can adapt their strategies accordingly.

In conclusion, the future of GraphQL Federation is marked by continuous improvement and adaptation. As the technology evolves, it will address emerging challenges, integrate with new platforms, and enhance its capabilities to meet the demands of modern applications. By staying abreast of these trends and actively participating in the community, developers and organizations can leverage the full potential of federated GraphQL and build scalable, efficient, and secure architectures. The dynamic nature of the technology landscape promises exciting opportunities and ongoing innovation in the realm of GraphQL Federation.

The future of GraphQL Federation also promises a deepening of its integration with modern development practices and tooling. As the ecosystem surrounding GraphQL continues to grow, there will likely be a greater emphasis on incorporating federation into continuous integration and continuous deployment (CI/CD) pipelines. This integration will facilitate automated testing, deployment, and monitoring of federated schemas, streamlining the development process and enhancing the reliability of services. The use of specialized tools and frameworks designed to support federated architectures within these pipelines will become more common, providing developers with sophisticated mechanisms for managing schema evolution and deployment.

Furthermore, the role of machine learning and artificial intelligence in GraphQL Federation is an area ripe for exploration. As AI and ML technologies advance, they could be leveraged to optimize query performance, automate schema stitching, and predict potential schema conflicts before they arise. For instance, machine learning algorithms could analyze historical query patterns to suggest optimizations or identify potential bottlenecks in federated queries. The integration of AI-driven insights into federated GraphQL systems could lead to more adaptive and self-tuning architectures, enhancing both performance and developer productivity.

Scalability and performance are expected to remain central themes as GraphQL Federation evolves. The increasing volume of data and the complexity of distributed systems will drive innovations aimed at improving scalability. This may involve new approaches to load balancing, more efficient data partitioning strategies, and enhanced caching mechanisms specifically designed for federated environments. Additionally, the development of new algorithms and protocols that can handle large-scale federated queries efficiently will be crucial for supporting the growing demands of modern applications.

Another significant trend is the growing focus on developer experience (DX) in federated GraphQL systems. As the technology matures, there will be a concerted effort to improve the ease of use and accessibility of federated GraphQL for developers. This includes the creation of more intuitive development tools, better documentation, and enhanced support for debugging and troubleshooting. Providing a smoother and more efficient developer experience will be key to fostering adoption and ensuring that federated GraphQL can be effectively utilized in diverse and complex environments.

Moreover, the adoption of federated GraphQL across various industries is likely to drive the emergence of industry-specific standards and best practices. As organizations in sectors such as finance, healthcare, and e-commerce increasingly deploy federated GraphQL, there will be a demand for specialized guidelines and tools tailored to the unique requirements of these industries. These sector-specific standards will help address regulatory compliance, data privacy concerns, and integration with legacy systems, ensuring that federated GraphQL can be effectively adapted to meet the needs of different domains.

In conclusion, the future of GraphQL Federation is marked by a blend of technological advancements, evolving practices, and a heightened focus on developer and operational efficiencies. The continued evolution of standards, the integration of emerging technologies, and the development of new tools and best practices will shape the next generation of federated GraphQL architectures. As the field progresses, staying informed about these trends and proactively adapting to new developments will be essential for leveraging the full potential of federated GraphQL and maintaining a competitive edge in the ever-evolving landscape of modern application development.

As the GraphQL ecosystem continues to advance, one notable area of growth is the increased focus on interoperability between federated GraphQL systems and other data management technologies. The need to seamlessly integrate federated GraphQL with various types of databases, messaging systems, and external APIs will drive the development of new standards and tools that facilitate these interactions. This trend will likely lead to the creation of more sophisticated connectors and adapters that simplify the process of integrating disparate systems, enhancing the overall flexibility and utility of federated GraphQL architectures.

Furthermore, the rise of serverless computing and its integration with GraphQL Federation represents another significant trend. Serverless architectures offer a way to run backend services without managing infrastructure, which can be particularly advantageous in a federated setup. The ability to scale individual federated services independently and deploy them without worrying about underlying infrastructure will likely encourage more organizations to adopt serverless models. This shift could lead to the development of new patterns and best practices for deploying federated GraphQL services in serverless environments, optimizing performance and cost efficiency.

In addition to technological advancements, there is also an increasing emphasis on governance and compliance within federated GraphQL systems. As data privacy regulations become more stringent globally, federated GraphQL implementations will need to incorporate robust governance frameworks to ensure compliance. This involves implementing mechanisms for data protection, access control, and audit logging. The development of standards and practices to address these requirements will be crucial for organizations that operate in regulated industries, ensuring that their federated GraphQL systems can meet legal and ethical standards.

Another anticipated development is the evolution of query language capabilities and the introduction of new features that enhance the expressiveness and efficiency of GraphQL queries. As federated GraphQL continues to mature, there may be innovations in the query language itself, including support for more advanced query patterns, improved syntax for complex operations, and enhancements that streamline the process of composing and executing queries across multiple services. These improvements will contribute to making federated GraphQL more powerful and user-friendly, catering to a broader range of use cases and developer needs.

The community-driven aspect of GraphQL Federation will likely play a significant role in its future evolution. As more organizations and developers contribute to the GraphQL ecosystem, there will be a continuous exchange of ideas, best practices, and open-source tools that drive innovation. This collaborative environment will foster the development of new features and improvements, ensuring that federated GraphQL remains at the forefront of data querying and management technologies.

In summary, the future of GraphQL Federation is poised to be shaped by advancements in integration, scalability, developer experience, and governance. Emerging trends such as the integration with serverless architectures, enhanced interoperability, and the evolution of query capabilities will drive the continued growth and refinement of federated GraphQL systems. By staying informed about these trends and actively participating in the community, developers and organizations can ensure that they remain well-positioned to leverage the full potential of federated GraphQL in their data management strategies.

CHAPTER 15: CASE STUDIES IN FEDERATED GRAPHQL DEPLOYMENTS

In the evolving landscape of software architecture, federated GraphQL has emerged as a powerful solution for managing complex, distributed systems. This chapter delves into real-world case studies of organizations that have successfully implemented federated GraphQL, offering a detailed examination of diverse deployment scenarios. By exploring these case studies, we aim to provide practical insights into the challenges encountered, the solutions devised, and the outcomes realized. These examples will serve as valuable reference points for anyone considering or currently engaged in federated GraphQL projects.

One notable case study involves a global e-commerce platform that adopted federated GraphQL to streamline its microservices architecture. The platform's initial setup was characterized by a monolithic approach, where different aspects of the e-commerce experience—such as product catalog, user management, and order processing—were tightly coupled. This architecture proved problematic as the company scaled, leading to issues with performance, flexibility, and maintainability. The transition to federated GraphQL allowed the organization to decouple its services into independently managed, domain-specific microservices.

The deployment began with a comprehensive analysis of the existing architecture to identify the boundaries of each microservice. Each service was then exposed via GraphQL, with federated GraphQL serving as the orchestration layer to unify these disparate schemas. The main challenge faced was ensuring consistent data integrity and managing inter-service dependencies. To address this, the team implemented a robust schema stitching strategy, using directives to specify relationships between different services and employing caching mechanisms to optimize data retrieval. The outcome was a significant improvement in performance and scalability, along with a more modular and maintainable codebase.

Another illustrative case study features a financial services firm that integrated federated GraphQL to enhance its data management and reporting capabilities. The firm's architecture initially comprised several legacy systems, each offering a RESTful API. This setup created difficulties in aggregating data for comprehensive reporting and analytics. The decision to adopt federated GraphQL was driven by the need to provide a unified query interface across these disparate systems while leveraging the existing REST APIs.

The integration process involved developing GraphQL gateways that interfaced with each RESTful service, transforming their responses into GraphQL-compatible formats. This approach required designing custom resolvers and leveraging tools to handle REST-to-GraphQL transformations efficiently. Key challenges included ensuring secure and consistent data access, particularly given the sensitive nature of financial data. To mitigate these issues, the team implemented stringent authentication and authorization mechanisms and established comprehensive monitoring to track data flow and identify anomalies. The successful deployment led to enhanced data accessibility and streamlined reporting processes, significantly improving operational efficiency.

A third case study revolves around a healthcare provider that utilized federated GraphQL to unify its diverse data sources and improve patient data management. The healthcare system comprised various subsystems, including electronic health records (EHR), laboratory results, and appointment scheduling. Integrating these systems into a cohesive GraphQL schema required careful consideration of data privacy regulations and the need for real-time updates.

The project began with an audit of the existing data sources and the development of a federated schema that could accommodate the unique requirements of each subsystem. Special attention was given to implementing real-time data synchronization and subscription mechanisms to ensure that updates across different systems were reflected promptly in the unified GraphQL layer. Security concerns were addressed through robust encryption and access controls, ensuring compliance with healthcare data protection standards. The end result was a more integrated and responsive system that enhanced the provider's ability to deliver coordinated and timely patient care.

In these case studies, several common themes emerge. Successful federated GraphQL implementations often involve a clear understanding of the existing architecture, meticulous planning, and careful consideration of data management and security. The deployment process generally includes defining service boundaries, integrating disparate data sources, and establishing robust mechanisms for data consistency and access control. Each organization faced unique challenges, but through targeted solutions and best practices, they were able to realize significant benefits in terms of performance, scalability, and operational efficiency.

These case studies highlight the versatility and effectiveness of federated GraphQL in addressing a wide range of deployment scenarios. Whether transitioning from a monolithic architecture, integrating legacy systems, or unifying diverse data sources, federated GraphQL offers a powerful framework for managing complex systems. The insights gained from these real-world examples provide valuable guidance for organizations embarking on their own federated GraphQL journeys, offering practical strategies and lessons learned to inform and optimize their implementations.

In another prominent case study, a leading media company undertook a federated GraphQL implementation to modernize its content delivery system. The company had an extensive array of content services spread across various domains, including video streaming, articles, and user-generated content. Prior to the federated approach, these services operated independently with distinct APIs, leading to inefficiencies in content aggregation and user experience inconsistencies.

The transition to federated GraphQL involved several strategic steps. Initially, the company mapped out the different domains and their respective data schemas, which were then exposed through GraphQL endpoints. The federated layer was introduced to provide a unified schema that aggregated these endpoints, enabling seamless data retrieval across services. One of the significant challenges was aligning the different schemas to ensure that the federated schema accurately reflected the underlying data models. This required meticulous schema design and transformation strategies to ensure data consistency and accuracy.

The solution implemented involved creating a centralized gateway service responsible for coordinating requests and resolving data from the various federated services. This gateway employed advanced query planning techniques to optimize data fetching, reducing the latency typically associated with cross-service queries. Additionally, the company integrated real-time data updates into the federated GraphQL setup, leveraging subscriptions to provide users with instant notifications on content changes. The outcome was a streamlined content delivery system that improved user engagement and satisfaction, as well as operational efficiencies through reduced data duplication and simplified data access.

A third case study highlights a healthcare organization that integrated federated GraphQL to enhance patient data management across its network of clinics and hospitals. The organization faced significant challenges with integrating diverse healthcare records and clinical data systems, which were previously managed through separate, proprietary systems. The goal was to provide a cohesive view of patient data while maintaining compliance with stringent data privacy regulations.

The implementation process began with a thorough analysis of the existing data sources and their respective schemas. The team designed a federated GraphQL schema that could integrate data from various sources, including electronic health records (EHRs), laboratory results, and patient management systems. To address compliance and security concerns, the team implemented rigorous access control mechanisms and data encryption techniques. Federated GraphQL's flexibility allowed the organization to create a unified query interface that could securely aggregate and present patient information across different systems.

One of the key challenges was ensuring that sensitive data was handled appropriately and that access controls were enforced consistently across the federated schema. The team used role-based access control (RBAC) and attribute-based access control (ABAC) strategies to manage permissions and ensure that only authorized users could access specific data. Additionally, they employed advanced auditing and logging techniques to monitor data access and modifications. The result was a more cohesive and user-friendly data management system that improved patient care by providing clinicians with a comprehensive view of patient history and facilitating better decision-making.

In each of these case studies, the deployment of federated GraphQL provided solutions to complex integration challenges and delivered tangible benefits. The adoption of federated GraphQL allowed organizations to streamline data access, enhance performance, and improve scalability. The flexibility and modularity of federated GraphQL proved instrumental in addressing the unique needs of diverse use cases, from content delivery to data management and real-time updates.

These case studies illustrate the practical applications of federated GraphQL in various industries and highlight the potential for this approach to drive innovation and efficiency. By examining these real-world examples, organizations can gain valuable insights into the strategies and best practices for implementing federated GraphQL in their own contexts. The lessons learned from these deployments underscore the importance of careful planning, robust schema design, and attention to performance and security considerations in achieving successful outcomes with federated GraphQL.

The final case study in this chapter involves a global e-commerce platform that adopted federated GraphQL to address issues related to scaling and maintaining a highly diverse set of microservices. This platform, which supports millions of users worldwide, faced performance bottlenecks and complexities arising from its various services, including product catalog, user management, and order processing.

Before the adoption of federated GraphQL, the platform used a traditional monolithic API approach, which quickly became cumbersome as the number of services grew. Each service had its own API, leading to significant overhead in managing and synchronizing these endpoints. The lack of a unified schema also meant that client applications had to make multiple requests to different endpoints, which complicated the development process and impacted performance.

The transition to federated GraphQL was driven by the need to simplify API management and improve performance. The company began by designing a federated schema that consolidated the disparate service schemas into a single, coherent schema. This required a deep understanding of each microservice's data model and interactions. A significant challenge was integrating these schemas while maintaining performance and consistency. The solution involved employing advanced query optimization techniques and introducing a sophisticated query planner that could efficiently handle the complexities of the federated schema.

To further enhance performance, the platform implemented caching strategies at multiple levels. This included caching responses at the federated gateway and employing distributed caching mechanisms to reduce latency. Additionally, the team leveraged real-time data capabilities to keep users informed about order statuses and inventory changes. This was achieved through GraphQL subscriptions, which provided a seamless way to push updates to clients in real-time.

The deployment of federated GraphQL led to notable improvements in both performance and maintainability. The unified schema simplified client development and improved the overall efficiency of data fetching. The caching strategies reduced the load on backend services and improved response times. Furthermore, the use of real-time subscriptions enhanced the user experience by providing timely updates, which was particularly valuable for users tracking order shipments and inventory levels.

In each of these case studies, the organizations faced unique challenges but found that federated GraphQL provided effective solutions. Whether it was consolidating diverse content services, integrating sensitive healthcare data, or scaling a global e-commerce platform, federated GraphQL demonstrated its flexibility and power in addressing complex requirements. The key to success in these implementations was a careful design of the federated schema, rigorous performance optimization, and a focus on maintaining data security and compliance.

These real-world examples offer valuable insights into the practical application of federated GraphQL. They highlight the importance of understanding the specific needs of your organization and tailoring the federated approach to address those needs effectively. As technology continues to evolve, staying informed about emerging trends and best practices will be crucial for leveraging federated GraphQL to its fullest potential.

CHAPTER 16: LEVERAGING GRAPHQL FEDERATION FOR MULTI-TENANT APPLICATIONS

In the landscape of modern software architecture, multi-tenant applications represent a significant paradigm shift, enabling multiple customers or groups to share the same application while maintaining isolation and data privacy. GraphQL federation, with its ability to unify disparate schemas into a single, cohesive API, offers powerful tools for managing multi-tenant environments. This chapter delves into the application of federated GraphQL in multi-tenant systems, focusing on data isolation, privacy, and scalability challenges.

Multi-tenant applications are characterized by their capacity to serve multiple clients from a single instance of the application, with each tenant's data being isolated and secured. This model introduces several complexities, particularly when integrating federated GraphQL, which aims to provide a unified API across various microservices. To effectively leverage GraphQL federation in a multi-tenant context, a robust strategy must be implemented to ensure data separation while maintaining the efficiency and coherence of API interactions.

The first crucial aspect of managing multi-tenant applications with federated GraphQL is data isolation. Each tenant's data must be securely partitioned to prevent unauthorized access and ensure privacy. One approach to achieving this is by incorporating tenant-specific context into the federated schema. This context allows resolvers to filter and handle requests based on the tenant's identity, ensuring that data is only accessible to the appropriate tenant. Implementing tenant-aware resolvers is essential for enforcing access controls and maintaining the integrity of data isolation across the federated services.

In practice, this often involves enhancing the schema definition to include tenant identifiers and leveraging middleware or context objects within resolvers to inject tenant-specific information. For instance, when a request is processed, the context object can carry tenant-specific metadata, such as tenant IDs or authentication tokens, which resolvers use to filter data accordingly. This approach ensures that all data queries are scoped correctly, adhering to the boundaries set for each tenant.

Scalability is another critical consideration when deploying federated GraphQL in multi-tenant applications. As the number of tenants grows, the federated system must handle an increasing volume of requests efficiently without compromising performance. One strategy to address this challenge is to implement query optimization techniques that can handle complex multi-tenant queries more efficiently. This may involve optimizing the query planner to reduce redundant data fetching and minimize the computational overhead of processing tenant-specific requests.

Additionally, caching strategies play a significant role in improving performance in multi-tenant environments. Implementing effective caching mechanisms can alleviate the load on backend services by storing frequently accessed data, thus reducing the need for repetitive queries. In a multi-tenant setup, caching strategies must be designed to handle tenant-specific data efficiently, ensuring that cached responses are correctly scoped and do not inadvertently expose data across tenants.

Securing multi-tenant federated GraphQL systems also requires careful consideration. Beyond data isolation, security measures must address potential vulnerabilities and ensure that tenant data is protected against unauthorized access. This involves implementing robust authentication and authorization mechanisms, such as OAuth or JSON Web Tokens (JWT), to control access to the federated API. Each request must be authenticated and authorized based on the tenant's context, ensuring that only authorized users can access or modify data.

Moreover, regular security audits and vulnerability assessments should be conducted to identify and address potential weaknesses in the system. Ensuring that all federated services adhere to best security practices and comply with relevant data protection regulations is essential for maintaining a secure multi-tenant environment.

In addition to the core aspects of data isolation, scalability, and security, managing multi-tenant applications with federated GraphQL also involves addressing operational concerns such as monitoring and debugging. Effective monitoring solutions are required to track the performance and health of the federated services, providing insights into potential issues and allowing for proactive management. This includes monitoring query performance, detecting anomalies, and analyzing tenant-specific usage patterns.

Similarly, debugging multi-tenant systems can be complex due to the need to trace issues across multiple tenants and services. Implementing comprehensive logging and tracing mechanisms is crucial for diagnosing and resolving issues in a federated environment. Distributed tracing tools can help track the flow of requests and identify bottlenecks or failures, while detailed logging provides visibility into tenant-specific interactions and errors.

By addressing these considerations, federated GraphQL can be effectively leveraged to build scalable, secure, and efficient multi-tenant applications. The ability to unify diverse data sources into a cohesive API, combined with robust strategies for data isolation, performance optimization, and security, makes federated GraphQL a powerful tool for modern multi-tenant architectures. As organizations continue to embrace multi-tenant models, the insights and practices outlined in this chapter will be instrumental in guiding the successful implementation and management of federated GraphQL systems.

The effective management of queries and responses in a multi-tenant GraphQL environment necessitates a deep understanding of how to optimize performance while maintaining data isolation. To address this, the federation layer must incorporate mechanisms that handle the complexity of querying across multiple tenants efficiently. One approach involves leveraging advanced caching strategies tailored for multi-tenant contexts.

Caching is essential for performance optimization, but in multi-tenant systems, the cache must be designed to respect tenant boundaries. This means implementing a cache layer that can store tenant-specific data without allowing cross-tenant data leakage. Techniques such as cache keys that incorporate tenant identifiers can ensure that cached responses are segregated by tenant, preventing one tenant's data from being inadvertently exposed to another.

Furthermore, the federated GraphQL architecture must support robust monitoring and debugging tools to manage the intricacies of multi-tenant systems. Monitoring tools should be capable of providing insights into tenant-specific performance metrics, such as query response times and error rates. This granularity allows for the identification of performance bottlenecks or issues affecting specific tenants, enabling targeted optimizations and quicker resolutions.

Implementing comprehensive logging strategies is also crucial. Logs should capture tenant-specific information along with standard operation data, providing a complete view of how each tenant interacts with the system. These logs become invaluable when diagnosing issues, tracking usage patterns, and ensuring compliance with data privacy regulations.

Security remains a paramount concern in multi-tenant applications, particularly when integrating federated GraphQL. Ensuring data protection involves several layers of security measures. Authentication and authorization mechanisms must be finely tuned to handle tenant-specific access controls. Federated GraphQL services should enforce stringent access control policies that verify the identity and permissions of users at every level of the request processing chain.

Moreover, encrypting data in transit and at rest is fundamental to safeguarding sensitive information. Implementing encryption protocols ensures that data is protected from unauthorized access both while being transmitted over the network and when stored within the system. For multi-tenant applications, this means ensuring that encryption keys are managed securely and that data encryption practices are consistently applied across all services involved in the federation.

When scaling multi-tenant federated GraphQL systems, it is also crucial to consider the architecture of the underlying infrastructure. Horizontal scaling, where additional instances of services are added to distribute the load, can be particularly effective. However, scaling strategies must be designed to accommodate the increased complexity introduced by multiple tenants. This might involve dynamic scaling solutions that adjust resources based on real-time demand and usage patterns, ensuring that the system remains responsive and efficient as the number of tenants grows.

To facilitate smooth scaling and avoid potential bottlenecks, consider employing microservices architecture within the federated system. Each microservice can handle different aspects of the application or different tenants, allowing for more granular control over resource allocation and service performance. This approach also enhances fault tolerance, as issues in one service or tenant do not necessarily impact the entire system.

Lastly, as the multi-tenant federated GraphQL system evolves, it is essential to stay informed about emerging standards and best practices. The GraphQL ecosystem is continually evolving, with new tools, libraries, and frameworks being developed to address various challenges, including those specific to multi-tenant environments. Engaging with the community, participating in discussions, and experimenting with new technologies can provide valuable insights and help ensure that the system remains at the forefront of innovation.

In summary, leveraging GraphQL federation in multi-tenant applications involves a careful balance of performance optimization, security, and scalability. By implementing robust data isolation strategies, optimizing query handling, and adhering to stringent security practices, organizations can successfully manage complex multi-tenant environments. Employing advanced caching techniques, monitoring tools, and scalable infrastructure will ensure that federated GraphQL systems continue to provide efficient and secure service as they grow. Keeping abreast of industry trends and best practices will further enhance the ability to adapt to new challenges and opportunities in the evolving landscape of GraphQL.

Scaling multi-tenant federated GraphQL systems involves both horizontal and vertical scaling strategies, tailored to the specific requirements and challenges of handling multiple tenants. Horizontal scaling, which involves adding more instances of services, can distribute the load and improve system resilience. For federated GraphQL, this might mean deploying additional instances of each service that handles tenant-specific data or query processing. This approach allows for the balancing of requests across multiple servers, reducing the risk of any single instance becoming a bottleneck.

Vertical scaling, on the other hand, involves increasing the resources (such as CPU and memory) allocated to individual instances. While vertical scaling can improve the performance of a single instance, it has its limits and is typically used in conjunction with horizontal scaling to optimize performance and resource utilization.

In practice, implementing horizontal scaling for federated GraphQL systems requires a thoughtful approach to load balancing. It is essential to ensure that incoming queries are distributed evenly across instances to prevent any one instance from being overwhelmed. Load balancers that are aware of the federated architecture can intelligently route requests based on the specific services required, ensuring efficient use of resources.

Additionally, a distributed caching layer can significantly enhance performance in a scaled federated GraphQL system.

This involves setting up caching mechanisms that are distributed across multiple instances, allowing for quick access to frequently queried data and reducing the load on backend services. Effective cache invalidation strategies must also be employed to ensure that updates are propagated across the cache, maintaining data consistency and accuracy.

Another aspect of scaling involves managing the state and synchronization of data across multiple instances. In a federated GraphQL setup, where multiple services might be managing different aspects of tenant data, it is crucial to have mechanisms in place to synchronize state changes and ensure consistency. Distributed databases or data stores that support replication and consistency models can be instrumental in this regard. These systems help maintain data integrity and availability, even as the number of tenants and the volume of data grow.

To further ensure the efficiency and scalability of federated GraphQL systems, it is beneficial to adopt automated scaling solutions. Auto-scaling mechanisms, which dynamically adjust the number of running instances based on current load and performance metrics, can help maintain optimal performance without manual intervention. Such systems can scale out to handle increased load and scale in during periods of lower activity, optimizing resource utilization and cost.

In terms of security, maintaining a multi-tenant environment with federated GraphQL requires continuous vigilance. Implementing strong isolation practices ensures that tenant data remains separate and secure. One effective strategy is to employ a multi-layered approach to data isolation, where access controls, encryption, and network segmentation work together to protect tenant data.

For example, network segmentation involves dividing the network into isolated segments, each handling different types of data or tenants. This approach can prevent unauthorized access and reduce the risk of cross-tenant data breaches. Access controls should enforce strict policies that limit data access based on tenant identity and permissions. These controls must be enforced at both the application and database levels to ensure comprehensive protection.

Encryption of data both in transit and at rest is another critical component of securing multi-tenant federated GraphQL systems. In-transit encryption, using protocols like TLS (Transport Layer Security), protects data as it travels between clients and servers. At-rest encryption ensures that data stored on disk remains secure, even if physical storage media are compromised. Proper key management practices, including regular key rotation and secure storage, are essential for maintaining the effectiveness of encryption measures.

Regular security audits and compliance checks are also vital in a multi-tenant environment. These practices help identify and address potential vulnerabilities before they can be exploited. Engaging in continuous monitoring and logging of security events allows for the early detection of suspicious activities and the prompt response to potential threats.

In summary, leveraging federated GraphQL for multi-tenant applications offers significant advantages, including improved data management, isolation, and querying efficiency. By implementing strategies for scaling, securing, and optimizing performance, organizations can effectively address the unique challenges of multi-tenant environments. Through a combination of horizontal and vertical scaling, distributed caching, automated scaling solutions, and robust security measures, federated GraphQL systems can deliver scalable and secure solutions to meet the needs of diverse and dynamic applications.

CHAPTER 17: ENHANCING SCHEMA MANAGEMENT WITH GRAPHQL FEDERATION

In federated GraphQL architectures, schema management is a critical aspect that can become increasingly complex as the number of services and the size of the schema grow. This complexity stems from the need to ensure consistency, versioning, and evolution of schemas across multiple services while maintaining a cohesive overall architecture. Effective schema management strategies are essential for the seamless operation and scalability of federated systems.

One of the fundamental aspects of schema management in a federated setup is schema versioning. Versioning allows teams to make incremental changes to their schemas without disrupting existing clients. In a federated environment, where multiple services contribute to a unified schema, versioning must be handled in a way that ensures compatibility across the entire system. This involves adopting practices that allow for backward and forward compatibility, so that changes to one part of the schema do not adversely affect other services or clients.

To implement effective schema versioning, it is crucial to establish a versioning strategy that aligns with the needs of your organization and the nature of the changes being made. Semantic versioning, where changes are classified into major, minor, and patch versions, can provide a structured approach to versioning. Major versions indicate breaking changes, minor versions introduce backward-compatible new features, and patch versions are used for backward-compatible fixes. By clearly defining these versions and their implications, teams can communicate changes effectively and ensure that all services adhere to the agreed-upon schema versions.

Another important aspect of schema management is schema evolution. As applications grow and requirements change, schemas must evolve to accommodate new features and modifications. In a federated GraphQL system, schema evolution must be handled in a way that ensures all services continue to operate smoothly. This involves not only updating the schema in each individual service but also coordinating these updates across the entire federation.

To facilitate schema evolution, it is beneficial to adopt a schema management tool or platform that supports schema stitching and federation. These tools can automate the process of merging schemas from multiple services, ensuring that changes are propagated consistently throughout the system. They also provide capabilities for validating schemas against predefined rules, which helps maintain schema integrity and consistency as changes are introduced.

Maintaining consistency across federated schemas requires rigorous testing and validation. Automated testing frameworks can be employed to ensure that schema changes do not introduce errors or inconsistencies. These frameworks can validate the schema against a set of predefined tests, checking for issues such as missing fields, incorrect types, or broken references. By integrating automated testing into the development workflow, teams can catch potential issues early and reduce the risk of disruptions in the federated system.

Another strategy for enhancing schema management is the use of schema documentation and visualization tools. These tools can provide a clear and comprehensive view of the entire schema, including its structure, relationships, and dependencies. By visualizing the schema, teams can better understand how different parts of the schema interact and identify potential areas for improvement. Documentation tools can also facilitate communication among team members and stakeholders by providing detailed explanations of schema elements and their usage.

Effective collaboration among teams is also crucial for managing schemas in a federated environment. Since multiple teams may be responsible for different services and schema components, it is essential to establish clear communication channels and coordination mechanisms. Regular meetings, shared documentation, and collaborative tools can help ensure that all teams are aligned on schema changes and their implications. Additionally, adopting a governance model that defines roles, responsibilities, and decision-making processes can help manage schema changes more effectively and avoid conflicts.

In addition to these practices, monitoring and observability play a vital role in schema management. By implementing monitoring tools that track schema usage, performance, and error rates, teams can gain insights into how changes to the schema impact the overall system. Observability tools can provide valuable data on query patterns, response times, and other metrics, helping teams identify and address issues proactively.

As federated GraphQL systems continue to evolve, staying

informed about emerging best practices and tools is essential for effective schema management. The field of GraphQL federation is rapidly advancing, with new standards, frameworks, and techniques being developed to address the challenges of schema management. By keeping up with these developments and continuously refining schema management practices, organizations can ensure that their federated GraphQL systems remain scalable, reliable, and adaptable to changing needs.

In the realm of federated GraphQL, ensuring schema consistency and coherence is paramount for maintaining a functional and efficient system. As schemas evolve and services grow, it's crucial to implement strategies that preserve the integrity of the federated architecture. This section delves into best practices and tools that support effective schema management in a federated environment.

One of the core practices for maintaining schema consistency is establishing a robust schema governance framework. Governance involves setting standards and procedures for schema design, approval, and deployment. It ensures that all changes to the schema are made in a controlled and predictable manner, reducing the risk of conflicts and inconsistencies. A governance framework typically includes guidelines for schema design, review processes, and change management protocols. By enforcing these standards, organizations can better manage the complexity of multiple federated schemas and ensure that all services adhere to common conventions and practices.

To support schema governance, various tools can be employed to automate and streamline schema management tasks. Schema validation tools, for instance, can check for inconsistencies and errors in schemas before they are deployed. These tools can validate schemas against predefined rules or against the schemas of other services to ensure compatibility. Integration with continuous integration/ continuous deployment (CI/CD) pipelines can further automate schema validation, providing early feedback on potential issues and preventing problematic changes from reaching production environments.

Another essential aspect of schema management is effective documentation. Comprehensive and up-to-date documentation is vital for understanding and maintaining federated schemas. It should provide clear explanations of schema structures, relationships between services, and the rationale behind schema design decisions. Tools that generate and maintain documentation from schema definitions can be invaluable, as they ensure that documentation evolves in tandem with the schema. This documentation serves as a reference for developers, helping them to understand the interactions between different parts of the federation and facilitating easier troubleshooting and development.

Schema management also benefits from the use of introspection and visualization tools. Introspection tools allow developers to query the schema for details about its structure and capabilities. These tools can provide insights into the types, fields, and relationships defined in the schema, aiding in the understanding and debugging of schema-related issues. Visualization tools can create graphical representations of schema relationships, making it easier to grasp the overall structure and identify potential areas of concern. By leveraging these tools, teams can gain a clearer view of their federated schemas and more effectively manage their evolution.

Collaboration and communication are critical components of effective schema management in a federated environment. Given that multiple teams or individuals may be responsible for different parts of the schema, establishing clear communication channels and collaboration processes is essential. Regular meetings, shared documentation, and collaborative platforms can help ensure that all stakeholders are aligned and informed about schema changes and their implications. This collaborative approach helps to prevent misunderstandings and ensures that schema updates are coordinated across the federation.

Finally, it is important to establish mechanisms for monitoring and auditing schema changes. Monitoring tools can track changes to schemas and their impact on system performance and stability. They can provide insights into how schema changes affect queries and data access patterns, helping to identify potential issues before they escalate. Auditing tools can log schema changes and their origins, providing a historical record that can be useful for troubleshooting and accountability. By monitoring and auditing schema changes, organizations can maintain greater control over their federated schemas and ensure that they continue to meet performance and reliability standards.

In summary, enhancing schema management in a federated GraphQL architecture involves a multifaceted approach that includes governance, automation, documentation, visualization, collaboration, and monitoring. By implementing these practices and utilizing the appropriate tools, organizations can effectively manage the complexity of federated schemas, ensuring consistency and coherence across their systems. This approach not only facilitates smoother schema evolution but also supports the overall stability and performance of federated GraphQL architectures.

As federated GraphQL environments scale, maintaining schema consistency becomes increasingly challenging. This section explores advanced strategies and practices for managing schema evolution and consistency across federated services.

Effective schema versioning is critical in a federated

architecture where multiple teams might be evolving their schemas independently. Versioning allows teams to introduce changes without disrupting existing clients. One common approach is to use semantic versioning (SemVer), where changes are classified into major, minor, and patch versions. Major versions indicate breaking changes, minor versions introduce new features in a backward-compatible manner, and patch versions include backward-compatible bug fixes. This method ensures that clients can choose when to adopt new versions and helps manage compatibility across federated services.

When dealing with schema evolution, backward compatibility is a crucial concern. Changes to a schema should be introduced in a way that does not break existing clients. One practice to achieve this is to deprecate fields and types rather than removing them outright. Deprecation involves marking elements as outdated while continuing to support them. Clients are notified through the deprecation annotations in the schema, and they can gradually migrate to newer elements. This practice gives consumers of the API time to adapt and avoids sudden disruptions.

Furthermore, integrating schema evolution tools can facilitate the management of schema changes. Tools that provide schema diffing capabilities compare different versions of a schema to highlight changes, identify potential issues, and guide the migration process. These tools can also automate tasks such as generating migration scripts or updating documentation, reducing manual effort and minimizing errors.

To ensure schema consistency, establishing a robust testing strategy is essential. Tests should cover schema validation, integration, and end-to-end scenarios. Schema validation tests confirm that changes adhere to the established schema standards and do not introduce conflicts. Integration tests verify that interactions between federated services work as expected. End-to-end tests ensure that the overall system behaves correctly with the updated schema. By implementing a comprehensive testing strategy, teams can catch issues early and ensure that schema changes do not adversely affect the federated architecture.

Monitoring and observability also play a significant role in schema management. Implementing monitoring solutions allows teams to track the impact of schema changes on performance and usage. Metrics such as query execution times, error rates, and request volumes can provide insights into how schema updates affect the system. Observability tools that support tracing and logging help diagnose issues and understand the interactions between different parts of the federation. By leveraging these tools, teams can proactively address performance bottlenecks and other issues related to schema changes.

Coordination and communication between teams are vital for effective schema management in a federated setup. Regular meetings and communication channels should be established to discuss schema changes, share insights, and align on versioning strategies. Tools that support schema collaboration, such as shared repositories or design systems, can enhance coordination and streamline the development process. Clear documentation and change logs can also aid in keeping all stakeholders informed and involved.

Lastly, considering future-proofing strategies can help manage schema complexity as federated systems evolve. This involves designing schemas with flexibility and extensibility in mind. Adopting design patterns that accommodate future changes, such as using interfaces and union types, can make it easier to introduce new features without disrupting existing functionality. Additionally, investing in ongoing education and training for development teams ensures that they are well-versed in best practices and emerging trends in schema management.

By implementing these strategies and leveraging appropriate tools, organizations can enhance their schema management practices, ensuring that their federated GraphQL systems remain robust, scalable, and efficient. As the field of GraphQL continues to advance, staying informed about emerging practices and tools will further support the ongoing success and evolution of federated architectures.

CHAPTER 18: OPTIMIZING QUERY PERFORMANCE IN FEDERATED ENVIRONMENTS

In the realm of federated GraphQL, optimizing query performance is crucial for maintaining responsive and efficient systems. Given the complexity of federated architectures, where multiple services may handle parts of a query, careful consideration of performance optimization strategies is necessary. This chapter delves into advanced techniques for enhancing query performance, including query batching, data fetching strategies, and resolver optimization.

To begin with, query batching is a powerful technique to improve performance in federated environments. In a federated setup, a single GraphQL query might require multiple calls to different services. Without batching, each of these calls could result in separate network requests, which can be inefficient and increase latency. By batching queries, you can group multiple requests into a single network operation. This approach reduces the overhead associated with multiple network round-trips and can significantly decrease the overall response time. Implementing query batching requires configuring your GraphQL gateway or client to aggregate requests and handle them in a unified manner.

Another critical aspect of optimizing query performance involves effective data fetching strategies. Data fetching refers to how the GraphQL server retrieves and processes the data needed to fulfill a query. In a federated setup, this often involves interacting with multiple underlying services. To enhance performance, it is essential to adopt strategies that minimize unnecessary data retrieval and streamline the fetching process. One approach is to use query optimization techniques such as data loader libraries, which batch and cache database requests to avoid redundant queries. Data loaders can aggregate requests for the same type of data and serve them efficiently, reducing the number of calls to the underlying data sources.

Furthermore, optimizing resolver performance is key to achieving efficient query execution in a federated environment. Resolvers are functions responsible for fetching and returning data for a specific field in a GraphQL query. In a federated setup, resolvers often interact with various services, and their performance can impact the overall query response time. To optimize resolvers, consider several strategies. First, ensure that resolvers are designed to handle requests efficiently by minimizing complex operations and avoiding unnecessary computations. Additionally, employing caching mechanisms within resolvers can help reduce the load on services and databases by storing frequently accessed data temporarily.

Effective schema design also plays a role in optimizing query performance. A well-designed schema can facilitate more efficient query execution by minimizing the complexity of queries and the amount of data processed. Consider designing schemas with a focus on avoiding deeply nested queries and excessive field selections. Simplifying the schema structure and using fragments effectively can help ensure that queries are more predictable and manageable.

Moreover, monitoring and profiling tools are invaluable for identifying performance bottlenecks in federated GraphQL systems. Implementing monitoring solutions allows you to track metrics related to query execution, such as latency, throughput, and error rates. Profiling tools can provide insights into the performance of individual resolvers and data fetching operations, helping you pinpoint areas that require optimization. By analyzing these metrics, you can make informed decisions on where to focus your optimization efforts.

In summary, optimizing query performance in federated GraphQL environments involves a combination of strategies, including query batching, efficient data fetching, resolver optimization, and thoughtful schema design. Implementing these techniques can lead to significant improvements in response times and overall system efficiency. As federated architectures continue to evolve, ongoing performance tuning and monitoring will be essential to maintaining a high level of responsiveness and user satisfaction.

In addition to query batching and optimizing resolver performance, efficient data fetching strategies are central to improving query performance in federated GraphQL environments. One effective method is leveraging the concept of data co-location, which involves grouping related data together to minimize the number of calls required to fulfill a query. By designing schemas and resolvers to access related data from a single service or batch requests when possible, you reduce the overhead associated with cross-service communication and improve response times.

Another technique is to utilize asynchronous data fetching where feasible. Asynchronous operations allow the server to handle multiple data retrieval tasks concurrently, rather than sequentially. This approach can be particularly beneficial in a federated setup, where queries might involve multiple services. By employing asynchronous techniques, you can enhance the efficiency of data retrieval and reduce the time it takes to aggregate responses from various services.

Caching strategies also play a pivotal role in optimizing performance. Implementing caching at various levels—such as within individual resolvers, across services, and at the GraphQL gateway—can significantly reduce the amount of redundant processing and data retrieval. For instance, employing an in-memory cache to store frequently accessed data or the results of previous queries can minimize the need for repeated database queries or network calls. Additionally, considering cache invalidation strategies ensures that stale data is not served, maintaining the accuracy of the responses.

In a federated GraphQL architecture, managing and optimizing the interaction between services is essential. Service-level caching and optimization techniques, such as implementing rate limiting and optimizing service queries, contribute to reducing the latency of individual services and improving overall query performance. When multiple services are involved, optimizing the performance of each service individually can have a cumulative positive effect on the federated system as a whole.

Analyzing query performance metrics and leveraging monitoring tools is also crucial for identifying bottlenecks and areas for improvement. By employing performance monitoring tools and establishing metrics for query execution times, response sizes, and service latencies, you gain insights into where optimizations are needed. Tools such as distributed tracing can provide detailed visibility into the flow of data across services, allowing for precise identification of performance issues and their resolution.

Another advanced technique involves query optimization at the gateway level. The gateway serves as the entry point for GraphQL queries and can apply optimization strategies such as query complexity analysis and query optimization rules. By analyzing the complexity of incoming queries and applying optimization rules, the gateway can prevent inefficient queries from being processed and ensure that resource usage is balanced across services.

Implementing intelligent query planning and execution strategies further enhances performance. Query planning involves analyzing and optimizing the structure of the query before execution, while intelligent execution strategies ensure that the query is executed in the most efficient manner. Techniques such as query decomposition, where complex queries are broken down into simpler sub-queries, can improve performance by allowing more efficient processing of individual components.

In summary, optimizing query performance in federated GraphQL environments involves a multifaceted approach that includes query batching, efficient data fetching strategies, resolver performance optimization, and effective caching. By adopting these techniques and continuously monitoring and analyzing performance metrics, organizations can achieve significant improvements in query efficiency and overall system responsiveness. This holistic approach not only enhances the performance of federated GraphQL queries but also ensures a scalable and efficient architecture capable of handling complex and high-demand scenarios.

Implementing efficient query performance strategies in federated GraphQL environments also involves dealing with the intricacies of network latency and inter-service communication. Given that federated GraphQL setups often involve multiple services, optimizing how these services communicate can have a significant impact on overall query performance. One approach to address this is by reducing the number of network hops required to fulfill a query. This can be achieved by minimizing the dependencies between services and ensuring that services handle as much of the query processing as possible on their end before returning results to the gateway.

Another important consideration is optimizing the data serialization and deserialization processes. In federated systems, data is often passed between services in serialized formats such as JSON. Efficiently handling these data transformations can help reduce overhead and improve response times. Using optimized libraries and techniques for serialization can minimize the performance impact of these processes. Additionally, ensuring that services use consistent and efficient data formats can reduce the complexity of data transformations and improve the overall efficiency of data handling.

Load balancing is another critical factor in optimizing performance within federated GraphQL environments. As the number of requests increases, distributing the load evenly across multiple instances of a service can prevent bottlenecks and ensure that no single instance becomes overwhelmed. Implementing effective load balancing strategies, such as round-robin or least-connection algorithms, can help maintain high availability and responsiveness. Additionally, monitoring the load distribution and adjusting the balance as needed based on real-time metrics can further enhance performance.

Concurrency control is also essential in optimizing query performance. In a federated setup, concurrent requests may be processed by multiple services simultaneously, leading to potential contention and conflicts. Employing concurrency control mechanisms, such as optimistic locking or versioning, can help manage these conflicts and ensure data consistency while maintaining high performance. By carefully managing concurrent access to shared resources, you can avoid performance degradation and ensure that queries are processed efficiently.

To further enhance query performance, consider leveraging modern hardware and infrastructure optimizations. Utilizing high-performance computing resources, such as in-memory databases or SSDs for faster data access, can significantly improve query execution times. Additionally, leveraging cloud-based infrastructure allows for dynamic scaling and resource allocation based on demand, which can help accommodate fluctuations in query volume and maintain optimal performance.

Finally, it's important to foster a culture of continuous performance optimization and improvement. Regularly reviewing and analyzing performance data, staying informed about advancements in GraphQL technologies, and iteratively applying optimization techniques can help maintain and improve the efficiency of your federated GraphQL setup. Encouraging a proactive approach to performance management ensures that your system remains responsive and scalable in the face of evolving demands and technological advancements.

By integrating these advanced techniques and best practices, you can effectively optimize query performance in federated GraphQL environments, leading to faster, more efficient, and reliable query execution.

CHAPTER 19: FEDERATION WITH GRAPHQL SUBSCRIPTIONS AND REAL-TIME FEATURES

Integrating real-time features within a federated GraphQL architecture presents unique challenges and opportunities. As organizations increasingly demand real-time capabilities, such as live data updates and interactive user experiences, incorporating these features into a federated GraphQL setup requires careful consideration of several factors. This chapter delves into the complexities of implementing GraphQL subscriptions and other real-time functionalities within a federated environment, focusing on strategies for managing real-time data and updates across distributed services.

GraphQL subscriptions are a powerful tool for enabling real-time communication between clients and servers. They allow clients to receive updates when data changes, which is particularly useful for applications that require live updates, such as messaging platforms, live dashboards, or collaborative tools. However, integrating subscriptions into a federated GraphQL setup introduces several layers of complexity, primarily due to the distributed nature of the services involved.

The first challenge in implementing real-time features in a federated GraphQL architecture is managing subscription requests and responses across multiple services. In a typical federated setup, each service manages a portion of the overall schema and may be responsible for different types of data. When a subscription request is issued, it must be routed to the appropriate service or services responsible for the relevant data. This requires a coordination mechanism to ensure that subscription requests are correctly routed and that updates are propagated to all relevant clients.

To handle subscription requests in a federated environment, it is essential to implement a robust subscription management system. This system should be capable of tracking active subscriptions, handling subscription lifecycles, and ensuring that updates are delivered to clients in a timely manner. One approach to managing subscriptions is to use a central subscription manager that coordinates with the individual federated services. This manager can handle the orchestration of subscription requests, track which services need to push updates, and ensure that all updates are delivered to clients efficiently.

Another significant aspect of integrating real-time features is handling the underlying data infrastructure. Federated GraphQL setups often rely on multiple data sources, including databases, third-party APIs, and other services. Ensuring that these data sources can support real-time updates and efficiently propagate changes is crucial. This may involve implementing change data capture mechanisms, real-time data streaming solutions, or other technologies that can handle data changes in real time. Additionally, services must be designed to efficiently handle incoming data updates and push these updates to subscribed clients.

Implementing real-time features also requires attention to scalability and performance. As the number of clients and subscription requests grows, the system must be able to handle increased loads without degradation in performance. Strategies for scaling real-time features include distributing subscription handling across multiple instances of services, using message brokers or event streams to manage updates, and optimizing the performance of data processing and delivery mechanisms. Additionally, employing efficient data structures and algorithms for managing subscriptions and updates can help maintain high performance as the system scales.

Security is another critical consideration when implementing real-time features in a federated GraphQL environment. Subscriptions can potentially expose sensitive data or allow unauthorized access if not properly secured. Implementing authentication and authorization mechanisms is essential to ensure that only authorized clients can access subscription data. Additionally, employing encryption for data transmission and secure handling of subscription tokens or credentials can help protect against unauthorized access and data breaches.

In summary, integrating real-time features with federated GraphQL involves addressing several key challenges, including managing subscription requests and responses across distributed services, ensuring the underlying data infrastructure can handle real-time updates, and maintaining scalability and performance. By implementing a central subscription management system, leveraging real-time data infrastructure technologies, and addressing security concerns, organizations can successfully incorporate real-time capabilities into their federated GraphQL architectures. This enables the creation of dynamic, interactive applications that can deliver live data updates and enhance user experiences.

The integration of real-time features, such as GraphQL subscriptions, into a federated GraphQL setup is not without its technical hurdles. One major challenge lies in ensuring that updates are propagated consistently and efficiently across the distributed architecture. As each federated service might handle a distinct segment of the schema, the synchronization of real-time data between services becomes critical.

A pivotal aspect of handling real-time updates in a federated environment involves managing the communication between various services. Since subscriptions can originate from any part of the schema, a strategy must be devised to route these subscriptions to the appropriate service or services. This routing ensures that each service can handle the subscription according to its specific responsibilities, thus avoiding any single point of failure or bottleneck.

To achieve efficient communication, consider implementing a publish-subscribe (pub-sub) model at the infrastructure level. In a pub-sub system, publishers send messages to a central channel, while subscribers receive updates from that channel. This model can be adapted for federated GraphQL environments by using a central pub-sub system that manages subscription events and distributes them to the appropriate federated services. This approach simplifies the orchestration of subscription events and ensures that each federated service remains decoupled yet synchronized.

Another crucial component is the use of message brokers or event streaming platforms, such as Apache Kafka or RabbitMQ. These tools can facilitate real-time data propagation across services by providing reliable message delivery and high throughput. By integrating a message broker with the federated GraphQL architecture, each service can publish updates to the broker, which then ensures that all interested parties, including other services and clients, receive timely updates. This setup also allows for better scalability and fault tolerance, as the message broker can handle large volumes of data and provide mechanisms for data recovery in case of failures.

In addition to managing real-time updates, it's essential to address the challenge of data consistency and synchronization across services. In a federated setup, each service might have its own data source and update frequency. To maintain consistency, services must implement mechanisms to detect and handle discrepancies in data states. Techniques such as event sourcing, where changes to data are recorded as a sequence of events, can be beneficial. This approach allows services to reconstruct the current state of data from historical events and ensures that all services operate on a consistent view of the data.

Furthermore, the performance of real-time features must be optimized to avoid latency issues. The latency in processing subscription requests and delivering updates can impact user experience, particularly in applications requiring low-latency interactions. Performance optimization can be achieved through various techniques, such as optimizing resolver functions, reducing the volume of data transferred, and minimizing the number of network hops involved in processing updates.

Efficient resolver design is a critical factor in optimizing performance. Resolvers should be designed to handle subscription queries and updates swiftly. This includes using efficient querying techniques, such as batching and caching, to reduce the load on backend systems. Additionally, leveraging asynchronous processing and concurrency can enhance the responsiveness of resolvers, ensuring that updates are handled promptly.

Data fetching strategies also play a significant role in optimizing performance. When dealing with real-time data, it is essential to minimize the amount of data fetched and processed. Techniques such as selective data fetching, where only the relevant data is retrieved, and incremental updates, where only the changes since the last update are transmitted, can improve efficiency. By focusing on the most pertinent data and minimizing unnecessary transfers, the system can better handle the demands of real-time features.

Lastly, the integration of monitoring and alerting mechanisms is vital for maintaining the health of real-time features. Monitoring tools can track the performance of subscription handling, data propagation delays, and system health, providing insights into potential issues. Setting up alerts for anomalies, such as unusually high latency or message delivery failures, ensures that problems are detected and addressed promptly, maintaining a smooth user experience.

In conclusion, integrating real-time features into a federated GraphQL architecture involves addressing various challenges, from managing subscription routing and ensuring data consistency to optimizing performance and monitoring system health. By implementing robust communication strategies, leveraging message brokers, and optimizing resolver and data fetching techniques, organizations can effectively incorporate real-time capabilities into their federated GraphQL setups, delivering interactive and responsive experiences to users.

The integration of real-time features into a federated GraphQL architecture extends beyond mere implementation; it necessitates thoughtful consideration of system design, performance, and fault tolerance. Each component of the system must be carefully engineered to handle real-time updates efficiently while maintaining the overall integrity and reliability of the federated environment.

A critical consideration in implementing GraphQL subscriptions in a federated setup is managing the connection lifecycle. Unlike standard queries and mutations, subscriptions involve maintaining a persistent connection between the client and server to push updates in real time. This persistent connection is generally achieved using WebSockets, which support bidirectional communication. In a federated architecture, each service handling a part of the schema must be capable of managing these WebSocket connections and delivering updates accordingly.

To address this, a unified strategy for managing WebSocket connections across services is essential. This often involves creating a gateway service or a dedicated subscription manager that acts as the central point of contact for all subscription requests. The gateway service routes subscription requests to the appropriate federated services and aggregates updates before pushing them to the clients. This approach helps in maintaining a single source of truth for managing WebSocket connections and ensures that updates are propagated accurately and promptly.

Moreover, optimizing the performance of real-time features requires attention to the efficiency of data processing and delivery. Each federated service must be optimized to handle the volume of real-time updates it processes. This involves implementing efficient data structures and algorithms for handling subscription events and minimizing the latency between data changes and client notifications. Techniques such as data caching and batching can be employed to reduce the overhead associated with real-time updates. Caching frequently accessed data helps in quickly serving subscription requests without redundant computations, while batching allows for grouping multiple updates into a single operation to improve throughput.

Additionally, the scalability of real-time features in a federated GraphQL setup is a significant concern. As the number of clients and the volume of real-time data increase, the system must scale accordingly to maintain performance. Horizontal scaling, where additional instances of services are deployed to handle increased load, is a common approach. For instance, multiple instances of the gateway service or subscription manager can be deployed to balance the load of WebSocket connections and subscription events. Similarly, federated services can be scaled independently based on their specific workloads and data processing requirements.

Fault tolerance and error handling are also critical in maintaining the reliability of real-time features. In a federated environment, failures in one service should not disrupt the entire system. Implementing strategies such as retries, fallbacks, and graceful degradation helps in managing errors and ensuring continuity of service. For instance, if a federated service fails to deliver an update, the system can retry the operation or provide alternative mechanisms to ensure that clients eventually receive the update. Monitoring and logging tools are valuable for detecting and diagnosing issues, enabling prompt responses to any disruptions in real-time data handling.

Security considerations are paramount when dealing with real-time features. Securing WebSocket connections involves implementing authentication and authorization mechanisms to prevent unauthorized access and ensure that clients can only access the data they are permitted to view. Encryption of WebSocket communication is also crucial to protect data in transit from potential interception. Additionally, adhering to best practices for data protection and privacy helps in safeguarding sensitive information during real-time updates.

In summary, integrating real-time features such as GraphQL subscriptions into a federated architecture requires a comprehensive approach to system design, performance optimization, and fault tolerance. By establishing a robust strategy for managing WebSocket connections, optimizing data processing, and ensuring scalability and security, organizations can effectively leverage real-time capabilities within their federated GraphQL environments. These considerations will not only enhance the user experience through timely updates but also contribute to the overall resilience and efficiency of the system.

CHAPTER 20: MANAGING GRAPHQL FEDERATION WITH CI/CD PIPELINES

The integration of GraphQL Federation with Continuous Integration and Continuous Deployment (CI/CD) pipelines is essential for ensuring that federated GraphQL services are reliable, scalable, and maintainable. This chapter explores the processes and strategies for incorporating federation into CI/CD workflows, focusing on automated testing, deployment strategies, and monitoring. The goal is to streamline the development and deployment of federated services, ensuring that changes are delivered smoothly and efficiently.

CI/CD pipelines provide a framework for automating the process of integrating code changes, testing them, and deploying them to production. In the context of federated GraphQL, this involves several key practices, starting with automated testing. Testing federated GraphQL services presents unique challenges due to the distributed nature of the system. Each service within the federation has its own schema and set of resolvers, and interactions between these services can be complex. Automated testing helps to address these challenges by ensuring that changes do not introduce regressions or break the functionality of the federation.

Unit tests are crucial for verifying the correctness of individual components within each federated service. These tests focus on ensuring that the resolvers, schema definitions, and business logic within a service are functioning as expected. For federated services, unit tests should be designed to cover not only the internal logic but also interactions with other services through mock federations. This approach ensures that each service is tested in isolation while still accounting for its role within the overall federation.

Integration tests, on the other hand, are essential for validating the interactions between services within the federation. These tests simulate the real-world scenarios in which services interact, verifying that the federation layer correctly composes schemas and resolves queries across services. Integration testing can be complex, as it requires setting up a test environment that mirrors the production federation setup. Automated tools can help in creating and managing these test environments, facilitating consistent and repeatable integration tests.

End-to-end testing goes a step further by testing the entire federated GraphQL system as a whole. This includes verifying that queries and mutations executed against the federated schema return the expected results and that the overall system performs correctly under load. End-to-end tests often involve running the full stack of federated services, including the gateway and individual services, and simulating real user interactions. These tests are critical for ensuring that the federation behaves correctly from the perspective of the end user.

Once automated testing is in place, the next step in managing GraphQL Federation with CI/CD is to develop robust deployment strategies. Deployment strategies for federated GraphQL services must account for the coordination required between different services and the gateway. One common approach is to use blue-green deployments, where two separate environments are maintained: the blue environment for the current version of the system and the green environment for the new version. Traffic is initially routed to the blue environment, and once the new version in the green environment is validated, traffic is switched over. This strategy helps in minimizing downtime and reducing the risk of deployment failures.

Another approach is canary deployments, where new versions of services are gradually rolled out to a small subset of users before being fully deployed. This allows for early detection of issues in the new version and provides an opportunity to roll back if necessary. Canary deployments are particularly useful for federated services as they help in identifying integration issues between services early in the deployment process.

Managing deployments in a federated GraphQL setup also requires careful coordination of schema changes. Schema changes can impact multiple services and the federation layer, so it is important to ensure that changes are compatible and do not introduce breaking changes. Strategies for managing schema changes include using versioning and deprecation strategies to handle changes incrementally and avoid disruptions. Schema versioning involves maintaining multiple versions of the schema and allowing clients to migrate to newer versions over time, while deprecation strategies involve marking old fields or types as deprecated and providing a timeline for their removal.

Monitoring and observability are crucial for maintaining the health and performance of federated GraphQL services. Monitoring tools can track metrics such as request latencies, error rates, and resource utilization across the federation. Observability tools, including distributed tracing and logging, help in diagnosing issues and understanding the behavior of the federation. Implementing comprehensive monitoring and observability practices enables teams to detect and address issues proactively, ensuring the continued reliability of the federated services.

In conclusion, integrating GraphQL Federation with CI/CD pipelines involves implementing automated testing to ensure the correctness and reliability of federated services, developing effective deployment strategies to manage changes and minimize disruptions, and maintaining robust monitoring and observability practices to ensure the ongoing health of the system. By leveraging these practices, teams can streamline their development and deployment processes, delivering high-quality federated GraphQL services with confidence.

As federated GraphQL systems evolve, deploying updates efficiently while maintaining service reliability becomes crucial. CI/CD pipelines play a key role in this process by automating deployment strategies and ensuring that changes are rolled out smoothly. Effective deployment strategies within a federated GraphQL environment must address the complexity introduced by multiple interconnected services.

Deployment pipelines for federated GraphQL systems should incorporate several critical stages. The first stage is the build phase, where the code for each federated service is compiled and packaged. This includes not only the individual service code but also any schema definitions and configuration files. During this phase, it is essential to ensure that the build process produces artifacts that are compatible with the overall federation setup. For instance, if schema definitions are updated, these changes must be validated to ensure compatibility with other services within the federation.

The second stage is the deployment phase, which involves rolling out updates to the federated services. In a federated environment, this process must be managed carefully to avoid disruptions. One common strategy is to use blue-green deployments, which involve deploying the new version of a service alongside the existing version. Traffic can then be switched gradually from the old version to the new version, allowing for a smooth transition and minimizing the risk of service interruptions. This approach also allows for quick rollbacks if issues are discovered during the deployment.

Another critical aspect of deployment in a federated setup is managing schema changes. Schema evolution can be challenging, particularly when introducing breaking changes. To mitigate this, versioning strategies should be employed. One approach is to maintain backward compatibility by ensuring that new schema versions do not break existing queries or mutations. Another approach is to use feature flags to control the rollout of new schema features. This allows teams to enable or disable features dynamically without requiring redeployment, providing greater flexibility and control over the deployment process.

Monitoring and observability are integral components of a CI/CD pipeline for federated GraphQL systems. Effective monitoring involves tracking the health and performance of both individual services and the overall federation. Metrics such as response times, error rates, and query performance provide valuable insights into the system's behavior and can help identify issues early. Tools such as Prometheus and Grafana can be used to collect and visualize these metrics, providing a comprehensive view of the system's performance.

In addition to metrics, logging is crucial for diagnosing issues in a federated setup. Centralized logging systems can aggregate logs from all federated services, making it easier to track down and resolve problems. Logs should include detailed information about request and response payloads, as well as any errors or exceptions encountered during processing. This level of detail helps in pinpointing issues that may arise from interactions between services.

Alerts and automated responses also play a significant role in maintaining service reliability. CI/CD pipelines should be configured to trigger alerts based on predefined thresholds for metrics or error rates. For example, if the response time for a particular query exceeds a certain threshold, an alert can be generated to notify the development team. Automated responses, such as rolling back a deployment or scaling up resources, can help address issues quickly and minimize the impact on users.

Another consideration in managing CI/CD for federated GraphQL systems is ensuring that the pipeline itself is resilient and scalable. As the number of services in the federation grows, the complexity of the CI/CD pipeline can increase. It is important to design the pipeline to handle this complexity, using modular and reusable components where possible. For instance, automated tests can be grouped by service or functionality, allowing for parallel execution and reducing overall pipeline run times.

To sum up, integrating GraphQL Federation with CI/CD pipelines involves a comprehensive approach to automated testing, deployment strategies, and monitoring. By employing advanced techniques in these areas, organizations can streamline their development and deployment processes, ensuring that federated GraphQL services are robust, reliable, and capable of evolving to meet changing needs. As the landscape of federated GraphQL continues to evolve, staying abreast of best practices and emerging tools will be essential for maintaining an effective CI/CD workflow.

In the deployment phase, ensuring smooth and reliable releases is paramount for maintaining the integrity of a federated GraphQL system. To achieve this, implementing sophisticated deployment strategies within your CI/CD pipeline is essential. One effective approach is to use feature flags or toggles, which allow teams to deploy new features or changes in a controlled manner. This technique enables you to release updates to specific user segments or gradually roll out changes, minimizing risk and allowing for incremental testing in production environments.

Feature flags are particularly useful in a federated GraphQL setup because they provide flexibility in managing updates across different subgraphs. For instance, if a new feature is introduced in one subgraph, it can be toggled on or off without affecting the entire system. This allows teams to test the feature in production with real user interactions while keeping it hidden from the general audience until it is fully validated. Furthermore, feature flags can help in coordinating deployments across multiple teams working on different subgraphs, ensuring that all changes are synchronized and compatible.

Another important aspect of deployment in a federated environment is managing schema migrations. As subgraphs evolve, schema changes must be carefully coordinated to avoid breaking the federation layer. Implementing a schema versioning strategy can help manage these changes. Each subgraph should adhere to versioned schemas, with clear documentation on the evolution of the schema over time. This strategy facilitates backward compatibility and ensures that older clients can continue to interact with the API without disruptions.

Automated deployment processes should include thorough validation steps to confirm that schema migrations and other updates do not introduce issues. This involves integrating schema checks and automated rollbacks into the deployment pipeline. If a deployment introduces a breaking change or causes unforeseen issues, automated rollback mechanisms can revert the system to a stable state, reducing downtime and mitigating risks associated with faulty releases.

In addition to automated testing and deployment, continuous monitoring is crucial for maintaining the health and performance of a federated GraphQL system. Monitoring tools should be integrated into the CI/CD pipeline to provide real-time insights into the system's behavior, performance metrics, and any errors or issues that arise. This includes setting up alerts for critical issues such as high error rates, performance degradation, or schema validation failures.

Effective monitoring involves not only tracking the health of individual subgraphs but also ensuring that the federation gateway is operating as expected. The gateway serves as the central hub for coordinating queries and mutations across subgraphs, so its performance and reliability are critical. Monitoring solutions should capture metrics such as query response times, error rates, and the load on the gateway. These metrics help identify performance bottlenecks and ensure that the federation layer remains responsive and reliable.

Additionally, logging plays a vital role in troubleshooting and debugging. Implementing comprehensive logging for both subgraphs and the gateway provides valuable insights into system behavior and helps diagnose issues that may arise during or after deployment. Logs should be aggregated and analyzed to identify patterns or anomalies that could indicate potential problems. Integrating logging with monitoring tools allows for more effective issue resolution by providing context and details about errors or performance issues.

To further enhance the CI/CD pipeline, consider incorporating canary deployments or blue-green deployments. Canary deployments involve releasing updates to a small subset of users before a full rollout. This approach allows teams to test changes in a real-world environment with a limited audience, enabling them to identify issues early and make necessary adjustments. Blue-green deployments, on the other hand, involve maintaining two production environments—one for the current version and one for the new version. This strategy allows for a seamless switch between versions and minimizes downtime during the deployment process.

Overall, managing GraphQL federation with CI/CD pipelines requires a comprehensive approach that integrates automated testing, deployment strategies, and continuous monitoring. By implementing these practices, teams can ensure that their federated services remain stable, performant, and resilient in the face of ongoing development and changes. As the complexity of federated systems continues to grow, maintaining a well-structured CI/CD pipeline will be essential for delivering high-quality GraphQL services that meet the needs of both developers and users.

CHAPTER 21: HANDLING SCHEMA EVOLUTION IN FEDERATED ARCHITECTURES

Schema evolution presents a significant challenge in federated GraphQL architectures, where multiple independent services, or subgraphs, collaborate through a unified API. In such environments, evolving schemas without causing disruptions or compatibility issues is essential for maintaining service reliability and minimizing downtime. This chapter delves into strategies for managing schema changes, including versioning techniques, ensuring backward compatibility, and handling schema migrations effectively.

One of the primary strategies for managing schema evolution is the implementation of a robust versioning system. Schema versioning enables teams to introduce changes incrementally while preserving the stability of the existing API. This approach involves assigning version numbers to different iterations of the schema, allowing clients and services to specify which version they interact with. In a federated architecture, each subgraph can independently evolve its schema and maintain versioned APIs. This isolation ensures that changes to one subgraph do not immediately impact others, thereby reducing the risk of breaking the overall federation.

Versioning can be approached in several ways, including semantic versioning, where each schema change is classified according to its impact—major, minor, or patch. Major changes that introduce breaking changes receive a new major version number, while minor and patch changes are reflected through incremental version updates. This method provides clarity on the nature and extent of schema changes and helps clients and services adapt accordingly.

Backward compatibility is another crucial aspect of schema evolution in federated environments. To ensure that existing clients continue to function correctly, schema changes should be designed to be backward-compatible. This means that new schema versions must accommodate existing queries and mutations without disrupting their current behavior. One common technique for achieving backward compatibility is to deprecate fields and types gradually rather than removing them outright. By marking certain elements as deprecated, developers signal to clients that these elements will eventually be phased out but will continue to be supported for a transitional period.

Deprecation allows clients time to adapt to new schema elements and ensures a smooth transition. This approach also helps avoid sudden disruptions, as clients can migrate their queries and mutations at their own pace. Additionally, employing clear documentation and communication strategies is vital in this process. Providing detailed information about deprecated features and their replacements enables clients to make informed decisions and reduces the risk of integration issues.

Handling schema migrations is another critical component

of schema evolution. Schema migrations involve the process of transitioning from one schema version to another while ensuring that data and functionality remain consistent throughout. In a federated architecture, this process requires careful coordination between multiple teams working on different subgraphs. To facilitate smooth migrations, adopting a phased rollout approach can be effective. This approach involves deploying schema changes incrementally, starting with a subset of services or clients before rolling out the changes more broadly.

Automated migration tools can assist in managing this process by providing features such as automated schema validation, data transformation, and rollback capabilities. These tools help ensure that schema migrations are executed smoothly and that any issues can be quickly addressed. Implementing comprehensive testing strategies is also essential to validate schema changes before they are deployed. Automated tests should cover various scenarios, including backward compatibility, data integrity, and performance impact.

Moreover, it is important to establish a clear governance process for schema changes within a federated architecture. This involves defining roles and responsibilities for managing schema evolution, setting up approval workflows, and ensuring that all stakeholders are involved in the decision-making process. Effective communication and collaboration between teams are crucial for coordinating schema changes and avoiding conflicts or inconsistencies.

In conclusion, managing schema evolution in federated GraphQL architectures requires a multifaceted approach that encompasses versioning techniques, backward compatibility, and effective schema migration strategies. By adopting these practices, organizations can ensure that their federated services remain robust and adaptable, providing a reliable API experience for clients while accommodating the continuous evolution of underlying schemas. Through careful planning and execution, schema evolution can be managed efficiently, minimizing disruptions and maintaining the overall integrity of the federated system.

Testing is a crucial component of managing schema evolution in federated architectures. Comprehensive testing helps ensure that schema changes do not introduce regressions or break existing functionality. In the context of federated GraphQL, this involves testing not only the individual services but also the interactions between them. A thorough testing strategy includes unit tests, integration tests, and end-to-end tests.

Unit tests are essential for validating changes within individual services. Each service should have a suite of unit tests that cover its specific logic and schema definitions. When schema changes are introduced, unit tests can help verify that the service behaves as expected and that new fields or types are correctly implemented. For example, if a new field is added to a type, unit tests should check that the field is accessible and that it returns the expected data.

Integration tests focus on the interactions between federated services. These tests ensure that changes in one service do not negatively impact others. Integration tests can be particularly challenging in a federated environment due to the need to simulate and validate interactions across multiple services. Mocking and stubbing techniques are often employed to create a controlled environment for testing integrations. By simulating responses from dependent services, integration tests can help identify issues related to schema changes and service interactions.

End-to-end tests provide a comprehensive check of the entire federated system. These tests validate the functionality of the complete data graph, ensuring that queries and mutations operate correctly across all services. End-to-end tests are typically more complex and time-consuming to set up but are invaluable for identifying issues that might not be apparent in unit or integration tests. They ensure that the federated architecture as a whole continues to function as expected after schema changes.

In addition to testing, monitoring plays a crucial role in managing schema evolution. Monitoring tools help track the performance and health of services, providing insights into how schema changes impact the system. Metrics such as response times, error rates, and resource utilization can indicate whether recent changes have introduced performance regressions or other issues. Implementing monitoring and alerting systems allows teams to quickly detect and address problems that arise from schema updates.

One effective way to manage schema evolution is through feature flags. Feature flags allow teams to deploy schema changes gradually and control their visibility. By using feature flags, teams can enable or disable specific features or schema changes for different users or environments. This approach provides greater flexibility and control over how schema changes are rolled out and allows for testing changes in production environments without exposing them to all users immediately.

Documentation is another critical aspect of managing schema evolution. Maintaining up-to-date documentation ensures that developers are aware of changes and understand how to work with the updated schema. Documentation should include information about new fields, deprecated fields, and any other modifications that have been made. Providing clear and comprehensive documentation helps reduce the risk of confusion and errors as developers adapt to schema changes.

Ultimately, effective schema evolution in federated

architectures requires a combination of careful planning, thorough testing, and ongoing monitoring. By employing versioning techniques, adopting a rolling migration strategy, and utilizing feature flags, teams can manage schema changes in a way that minimizes disruption and maintains service quality. Testing and monitoring are essential for ensuring that schema updates do not introduce issues, and up-to-date documentation helps facilitate a smooth transition for developers and users alike.

As organizations continue to evolve their federated GraphQL systems, they must remain vigilant and adaptable. Schema evolution is an ongoing process that requires continuous attention and adjustment. By following best practices and leveraging the right tools and strategies, teams can successfully navigate the complexities of schema evolution and maintain a robust and scalable federated architecture.

Managing schema migrations in a federated architecture involves careful coordination and communication between teams responsible for different services. When a schema change is necessary, it is crucial to follow a structured approach to ensure that updates are applied seamlessly across the federated system without causing disruptions.

One common approach to schema migration is the use of a migration plan, which outlines the steps required to transition from the current schema to the new one. This plan should include details on how the changes will be implemented, the timeline for deployment, and any dependencies or potential conflicts with other services. A well-defined migration plan helps teams anticipate and address issues before they arise, minimizing the risk of downtime or data inconsistencies.

Schema versioning is another important aspect of managing schema evolution. Versioning allows for the gradual rollout of changes while maintaining compatibility with existing clients. By adopting a versioning strategy, teams can ensure that new features or modifications are introduced in a controlled manner, allowing clients to adapt to changes at their own pace. There are several versioning approaches, including semantic versioning and date-based versioning, each with its own advantages and considerations. Semantic versioning, for example, uses version numbers to indicate the level of changes (e.g., major, minor, patch), while date-based versioning uses timestamps to track changes.

Backward compatibility is a key consideration when evolving schemas. Ensuring that changes do not break existing clients or services is essential for maintaining system stability. One approach to achieving backward compatibility is to introduce changes in a non-breaking manner, such as adding new fields or types without removing or modifying existing ones. Another approach is to use deprecation annotations to signal the eventual removal of deprecated features while providing clients with ample time to migrate to new alternatives. By communicating deprecation plans clearly and providing appropriate documentation, teams can help clients transition smoothly to updated schemas.

Testing plays a crucial role in validating schema migrations and ensuring backward compatibility. Comprehensive testing should cover various aspects of the schema evolution, including regression testing, integration testing, and performance testing. Regression testing verifies that existing functionality remains intact after schema changes, while integration testing ensures that interactions between federated services continue to work as expected. Performance testing helps identify any potential impact on system performance resulting from schema updates. By conducting thorough testing, teams can identify and address issues before they affect end-users.

Collaboration and communication between teams are essential for successful schema evolution in a federated environment. Regular meetings and updates help ensure that all stakeholders are informed of upcoming changes, potential impacts, and timelines. Establishing clear communication channels and fostering a culture of collaboration can help teams work together effectively to address challenges and coordinate schema updates.

In addition to the technical aspects of schema management, it is important to consider the impact on clients and users. Providing clear documentation and guidance on schema changes helps clients understand how to adapt to new features or modifications. Documentation should include information on new fields or types, deprecated features, and any changes in behavior. Additionally, providing examples and use cases can help clients implement and test changes more effectively.

Overall, managing schema evolution in federated architectures requires a comprehensive approach that includes versioning, backward compatibility, migration planning, testing, and collaboration. By following best practices and leveraging effective tools and techniques, teams can ensure that schema changes are implemented smoothly and that the federated system remains stable and reliable. This proactive approach to schema management helps organizations adapt to evolving requirements and maintain high-quality services in a dynamic and distributed environment.

CHAPTER 22: FEDERATED GRAPHQL AND API GATEWAY INTEGRATION

In the evolving landscape of microservices and distributed architectures, API gateways serve as a crucial component in managing and optimizing federated GraphQL services. By acting as a single entry point for client requests, API gateways provide a range of functionalities that enhance the effectiveness and security of federated GraphQL implementations. This chapter delves into the integration of GraphQL Federation with API gateways, exploring various use cases, benefits, and configuration strategies to maximize the potential of this combination.

API gateways are designed to handle multiple cross-cutting concerns, such as request routing, authentication, rate limiting, and caching. When integrated with federated GraphQL architectures, they offer several advantages. One of the primary benefits is the ability to aggregate and route requests to the appropriate federated services efficiently. This aggregation simplifies client interactions by providing a unified endpoint through which all requests pass, thereby masking the complexity of the underlying federated service structure.

Integrating API gateways with federated GraphQL services also facilitates enhanced security. API gateways can enforce authentication and authorization policies at a centralized point before requests are forwarded to the federated services. This setup ensures that sensitive operations are protected and that access control measures are consistently applied across the entire system. For example, OAuth2 or JWT (JSON Web Token) mechanisms can be utilized to validate and authorize user requests before they reach the GraphQL services, thus safeguarding data and ensuring compliance with security policies.

Another key benefit of using API gateways with federated GraphQL is the ability to implement rate limiting and traffic management. API gateways can monitor and control the rate of incoming requests to prevent abuse and ensure equitable resource distribution among services. This is particularly important in a federated setup where multiple services are involved, as it helps maintain the stability and performance of the entire system. Rate limiting policies can be configured to apply globally or on a per-service basis, depending on the needs of the application.

Caching is another area where API gateways can significantly impact performance. By caching responses from federated services, API gateways can reduce the number of direct calls to the underlying services, thereby alleviating their load and improving response times. This caching can be applied at various levels, including query results and aggregated responses, and can be fine-tuned to balance between freshness and performance. The configuration of caching strategies should align with the specific needs of the application, taking into account factors such as data volatility and query complexity.

In terms of configuration, integrating API gateways with federated GraphQL services typically involves setting up routing rules and defining how requests are translated into queries that are distributed across the federated services. API gateways need to be aware of the federated schema and the service endpoints to accurately direct requests. This often requires defining mappings between GraphQL operations and the corresponding backend services, which can be managed through configuration files or via the API gateway's management interface.

One practical approach to managing this integration is to use schema stitching or schema federation techniques within the API gateway. Schema stitching involves combining multiple GraphQL schemas into a single schema that the API gateway can present to clients. This method allows for seamless interaction with federated services, as the gateway handles the schema composition and query distribution. On the other hand, schema federation enables a more modular approach where each federated service maintains its schema, and the API gateway consolidates these schemas into a unified endpoint. Both approaches have their advantages, and the choice between them depends on factors such as the complexity of the schema and the operational requirements of the system.

Monitoring and observability are also critical aspects of integrating API gateways with federated GraphQL services. API gateways provide valuable insights into request patterns, performance metrics, and error rates. These insights can be used to identify bottlenecks, troubleshoot issues, and optimize the performance of the federated system. Implementing logging and monitoring solutions that capture detailed metrics and logs from the API gateway helps maintain operational visibility and supports proactive management of the federated services.

In summary, API gateways play a pivotal role in enhancing the functionality and security of federated GraphQL services. They offer a range of benefits, including efficient request routing, centralized security enforcement, rate limiting, and caching. Proper configuration and integration of API gateways with federated GraphQL systems require careful planning and execution, with attention to schema management, routing rules, and monitoring practices. By leveraging the capabilities of API gateways, organizations can streamline their federated GraphQL architectures, improve performance, and maintain robust security measures.

When integrating API gateways with federated GraphQL services, it is essential to address several technical considerations to ensure a seamless and efficient operation. One of these considerations is the management of request and response transformations. API gateways can be configured to modify requests before they reach the federated services and to adjust responses before they are returned to clients. This capability is particularly useful in adapting responses from various federated services to a unified format that meets the client's expectations. For instance, an API gateway can map different fields or consolidate responses from multiple services into a single coherent output, thus enhancing the client-side experience.

Additionally, API gateways can facilitate more granular monitoring and logging of federated GraphQL traffic. By centralizing the logging of requests and responses, API gateways provide valuable insights into the interactions between clients and federated services. This centralized monitoring can help identify performance bottlenecks, troubleshoot issues, and analyze usage patterns. For example, detailed logs can reveal which federated services are experiencing high traffic or encountering errors, enabling targeted optimizations and proactive maintenance.

Another significant advantage of API gateways is their support for API versioning. In a federated GraphQL environment, where multiple services are updated independently, managing different versions of the API becomes crucial. API gateways can handle versioning by routing requests to the appropriate version of a service based on the version specified in the request. This capability allows for smooth transitions between different versions of the federated services, reducing the risk of breaking changes and maintaining backward compatibility.

Configuring API gateways for federated GraphQL involves several steps, including setting up routing rules, defining authentication and authorization policies, and configuring caching and rate limiting. Routing rules are used to direct incoming requests to the correct federated services based on the GraphQL operations requested. For example, a request for user data might be routed to a user service, while a request for product information might be sent to a product service. Properly defining these rules ensures that each request is handled by the appropriate service, optimizing performance and accuracy.

Authentication and authorization policies must be carefully configured to protect the federated GraphQL services from unauthorized access. API gateways can integrate with identity providers to enforce security protocols and validate tokens. This setup ensures that only authorized users can access sensitive data or perform specific actions within the federated services. In addition, API gateways can apply fine-grained authorization rules based on user roles or request attributes, providing a robust security model.

Caching and rate limiting configurations require careful planning to balance performance with resource usage. Caching strategies should be designed to improve response times while ensuring that clients receive up-to-date information. API gateways typically support various caching mechanisms, such as in-memory caching or distributed caches, which can be tailored to the specific needs of the federated services. Rate limiting policies should be established to prevent abuse and ensure fair usage, taking into account the individual capacities of the federated services and the overall system load.

Integrating API gateways with federated GraphQL services also involves handling cross-cutting concerns such as error handling and resiliency. API gateways can be configured to implement retry logic, fallback mechanisms, and circuit breakers to enhance the robustness of the system. For example, if a federated service becomes unavailable, the API gateway can automatically retry the request or route it to a fallback service. These resiliency features help maintain the reliability and availability of the federated GraphQL system.

In conclusion, the integration of API gateways with federated GraphQL services provides a range of benefits that enhance functionality, security, and performance. By effectively managing request routing, implementing security policies, and leveraging caching and rate limiting, API gateways play a vital role in optimizing the operation of federated architectures. Proper configuration and management of these components ensure that federated GraphQL services are robust, efficient, and capable of delivering a seamless experience to clients.

To leverage the full potential of API gateways in a federated GraphQL environment, it is important to explore additional advanced features such as caching and request throttling. Caching can significantly enhance the performance of federated GraphQL services by reducing redundant requests to backend services and improving response times. API gateways can be configured to cache responses from federated services based on various criteria, such as query parameters or request headers. This approach minimizes the load on backend services, as frequently requested data is served from the cache, rather than being retrieved from the database or other service endpoints each time.

The configuration of caching policies requires careful consideration of cache invalidation strategies to ensure that stale data does not persist. API gateways often support various cache expiration settings, including time-based expiration and event-based invalidation. Time-based expiration automatically clears cached data after a specified period, while event-based invalidation involves triggering cache refreshes in response to changes in the underlying data. Combining these strategies can help maintain data consistency while optimizing performance.

Request throttling is another crucial feature provided by API gateways. Throttling controls the rate at which requests are processed, preventing overloading of federated services and ensuring fair usage across all clients. By implementing rate limits at the API gateway level, organizations can protect their services from abuse and maintain a high level of availability. Throttling policies can be configured based on various parameters, such as the number of requests per minute or the number of concurrent connections. Additionally, API gateways can provide detailed metrics and alerts on throttling events, helping teams to monitor and adjust their policies as needed.

Incorporating API gateways into a federated GraphQL setup also enhances security through features like IP whitelisting, bot protection, and DDoS mitigation. IP whitelisting restricts access to federated services based on IP addresses, allowing only trusted sources to interact with the services. Bot protection mechanisms help prevent automated scripts and bots from overwhelming the services with malicious traffic. DDoS (Distributed Denial of Service) mitigation techniques are employed to defend against large-scale attacks aimed at disrupting service availability. By employing these security features, organizations can safeguard their federated GraphQL services from potential threats and ensure a secure user experience.

Integrating an API gateway with federated GraphQL services requires a thorough understanding of the gateway's capabilities and how they align with the architectural goals of the federated system. Each gateway solution offers different features and configurations, and selecting the right gateway involves evaluating factors such as ease of integration, support for GraphQL, and the ability to handle specific requirements like authentication, caching, and throttling. Furthermore, as federated systems evolve, it is essential to continuously monitor the performance and effectiveness of the API gateway, making adjustments as needed to accommodate new services or changing traffic patterns.

API gateway integration also facilitates better management of service interdependencies within a federated GraphQL architecture. By providing a centralized entry point for all requests, API gateways help to decouple frontend applications from the complexity of interacting with multiple backend services. This decoupling simplifies client-side development and enhances maintainability, as changes to backend services can be managed transparently without affecting the frontend code. Additionally, API gateways support service discovery and load balancing, ensuring that requests are distributed efficiently across multiple instances of a service, thus improving scalability and reliability.

In summary, API gateways play a pivotal role in optimizing and securing federated GraphQL environments. Through advanced features like request transformation, centralized logging, caching, throttling, and security measures, API gateways enhance the functionality and performance of federated services. The integration of an API gateway into a federated GraphQL setup not only streamlines the management of service interactions but also provides robust tools for handling real-time data, monitoring, and scaling. As organizations continue to adopt and expand their use of federated GraphQL, the effective utilization of API gateways will be instrumental in achieving a seamless and high-performance architecture.

CHAPTER 23: SECURING FEDERATED GRAPHQL ENDPOINTS

As the adoption of federated GraphQL architectures grows, ensuring the security of these systems becomes increasingly critical. In a federated setup, where multiple services collaborate to provide a unified GraphQL schema, the security measures must address both individual service endpoints and the interactions between them. This chapter delves into advanced security practices for federated GraphQL environments, encompassing authentication mechanisms, authorization strategies, and securing communication between services.

Authentication is a foundational aspect of securing federated GraphQL endpoints. It verifies the identity of users or systems attempting to access the services. In a federated GraphQL architecture, where multiple services may handle different parts of the schema, implementing consistent authentication across all services can be challenging. One common approach is to use a centralized authentication service, which issues tokens upon successful user authentication. These tokens, such as JSON Web Tokens (JWTs), are then used to authenticate requests across federated services. Each service in the federation can validate the token to ensure that requests are coming from authenticated users.

Implementing robust authentication mechanisms involves not only choosing the right token format but also ensuring secure token storage and handling. Tokens should be stored securely on the client side and transmitted over HTTPS to prevent interception. Additionally, token expiration and refresh mechanisms must be configured to balance security with user convenience. Short-lived tokens can mitigate the risk of token theft, while refresh tokens provide a way to obtain new access tokens without requiring users to reauthenticate frequently.

Authorization, on the other hand, determines what authenticated users are allowed to do within the federated GraphQL system. In a federated environment, authorization can be more complex due to the distributed nature of the services. Each service might have its own set of authorization rules, which must be coordinated to ensure consistent access control across the entire schema. One approach to managing authorization in federated GraphQL is to implement role-based access control (RBAC) or attribute-based access control (ABAC) at the service level. RBAC assigns roles to users, and each role has specific permissions within the service, while ABAC evaluates attributes of the user and the request to make authorization decisions.

To simplify authorization management, some federated GraphQL systems use a global authorization service that enforces policies across all services. This service can interact with individual services to determine whether a request should be allowed based on the user's roles, attributes, or permissions. By centralizing authorization logic, organizations can maintain consistency and reduce the complexity of managing access control in a federated setup.

Securing communication between services is another crucial aspect of safeguarding federated GraphQL architectures. Since federated services often communicate over networks, protecting this communication from eavesdropping and tampering is essential. Implementing Transport Layer Security (TLS) is a fundamental practice for encrypting data in transit between services. TLS ensures that data exchanged between services is encrypted and that the communication channel is secure from potential attackers.

In addition to TLS, organizations should consider mutual TLS (mTLS) for enhanced security. mTLS requires both the client and server to authenticate each other using certificates, adding an extra layer of trust to the communication process. This mutual authentication helps prevent unauthorized services from interacting with the federated system and ensures that only legitimate services can participate in the federation.

Another aspect of securing service-to-service communication is ensuring proper service discovery and verification. In a federated architecture, services may dynamically discover and interact with one another. To prevent unauthorized services from joining the federation, it is important to use mechanisms such as service registration and discovery tools that support secure communication and verification processes. These tools can validate the identity of services before allowing them to participate in the federation.

Monitoring and auditing play a significant role in maintaining the security of federated GraphQL endpoints. By implementing comprehensive logging and monitoring solutions, organizations can track access patterns, detect suspicious activities, and respond to potential security incidents. Logs should capture relevant information such as authentication attempts, authorization decisions, and communication between services. Regular audits of these logs can help identify vulnerabilities, ensure compliance with security policies, and provide insights into potential areas for improvement.

In summary, securing federated GraphQL endpoints involves a multi-faceted approach that includes implementing robust authentication and authorization mechanisms, securing communication channels, and employing effective monitoring and auditing practices. By addressing these security aspects, organizations can protect their federated GraphQL systems from various threats and ensure that their services operate securely and reliably.

Securing communication between federated GraphQL services is equally crucial, as it ensures that data exchanged between services remains confidential and tamper-proof. In a federated setup, where multiple services interact, encryption plays a pivotal role in safeguarding data in transit. Using Transport Layer Security (TLS) is a fundamental practice to protect data from being intercepted or altered during transmission. TLS provides a secure channel by encrypting the data exchanged between clients and services, as well as between services themselves.

In addition to encryption, securing inter-service communication often involves implementing mutual authentication. This technique ensures that not only the client authenticates to the service but also that services authenticate to each other. Mutual authentication can prevent unauthorized services from interacting with the federated system, thus mitigating risks associated with service impersonation. Techniques such as mTLS (mutual TLS) are commonly used to establish this level of trust between services.

Another aspect of securing federated GraphQL endpoints

involves securing the API gateway or federation gateway, which acts as a central point of contact for clients. The gateway often handles routing requests to the appropriate services and consolidates responses. Therefore, it must be protected from potential attacks such as denial-of-service (DoS) or distributed denial-of-service (DDoS) attacks. Implementing rate limiting and traffic monitoring can help mitigate these risks. Rate limiting restricts the number of requests a client can make in a given period, while traffic monitoring helps identify unusual patterns that could indicate an attack.

Furthermore, securing API endpoints requires robust input validation to prevent malicious data from compromising the system. Since GraphQL allows clients to specify queries, it is essential to validate inputs rigorously to avoid injection attacks or excessive resource consumption. Implementing schema validation and query complexity analysis can help in identifying and blocking potentially harmful requests. Schema validation ensures that the incoming queries adhere to the defined schema, while query complexity analysis evaluates the potential impact of queries on system resources.

Logging and monitoring are critical components of a security strategy, providing visibility into the operations of federated GraphQL services. Detailed logs can help detect and respond to suspicious activities or breaches. Effective logging should capture not only request and response details but also authentication and authorization events. Implementing centralized logging solutions can facilitate the aggregation and analysis of logs from multiple services, enhancing the ability to identify and address security incidents.

In addition to these measures, regular security assessments and audits are vital to maintaining a secure federated GraphQL architecture. Periodic vulnerability scans and penetration testing can uncover potential weaknesses in the system, allowing for timely remediation. Security assessments should cover all aspects of the federated setup, including authentication mechanisms, inter-service communication, and API gateway configurations.

Implementing a comprehensive security framework for federated GraphQL requires a combination of these practices, tailored to the specific needs and architecture of the system. By focusing on robust authentication, rigorous authorization, encrypted communication, and proactive monitoring, organizations can significantly enhance the security posture of their federated GraphQL environments. As the landscape of security threats evolves, continuous adaptation and improvement of security practices will be essential to safeguarding federated services against emerging risks.

Ensuring robust authorization in federated GraphQL environments involves implementing fine-grained access control mechanisms. Given that federated GraphQL setups often aggregate data from various services, it is imperative to control who can access what data and operations. This can be achieved through role-based access control (RBAC) or attribute-based access control (ABAC). RBAC assigns permissions based on predefined roles, such as admin or user, while ABAC evaluates access based on attributes associated with the user, the resource, and the environment.

In practice, these strategies can be implemented through middleware or custom resolvers. Middleware can intercept requests to enforce authorization policies before they reach the resolver functions. For instance, a middleware layer can check the user's roles or attributes and validate whether they have the necessary permissions to execute a particular query or mutation. Similarly, custom resolvers can be tailored to include authorization logic specific to the data they handle, ensuring that sensitive operations are adequately protected.

Another critical aspect of securing federated GraphQL endpoints involves managing secrets and credentials. Since federated systems often involve multiple services and components, securely storing and handling secrets, such as API keys or tokens, is essential. Utilizing secrets management tools or services can enhance security by ensuring that secrets are encrypted and access is controlled. These tools often provide features such as automated secrets rotation and audit logging, which contribute to a more secure environment.

It is also beneficial to integrate security best practices into the development lifecycle through practices such as security code reviews and automated security testing. Security code reviews involve systematically analyzing the code for vulnerabilities, while automated security testing tools can scan for common issues such as vulnerabilities in dependencies or insecure coding practices. These practices help identify and address potential security issues early in the development process, reducing the risk of vulnerabilities in production systems.

Compliance with industry standards and regulations is another important consideration when securing federated GraphQL endpoints. Depending on the nature of the data being handled, organizations may need to adhere to regulations such as GDPR, HIPAA, or PCI DSS. Compliance often involves implementing specific security controls, such as data encryption or audit trails, to meet regulatory requirements. Regular security assessments and audits can help ensure that these controls are effective and that the system remains compliant over time.

Finally, security awareness and training for development and operations teams play a crucial role in maintaining a secure federated GraphQL environment. Providing regular training on security best practices and emerging threats helps ensure that team members are aware of potential risks and know how to address them. This proactive approach contributes to a culture of security, where everyone involved in managing and developing federated services understands their role in safeguarding the system.

In summary, securing federated GraphQL endpoints requires a multifaceted approach that encompasses robust authentication and authorization mechanisms, secure communication practices, effective logging and monitoring, and adherence to industry standards and regulations. By integrating these advanced security practices, organizations can protect their federated architectures from potential threats and ensure that their data and services remain secure.

CHAPTER 24: ADVANCED QUERY PLANNING AND EXECUTION IN FEDERATION

In the realm of federated GraphQL architectures, optimizing query planning and execution is essential for ensuring high performance and efficient data retrieval. As federated systems aggregate data from multiple sources, the complexity of query planning increases significantly. This chapter explores advanced techniques for optimizing query planning and execution in federated GraphQL environments, focusing on distributed query processing and various optimization strategies.

The foundational element of query optimization in a federated GraphQL setup lies in understanding the nature of distributed query processing. Unlike monolithic GraphQL servers, which handle all queries within a single service, federated systems must coordinate query execution across multiple services. This distribution introduces challenges related to query aggregation, data fetching, and response composition. Efficiently managing these aspects is crucial for minimizing latency and improving overall system performance.

A primary technique for optimizing query execution is query planning. In a federated architecture, the query planning phase involves determining how to split a query into sub-queries that can be executed by different services. The complexity of this phase grows with the number of federated services and the intricacy of the queries. Advanced query planners must analyze the query structure, identify relevant services, and establish an efficient execution plan that balances load and minimizes cross-service communication.

One effective approach to advanced query planning is leveraging query optimization algorithms. These algorithms can analyze the query graph to determine the most efficient way to fetch and aggregate data. Techniques such as query rewriting, which involves transforming a query into a more efficient form, and cost-based optimization, which assesses different execution plans based on their resource consumption, are integral to this process. By applying these algorithms, federated systems can reduce query execution times and improve responsiveness.

Distributed query processing is another critical aspect of query optimization in federated environments. This involves dividing a query into multiple sub-queries that are executed concurrently across different services. Efficient distribution requires not only partitioning the query but also managing the communication and synchronization between services. Techniques such as parallel execution and pipelining can enhance performance by allowing simultaneous data retrieval and processing.

Parallel execution involves executing multiple sub-queries at the same time, thereby reducing the overall query processing time. This requires careful coordination to handle potential issues such as data dependencies and synchronization. Pipelining, on the other hand, involves processing data in stages, where each stage produces results that are consumed by the next stage. This technique can be particularly useful for queries that involve complex transformations or aggregations.

To further optimize query performance, caching mechanisms can be employed. Caching can significantly reduce the load on backend services by storing frequently requested data and serving it directly from the cache. In a federated GraphQL setup, caching strategies must be designed to work across multiple services and handle the potential for cache invalidation. Techniques such as query result caching, where the results of specific queries are stored, and data caching at the service level can help mitigate performance bottlenecks.

Another advanced technique involves leveraging batch data fetching. In federated environments, requests for data from multiple services can be batched to minimize the number of network round-trips. Batch fetching involves grouping multiple requests into a single query, which is then executed in one go. This reduces overhead and improves efficiency, particularly for queries that involve fetching data from multiple sources.

In addition to these techniques, monitoring and profiling tools play a vital role in optimizing query performance. These tools provide insights into query execution times, service response times, and overall system performance. By analyzing this data, developers and operations teams can identify performance bottlenecks, optimize query plans, and make informed decisions about resource allocation.

Advanced query planning and execution strategies must also consider scalability. As federated systems grow and handle an increasing volume of queries, scalability becomes a critical concern. Techniques such as load balancing, sharding, and horizontal scaling can help manage increasing query loads and ensure that the system remains responsive under heavy usage.

Finally, integrating query optimization strategies with continuous integration and continuous deployment (CI/CD) practices can enhance the overall efficiency of federated GraphQL systems. Automated testing and deployment pipelines can ensure that performance improvements are consistently applied and that optimizations are verified in real-world scenarios.

In conclusion, optimizing query planning and execution in federated GraphQL environments involves a combination of advanced techniques and strategic approaches. By employing query optimization algorithms, distributed query processing, caching, batch data fetching, and leveraging monitoring tools, organizations can significantly enhance the performance and efficiency of their federated systems. As federated architectures continue to evolve, these techniques will remain essential for managing complex queries and ensuring a high-performance GraphQL experience.

The effectiveness of distributed query processing is closely linked to how well sub-queries are managed and coordinated. When executing sub-queries in parallel, it is essential to address potential challenges such as network latency and the order of data arrival. One approach to mitigating these issues is through the implementation of asynchronous processing techniques, which allow for non-blocking operations and better resource utilization. Asynchronous processing ensures that while waiting for data from one service, other operations can continue, thus enhancing overall system efficiency.

Another critical consideration in advanced query planning is the role of caching mechanisms. Caching can significantly reduce the load on federated services by storing frequently accessed data closer to where it is needed. In a federated environment, caching strategies must be carefully designed to avoid stale data and ensure cache coherence. Techniques such as query result caching and service-level caching can be employed to optimize performance. Query result caching involves storing the results of previously executed queries, while service-level caching focuses on caching data at the individual service level. Both methods can reduce the need for redundant data fetching and speed up query responses.

Moreover, optimizing resolver performance is crucial for efficient query execution. Resolvers are responsible for fetching and returning the data for a specific field in a query. In a federated setup, each service may have its own set of resolvers, which must be optimized to handle high-throughput requests effectively. Techniques for optimizing resolvers include minimizing the number of database queries, leveraging batch processing to handle multiple requests in a single operation, and implementing efficient data retrieval strategies. By optimizing resolvers, federated systems can improve query performance and reduce overall latency.

To further enhance query planning and execution, it is beneficial to incorporate monitoring and profiling tools. These tools provide valuable insights into query performance, allowing for the identification of bottlenecks and areas for improvement. Monitoring tools can track metrics such as query execution times, service response times, and resource utilization. Profiling tools, on the other hand, offer detailed analysis of query execution paths, helping to pinpoint inefficiencies and optimize query processing. By leveraging these tools, teams can continuously assess and refine their query optimization strategies.

In addition to these techniques, it is essential to consider the impact of schema design on query performance. A well-designed schema can simplify query planning and execution by ensuring that data relationships are clearly defined and easily accessible. In a federated architecture, schema design should focus on minimizing the complexity of cross-service queries and reducing the need for extensive data aggregation.

Techniques such as schema stitching, where schemas are combined into a unified schema, can help streamline query processing and improve overall performance.

Furthermore, advanced query planning must address the challenge of schema evolution. As schemas evolve over time, maintaining performance while accommodating changes can be challenging. Techniques such as versioning, where different versions of the schema are supported simultaneously, and incremental updates, where only the changed parts of the schema are updated, can help manage schema evolution without disrupting query performance. By implementing these techniques, federated systems can ensure that query planning and execution remain efficient despite ongoing schema changes.

Lastly, optimizing query execution in a federated environment requires a holistic approach that considers both technical and architectural aspects. By combining advanced query planning techniques, efficient distributed query processing, caching strategies, resolver optimization, and monitoring tools, federated systems can achieve significant improvements in query performance. As federated architectures continue to evolve, ongoing research and development in query optimization will play a crucial role in addressing emerging challenges and enhancing the overall efficiency of federated GraphQL systems.

Through these advanced techniques and strategies, organizations can effectively manage complex queries in a federated setup, ensuring that their GraphQL services are both performant and scalable. As federated systems grow and become more intricate, the ability to optimize query planning and execution will remain a key factor in delivering high-quality, responsive services.

Another important aspect of advanced query planning in federated GraphQL is the management of distributed query execution. In a federated environment, queries often span multiple services, each responsible for different parts of the schema. Efficiently handling these distributed queries requires a well-coordinated approach to query planning and execution.

One strategy to improve distributed query execution is to implement query federation-specific optimizations. These optimizations include techniques for reducing cross-service communication overhead and improving data locality. For instance, minimizing the number of service calls required for a single query can be achieved by analyzing query patterns and consolidating data requests where possible. This approach reduces the latency associated with service-to-service communication and enhances overall query performance.

Additionally, distributed query execution can benefit from parallelism. By executing multiple sub-queries concurrently, the overall time required to fulfill a query can be significantly reduced. However, achieving effective parallelism requires careful coordination to ensure that concurrent queries do not overwhelm the system or cause contention. Techniques such as load balancing and request throttling can be employed to manage concurrency and maintain system stability.

To further optimize query execution, it is important to consider the role of data partitioning and sharding. Data partitioning involves dividing large datasets into smaller, more manageable chunks, while sharding distributes data across multiple servers or databases. These techniques can improve query performance by enabling more efficient data access and reducing the load on individual services. In a federated GraphQL setup, data partitioning and sharding can be applied to optimize data retrieval and processing, ensuring that queries are executed efficiently across distributed services.

Another key aspect of advanced query planning is the

handling of complex queries that involve multiple layers of nested fields or deep relationships. Complex queries can be particularly challenging in a federated environment, where data may be distributed across various services. To address this challenge, techniques such as query flattening and query optimization can be employed. Query flattening involves restructuring complex queries into simpler, more manageable components, while query optimization focuses on identifying and eliminating inefficiencies in query execution.

In addition to these techniques, it is crucial to incorporate effective error handling and fault tolerance mechanisms. Federated systems are inherently more complex and may be prone to various types of failures, such as network issues or service outages. Implementing robust error handling strategies, such as retries, fallbacks, and circuit breakers, can help mitigate the impact of failures and ensure that queries are processed reliably. By designing for fault tolerance, federated systems can maintain high levels of performance and availability even in the face of disruptions.

Finally, the role of metadata and schema introspection in query planning and execution cannot be overlooked. Metadata provides valuable information about the schema and its structure, which can be used to enhance query planning and execution. Schema introspection allows for dynamic query analysis and optimization based on the current state of the schema. By leveraging metadata and introspection capabilities, teams can gain deeper insights into query behavior and optimize their systems accordingly.

In summary, advanced query planning and execution in federated GraphQL environments involve a combination of strategies aimed at optimizing performance and handling complex queries. By employing techniques such as distributed query processing, parallelism, data partitioning, query flattening, and effective error handling, teams can ensure that their federated systems operate efficiently and reliably. Furthermore, incorporating monitoring and profiling tools, as well as leveraging metadata and schema introspection, can provide valuable insights for continuous improvement and optimization. Through these advanced techniques, federated GraphQL systems can achieve enhanced query performance and scalability, meeting the demands of modern, data-driven applications.

CHAPTER 25: FEDERATION AND EVENT-DRIVEN ARCHITECTURES

Event-driven architectures offer a powerful complement to federated GraphQL setups, enabling real-time data synchronization and enhanced system responsiveness. In this chapter, we will explore the integration of event-driven patterns with GraphQL Federation, focusing on how event sourcing, message queues, and asynchronous events can be utilized to enhance the capabilities of a federated system.

Event-driven architectures are based on the principle of decoupling components through asynchronous communication. This model can be particularly beneficial in federated GraphQL systems, where multiple services interact to provide a cohesive API. By leveraging event-driven patterns, these interactions can be managed more efficiently, leading to improved scalability and responsiveness.

One foundational concept in event-driven architectures is event sourcing. This technique involves persisting the state of an application as a series of events, rather than storing the current state directly. Each event represents a change in the system and is recorded in an event log. This approach allows for a complete history of changes to be maintained, facilitating easier debugging, auditing, and replay of events.

In the context of GraphQL Federation, event sourcing can be employed to handle changes across distributed services. For example, when a mutation occurs in one service, an event can be published to an event stream. Other services can then subscribe to this stream to receive updates and synchronize their state accordingly. This method ensures that all services remain consistent with the latest changes, even in a dynamic federated environment.

Message queues play a critical role in managing event-driven communication within federated systems. A message queue is a buffer that temporarily holds messages (or events) until they can be processed by the appropriate services. By utilizing message queues, services can communicate asynchronously, which helps to decouple them and manage load more effectively.

When integrating message queues with federated GraphQL, it is important to consider how messages will be routed and consumed. Each service in the federation may need to interact with one or more message queues to handle incoming events. Implementing a reliable messaging infrastructure involves setting up proper queue management, ensuring message durability, and configuring appropriate retry mechanisms for failed message processing.

Asynchronous event handling is another key aspect of integrating event-driven architectures with GraphQL Federation. Asynchronous processing allows services to handle events in a non-blocking manner, which can significantly improve the overall performance and responsiveness of the system. For example, when a user triggers a mutation, the service handling the mutation can immediately acknowledge the request while the actual processing occurs asynchronously.

In a federated GraphQL setup, asynchronous event handling can be particularly useful for managing long-running operations or tasks that do not need to be completed immediately. By offloading such tasks to background processes, services can remain responsive to user requests while continuing to process events in the background.

To effectively manage asynchronous events, it is essential to implement proper coordination and synchronization mechanisms. This involves ensuring that events are processed in the correct order and that services can handle eventual consistency. For instance, if a service receives an event that requires updating multiple dependent services, it must be able to manage the order of updates and handle any potential conflicts or inconsistencies.

Moreover, integrating event-driven patterns with federated GraphQL requires addressing potential challenges related to event schema evolution and data consistency. As the system evolves, the structure of events may change, necessitating updates to event schemas and corresponding handlers. This requires careful versioning and migration strategies to ensure that all services can handle both old and new event formats without disrupting the overall system.

By incorporating event-driven architectures into a federated GraphQL setup, organizations can achieve greater flexibility and responsiveness in their systems. The combination of event sourcing, message queues, and asynchronous processing provides a robust framework for managing real-time data and maintaining consistency across distributed services. This integration enhances the capabilities of GraphQL Federation, allowing for more dynamic and scalable applications.

As we move forward in this chapter, we will delve deeper into specific techniques and best practices for implementing event-driven patterns within federated GraphQL environments.

We will explore practical examples and case studies that illustrate how these approaches can be effectively applied to achieve a well-coordinated and high-performance federated architecture.

In a federated GraphQL architecture, integrating event-driven patterns necessitates a careful approach to ensure seamless interaction between services. Event sourcing, as previously discussed, provides a robust mechanism for persisting changes, but its effective implementation requires careful consideration of how events are structured and propagated.

When utilizing event sourcing within a federated GraphQL environment, it is crucial to define a consistent event schema. This schema should be agreed upon by all services involved in the federation. By standardizing the format of events, services can more easily interpret and process events without needing complex transformations. This standardization also aids in maintaining the consistency and reliability of the event stream, which is essential for ensuring that all services in the federation remain synchronized.

Message queues facilitate the asynchronous handling of events, providing a mechanism for buffering and routing events between services. In a federated setup, each service may interact with multiple queues to handle different types of events. For example, a user service might publish user-related events to one queue, while an order service publishes order-related events to another. Each service subscribes to the relevant queues to receive and process events pertinent to its domain. This segregation of queues helps manage event traffic more efficiently and ensures that each service processes only the events it is concerned with.

One of the primary advantages of using message queues is the ability to decouple services. This decoupling means that a service producing an event does not need to know which services will consume it, nor do consumers need to be aware of the specifics of the producers. This loose coupling enhances the flexibility and scalability of the federated system, as new services can be added or existing services modified without disrupting the overall architecture.

Handling asynchronous events requires a robust strategy for managing eventual consistency. Since events are processed out of order and at different times, there can be temporary inconsistencies between services. To address this, services must be designed to handle eventual consistency by reconciling their state based on the latest events received. Techniques such as idempotent processing and compensating transactions can be employed to ensure that the system remains consistent despite the inherent asynchrony.

Moreover, ensuring that events are processed reliably is crucial for maintaining the integrity of the federated system. This involves implementing mechanisms for tracking event delivery, handling failures, and retrying failed events. Many messaging systems provide built-in support for such features, including message acknowledgments, dead-letter queues, and configurable retry policies. By leveraging these features, you can build a resilient event-driven architecture that handles failures gracefully and maintains data integrity.

In a federated GraphQL environment, integrating real-time updates with event-driven patterns can enhance the responsiveness of the system. GraphQL subscriptions, which enable clients to receive real-time updates, can be paired with event-driven mechanisms to push updates to clients as soon as relevant events occur. This approach ensures that clients receive the most current data without needing to continuously poll the server.

Implementing real-time updates involves configuring your GraphQL server to handle subscriptions and connect it to your event-driven infrastructure. When an event is published, the server processes the event and pushes updates to subscribed clients. This setup requires careful orchestration to manage the flow of events and ensure that updates are delivered efficiently and accurately.

Additionally, security considerations must be addressed when integrating event-driven patterns with federated GraphQL. Event data should be encrypted during transmission to protect sensitive information. Authentication and authorization mechanisms should be in place to ensure that only authorized services can publish or consume events. Furthermore, access controls should be enforced to prevent unauthorized access to event data or manipulation of event streams.

To summarize, integrating event-driven architectures with federated GraphQL setups offers numerous benefits, including improved scalability, responsiveness, and flexibility. By implementing event sourcing, utilizing message queues, and handling asynchronous events effectively, you can enhance the performance and reliability of your federated system. Real-time updates via GraphQL subscriptions can further augment the user experience by delivering timely information. However, this integration requires careful planning and execution, particularly in areas such as event schema standardization, reliable message processing, eventual consistency, and security. With these considerations in mind, you can build a robust federated GraphQL architecture that leverages the strengths of event-driven approaches to deliver a dynamic and responsive system.

Incorporating event-driven patterns into a federated GraphQL architecture can greatly enhance its responsiveness and flexibility, but it requires careful coordination and integration. As the federated system grows, managing and processing events efficiently becomes increasingly important. To achieve this, a few key considerations must be addressed: the management of event schemas, the implementation of message queues, and the handling of asynchronous events.

The management of event schemas involves designing a standardized format that all services in the federation can understand. This standardization is critical to ensure that events are consistently produced and consumed across different services. When defining event schemas, it is beneficial to adopt a common language or format that all services agree upon, which facilitates smooth communication and integration. Additionally, versioning of event schemas may be necessary to handle changes in the structure of events over time. Versioning allows for backward compatibility and smooth transitions when schemas evolve, ensuring that different versions of services can coexist without causing disruptions.

Message queues are central to the event-driven architecture, providing a means to decouple services and handle asynchronous communication. Each service may publish events to a message queue, which acts as a buffer and ensures that events are delivered to the appropriate consumers in a reliable manner. The choice of message queue technology can impact the performance and reliability of the system. It is essential to select a message queue that supports features such as message persistence, ordering, and acknowledgment to ensure that events are not lost or processed out of order.

To integrate message queues with federated GraphQL services, each service should be designed to interact with its relevant queues. Services publish events to queues and subscribe to queues that provide the events they need to process. For example, an e-commerce system may have separate queues for order events, inventory updates, and user activities. By subscribing to the appropriate queues, services can stay informed about changes in other parts of the system and react accordingly.

Handling asynchronous events introduces challenges related to consistency and reliability. Since events are processed at different times, there is a need for mechanisms to manage eventual consistency. Services must be designed to reconcile their state based on the events they receive, which may involve applying compensating actions or retrying failed operations. Implementing idempotent processing is crucial, ensuring that applying the same event multiple times does not produce inconsistent results. This is especially important in a distributed system where duplicate events or out-of-order processing can occur.

In addition to managing eventual consistency, monitoring and tracing are vital to ensuring the smooth operation of an event-driven federated GraphQL system. Monitoring tools can track the flow of events through the system, identifying bottlenecks or failures in real-time. Tracing allows for a detailed view of event processing, helping to diagnose issues and optimize performance. By combining these tools with alerting mechanisms, administrators can quickly respond to and address any issues that arise.

Security considerations also play a significant role in integrating event-driven patterns with GraphQL Federation. Events often contain sensitive information, so it is important to implement appropriate security measures to protect data both in transit and at rest. Encryption can be used to secure event payloads, while access controls ensure that only authorized services can publish or consume events. Additionally, auditing and logging should be implemented to track event handling and detect any potential security breaches.

To further enhance the federated architecture, it is beneficial to incorporate event-driven patterns into the schema design. For example, services can define subscriptions in GraphQL schemas that correspond to events published by other services. This allows clients to subscribe to real-time updates and receive notifications when relevant events occur. By integrating event-driven patterns directly into the GraphQL layer, the system can provide a more seamless and responsive experience for users.

In summary, integrating event-driven architectures with federated GraphQL involves carefully managing event schemas, utilizing message queues, and addressing the challenges of asynchronous processing. By adopting these practices, organizations can build robust, scalable systems that leverage the strengths of both federated GraphQL and event-driven patterns. This approach not only improves the responsiveness of the system but also enhances its ability to handle complex interactions and maintain consistency across distributed services.

CHAPTER 26: TROUBLESHOOTING COMMON ISSUES IN FEDERATED GRAPHQL

Maintaining a federated GraphQL environment presents unique challenges, and effective troubleshooting is key to ensuring system reliability and performance. Federated architectures, while powerful, can be complex, making it essential to identify and resolve issues promptly to maintain smooth operation. This chapter explores common problems encountered in federated GraphQL setups, offering practical solutions and tips to diagnose and address these issues.

One of the primary challenges in federated GraphQL is managing schema stitching and schema consistency. When federating multiple GraphQL services, each service maintains its own schema, which must be stitched together into a unified schema. This integration can lead to conflicts, especially if different services define overlapping types or fields with different names or definitions. Inconsistent schemas can result in runtime errors or unexpected behavior when queries are executed.

To troubleshoot schema-related issues, start by validating

the schemas of all federated services individually. Tools like GraphQL's schema validation or introspection can help ensure that each schema adheres to expected standards. When stitching schemas, pay close attention to how types and fields are resolved. Utilizing schema validation tools can also help catch discrepancies early in the development process.

Another common issue is related to resolver performance and efficiency. Resolvers, which handle the actual data fetching for GraphQL queries, can become bottlenecks if not optimized properly. In a federated setup, this problem is compounded by the need to coordinate between multiple services. Performance issues often manifest as slow query responses or high latency.

To address resolver performance problems, first profile and monitor the resolver execution times. Tools such as Apollo Studio or GraphQL tracing can provide insights into which resolvers are taking the most time and why. Once the problematic resolvers are identified, review their implementation to ensure they are optimized for performance. This might involve reducing the number of database queries, using batching and caching techniques, or optimizing the data retrieval logic.

Network issues can also pose significant challenges in a federated GraphQL architecture. Since federated systems involve communication between multiple services, network latency or failures can impact the overall performance and reliability of the system. Problems such as timeouts, dropped connections, or incorrect data responses can often be traced back to network issues.

To troubleshoot network-related problems, start by examining the connectivity and latency between services. Use network monitoring tools to detect and analyze any anomalies in traffic patterns or connection stability. Implementing robust error handling and retry logic in your services can also help mitigate the impact of transient network issues.

Another frequent issue in federated GraphQL setups is managing and maintaining authentication and authorization. In a federated environment, each service may have its own authentication and authorization mechanisms, leading to complexities in ensuring consistent access control across the entire system. Issues can arise if tokens or credentials are not passed correctly between services or if authorization policies are inconsistently enforced.

To address these challenges, ensure that authentication and authorization mechanisms are clearly defined and uniformly applied across all services. Use centralized authentication services or token validation systems to manage and validate user credentials consistently. Regularly audit and review access control policies to ensure they are enforced correctly across the federated architecture.

Data consistency and synchronization can also be problematic, especially when services have their own independent data stores. Federated systems must manage data integrity and consistency across multiple services, which can be challenging when services update or delete data asynchronously.

To troubleshoot data consistency issues, implement strategies for data synchronization and consistency checks. Use event sourcing or change data capture mechanisms to keep services informed about data changes in real-time. Ensure that services are designed to handle eventual consistency and that they can reconcile data discrepancies when they arise.

In summary, troubleshooting common issues in federated GraphQL environments requires a systematic approach to diagnosing and resolving problems. By focusing on schema consistency, resolver performance, network stability, authentication and authorization, and data consistency, you can effectively maintain and optimize a federated GraphQL system. Implementing best practices for validation, monitoring, and error handling will help ensure that your federated architecture remains robust and responsive, providing a seamless experience for users and developers alike.

Another crucial aspect of troubleshooting in a federated GraphQL environment is handling errors and debugging effectively. In federated setups, errors can originate from any of the services involved, and pinpointing the source of an issue can be complex. Error messages returned from GraphQL queries may not always provide sufficient detail about the underlying problem, particularly if the error is related to the integration between services rather than a specific service itself.

To tackle error handling, start by ensuring that each service in your federation has comprehensive error logging and reporting in place. Implementing structured logging can help provide more context for errors, making it easier to trace issues across service boundaries. Additionally, ensure that error messages and stack traces are sufficiently detailed to aid in debugging. Tools like Apollo Engine or Datadog can aggregate logs and provide insights into error patterns, helping you identify and address recurring issues.

When dealing with authorization and authentication issues, the complexity increases in a federated environment due to the involvement of multiple services, each potentially handling its own security measures. Problems often arise when a service's authorization logic is misconfigured or does not align with the rest of the federated system. Users might experience unexpected access denials or unauthorized data exposure.

To address these issues, verify that each service's

authorization rules are correctly implemented and that they comply with the overall security policies of the federated system. Ensure that tokens or credentials used for authentication are correctly passed between services and validated appropriately. Consider implementing centralized authentication mechanisms, such as OAuth or JWT, to streamline authorization across services and reduce the potential for configuration errors.

Performance issues related to query execution can also be challenging to diagnose in a federated architecture. Queries that involve multiple services might experience slower response times if one or more services are underperforming or experiencing high load. Understanding how different services contribute to query execution and identifying which service is the bottleneck is essential for effective troubleshooting.

Profiling tools that provide insights into query performance at both the federated and individual service levels can be valuable. These tools can help you analyze the execution time of each part of a query, allowing you to identify which service is causing delays. Once identified, investigate the performance characteristics of that service, such as database query efficiency or network latency, and optimize accordingly. Additionally, consider implementing query optimization techniques, such as query batching or caching, to reduce load and improve response times.

Data consistency issues can also pose significant challenges in a federated GraphQL setup. Since data is distributed across multiple services, maintaining consistency and ensuring that updates are correctly reflected across all services is crucial. Problems may arise if a service updates its data but fails to propagate those updates to other services, leading to inconsistent or outdated information being returned in queries.

To manage data consistency, implement strategies such as eventual consistency or use data synchronization mechanisms to keep services in sync. Ensure that each service correctly handles data updates and propagates changes as needed. Additionally, consider implementing data validation and integrity checks to detect and address discrepancies.

Lastly, network security issues can impact the stability and security of a federated GraphQL environment. Federated systems often involve complex network interactions between services, increasing the potential for security vulnerabilities or attacks. Ensuring secure communication between services and protecting against common network threats is essential.

Utilize network security best practices, such as encryption, to safeguard data in transit between services. Implement firewalls and intrusion detection systems to protect against unauthorized access and monitor network traffic for suspicious activity. Regularly review and update security policies to address emerging threats and vulnerabilities.

In conclusion, troubleshooting common issues in a federated GraphQL environment requires a comprehensive approach, addressing schema integration, resolver performance, network reliability, error handling, authorization, and data consistency. By employing effective strategies for each of these areas, you can maintain a robust and reliable federated GraphQL system, ensuring smooth operation and a positive user experience.

Addressing issues related to schema management in a federated GraphQL environment involves navigating complexities arising from the integration of multiple schemas. Schema conflicts or inconsistencies can emerge when different services define overlapping types or fields, leading to unexpected behavior or errors in query results. These conflicts might result in issues such as type mismatches or incorrect data being returned.

To resolve schema-related problems, begin by maintaining a clear and well-documented schema for each service within your federation. Use schema validation tools to ensure that schemas are correctly composed and that there are no conflicts between them. Tools like GraphQL Schema Stitching or Apollo Federation provide capabilities to validate and merge schemas, ensuring compatibility and consistency across the federated setup. Regularly review and update schemas to address any changes or additions made to the services, and conduct thorough integration testing to confirm that the federated schema works as expected.

Another critical area of concern is managing service failures or downtimes. In a federated GraphQL environment, the failure of one service can impact the overall system, potentially causing disruptions in query responses or leading to cascading failures across services. Implementing robust service monitoring and health checks is essential for detecting and addressing these issues proactively. Tools such as Prometheus or Grafana can monitor the health of services and alert you to any performance or availability issues.

Designing for resilience involves implementing strategies such as circuit breakers or fallback mechanisms. Circuit breakers can prevent requests from reaching a failing service, while fallback mechanisms can provide default responses or alternative data sources in case of service unavailability. Additionally, consider using retries with exponential backoff to handle transient errors gracefully, reducing the likelihood of service degradation affecting the end-user experience.

When dealing with complex interactions between services, especially those involving asynchronous processes or inter-service communication, issues such as message delivery failures or data consistency problems can arise. To manage these challenges, ensure that your inter-service communication mechanisms, such as message queues or event streams, are reliably configured and monitored. Implementing retry policies and dead-letter queues can help handle message processing failures and ensure that no messages are lost.

Data consistency across services is another concern, particularly when services maintain their own databases or caches. Employ strategies such as eventual consistency or distributed transactions to manage data consistency issues. Event sourcing can be a valuable approach for capturing changes to data and ensuring that all services stay synchronized. By tracking and replaying events, you can address discrepancies and maintain data integrity throughout the federated system.

Finally, addressing issues related to security and compliance in a federated GraphQL environment requires a comprehensive approach. Ensuring that data protection regulations and security policies are consistently applied across all services is essential. Implement access controls and encryption mechanisms to protect sensitive data both in transit and at rest. Regular security audits and vulnerability assessments can help identify and mitigate potential risks, maintaining a secure environment for your federated GraphQL setup.

In conclusion, effective troubleshooting in federated GraphQL environments involves a multifaceted approach that addresses schema conflicts, service failures, performance issues, and security concerns. By implementing robust monitoring and validation mechanisms, designing for resilience, and ensuring data consistency, you can maintain a stable and reliable federated architecture. Embracing these practices will enhance your ability to diagnose and resolve issues promptly, ensuring a seamless experience for users and maintaining the integrity of your federated GraphQL services.

CHAPTER 27: FEDERATED GRAPHQL FOR MOBILE AND WEB APPLICATIONS

In an era where applications are increasingly expected to deliver seamless and responsive user experiences across multiple platforms, federated GraphQL emerges as a powerful tool to streamline data management and enhance performance. This chapter explores the design and implementation of federated GraphQL solutions tailored for mobile and web applications, focusing on optimizing performance and user experience for diverse client environments.

For mobile and web applications, the implementation of GraphQL Federation involves several key considerations. These considerations are crucial for ensuring that federated GraphQL services meet the performance and usability expectations of users across different devices and network conditions. By addressing these considerations, developers can leverage the full potential of federated GraphQL to provide a unified and efficient data interface.

One of the primary advantages of using GraphQL Federation

is its ability to consolidate data from multiple sources into a single, coherent schema. This feature is particularly beneficial for mobile and web applications, where the need for rapid and efficient data retrieval is paramount. By federating GraphQL services, developers can simplify client-side data fetching, reduce the complexity of handling multiple APIs, and provide a more intuitive querying experience for developers and users alike.

When designing federated GraphQL solutions for mobile and web clients, performance optimization is a critical aspect. Mobile devices, in particular, often operate under constrained network conditions and limited processing power. As a result, optimizing query performance and minimizing the amount of data transferred are essential for ensuring a smooth user experience. Implementing efficient query batching and minimizing unnecessary data retrieval can help address these performance challenges.

For web applications, performance considerations include optimizing query execution and handling responses efficiently. Web applications often need to handle larger volumes of data and more complex interactions compared to mobile applications. As such, ensuring that federated queries are optimized for web environments is essential. This can involve techniques such as leveraging caching mechanisms, optimizing resolver functions, and employing pagination strategies to manage large datasets.

In addition to performance considerations, designing federated GraphQL solutions for mobile and web applications requires attention to user experience. Both mobile and web clients demand responsive and fluid interactions, which can be achieved through efficient data fetching and real-time updates. Implementing features such as subscription support for real-time data and ensuring that queries are designed to fetch only the necessary data can enhance the user experience and provide a more engaging application.

Another important consideration when implementing federated GraphQL for mobile and web applications is error handling and recovery. Federated systems introduce additional complexity, and handling errors gracefully is crucial for maintaining application stability. Implementing robust error handling strategies, such as providing fallback mechanisms and informative error messages, can help ensure that users receive a consistent experience even in the face of failures.

To further enhance the user experience, developers should also consider how to integrate federated GraphQL solutions with existing client-side frameworks and libraries. Many popular frameworks, such as React and Angular for web applications, and Swift or Kotlin for mobile applications, offer built-in support for GraphQL or have libraries that facilitate integration. Leveraging these tools can streamline the development process and ensure that the federated GraphQL solution aligns with the best practices of the chosen framework.

Security is another crucial aspect of implementing federated GraphQL solutions for mobile and web applications. Ensuring that data is securely transmitted and accessed is essential for protecting user information and maintaining application integrity. Implementing proper authentication and authorization mechanisms, such as OAuth or JWT, and securing communication channels with HTTPS are fundamental practices for safeguarding data in a federated environment.

In conclusion, applying GraphQL Federation to mobile and web applications presents a range of opportunities and challenges. By focusing on performance optimization, user experience, error handling, and integration with client-side frameworks, developers can create federated GraphQL solutions that enhance the efficiency and effectiveness of data management across diverse platforms. Addressing these considerations thoughtfully will lead to a more cohesive and responsive application experience for users, whether they are accessing the application from a mobile device or a web browser.

To further enhance the integration of federated GraphQL with mobile and web applications, a deeper understanding of the specific needs and constraints of each platform is essential. Mobile and web environments present distinct challenges, which must be addressed to optimize the performance and usability of federated GraphQL solutions.

In mobile applications, one of the primary concerns is managing network connectivity, which can vary significantly between different conditions and locations. Mobile networks are often less reliable and have higher latency compared to wired connections used by web applications. To mitigate these issues, developers should consider implementing strategies such as offline support and adaptive loading techniques. For instance, employing local caching mechanisms can help ensure that users have access to critical data even when connectivity is poor. Additionally, mobile clients should be designed to handle intermittent network failures gracefully, retrying requests as needed without negatively impacting the user experience.

Another crucial aspect of mobile application performance is optimizing data transfer. Mobile devices often have limited bandwidth, so it is essential to minimize the volume of data sent over the network. This can be achieved through various methods, such as request coalescing and query optimization. By grouping multiple requests into a single query or using GraphQL's ability to fetch only the required fields, developers can reduce the amount of data transmitted and improve the overall efficiency of data fetching.

On the web front, performance optimization also plays a significant role but manifests differently due to the nature of web environments. Web applications typically handle a more extensive range of interactions and data types, often requiring more sophisticated caching strategies and data management approaches. Implementing server-side caching, client-side caching, and efficient data prefetching strategies can significantly enhance the performance of web applications. For example, using tools like Apollo Client for caching can help minimize redundant network requests and speed up data retrieval.

Web applications also benefit from the ability to use advanced GraphQL features such as fragments and directives to optimize queries. Fragments allow developers to define reusable pieces of queries, which can help reduce duplication and improve maintainability. Directives, on the other hand, can be used to conditionally include or exclude parts of queries, providing more flexibility and control over data fetching.

In both mobile and web contexts, real-time data and updates are increasingly important for creating dynamic and responsive user experiences. Integrating GraphQL subscriptions for real-time updates is one effective way to handle asynchronous events and provide users with the latest information without requiring manual refreshes. However, managing subscriptions in a federated environment introduces additional complexity. Developers need to ensure that subscription handling is consistent across different services and that the system can efficiently manage real-time data streams.

Another consideration is the design of the federated schema to accommodate platform-specific needs. For mobile applications, schema design should prioritize efficient querying and minimize the amount of data required for each request. For web applications, the schema might need to support more complex interactions and larger datasets, requiring additional attention to query optimization and response handling.

Furthermore, security and authentication are paramount when designing federated GraphQL solutions for mobile and web applications. Both platforms require robust mechanisms to protect sensitive data and ensure secure communication. Implementing secure authentication methods, such as OAuth or JSON Web Tokens (JWT), and enforcing proper authorization checks within federated services are essential practices to safeguard against unauthorized access and data breaches.

In summary, the successful application of federated GraphQL in mobile and web environments involves addressing specific performance, usability, and security challenges. By leveraging the capabilities of GraphQL Federation to streamline data management and optimize queries, developers can create more responsive, efficient, and secure applications. The careful consideration of platform-specific needs, coupled with advanced techniques for performance optimization and real-time data handling, will ensure that federated GraphQL solutions meet the demands of modern mobile and web applications.

As federated GraphQL setups expand to accommodate mobile and web applications, ensuring a seamless user experience across diverse platforms becomes increasingly critical. The integration of real-time data and handling asynchronous events are pivotal aspects that affect the overall performance and responsiveness of these applications.

For mobile applications, leveraging GraphQL subscriptions for real-time updates introduces several advantages. Real-time capabilities are particularly useful in scenarios where timely data synchronization is crucial, such as in messaging apps, live sports tracking, or collaborative platforms. Subscriptions enable mobile clients to receive updates automatically when the underlying data changes, providing a dynamic and engaging user experience. However, managing real-time subscriptions on mobile devices requires careful consideration of network constraints and battery usage. Implementing efficient subscription management strategies—such as using WebSocket connections only when necessary and optimizing the frequency of updates—can help mitigate these issues. Additionally, providing users with control over their notification preferences and update frequency can enhance the user experience while preserving battery life.

In web applications, real-time updates are similarly valuable, especially for applications that involve live data feeds or interactive features. Web applications can benefit from advanced subscription management techniques, including implementing server-side events or using frameworks like Apollo Client that support real-time subscriptions with GraphQL. By optimizing the use of WebSockets or HTTP2/3 for real-time communication, web applications can achieve low-latency updates and reduce the overhead associated with traditional polling methods.

When designing federated GraphQL solutions for both mobile and web platforms, it is essential to consider the impact of data consistency and synchronization. Ensuring that data remains consistent across different clients and platforms requires implementing robust synchronization mechanisms. This can involve strategies such as conflict resolution and optimistic UI updates. For example, in cases where multiple clients may concurrently update the same data, implementing conflict resolution policies ensures that changes are accurately reflected across all clients. Optimistic UI updates, on the other hand, provide immediate feedback to users while changes are being processed in the background, enhancing the perceived responsiveness of the application.

To further optimize performance, developers should focus on efficient query design and response handling. This involves crafting GraphQL queries that minimize the amount of data fetched and ensure that responses are tailored to the needs of the client. For mobile applications, where data transfer is often constrained by network bandwidth and latency, optimizing queries to fetch only necessary fields can significantly reduce the payload size and improve responsiveness. Similarly, in web applications, leveraging caching mechanisms—such as browser caching or server-side caching—can help reduce the load on the server and accelerate data retrieval.

Another consideration is the adaptation of the GraphQL schema to accommodate the specific requirements of different platforms. Mobile and web applications may have different data usage patterns and performance constraints, necessitating variations in the GraphQL schema to optimize for each platform. For instance, mobile applications might benefit from schemas that support pagination and batching to handle large datasets efficiently, while web applications might require schemas that support more complex queries and real-time interactions.

In conclusion, integrating federated GraphQL with mobile and web applications involves a nuanced approach to optimizing performance, managing real-time data, and ensuring consistent user experiences across platforms. By addressing the unique challenges and requirements of each environment —such as network constraints in mobile and advanced caching strategies in web applications—developers can leverage the full potential of GraphQL Federation. Emphasizing efficient query design, real-time updates, and platform-specific optimizations ensures that federated GraphQL solutions deliver a seamless and engaging experience for users, regardless of the device or platform they are using.

CHAPTER 28: BUILDING A GRAPHQL FEDERATION ECOSYSTEM

Building a comprehensive GraphQL Federation ecosystem requires a thorough understanding of the various tools, libraries, and frameworks that can enhance and support federated architectures. This chapter will delve into the components essential for constructing a robust federated environment, focusing on integration strategies and practical applications that can streamline development and ensure scalability.

At the core of a federated GraphQL ecosystem are the fundamental libraries and frameworks that facilitate the creation and management of federated schemas. GraphQL tools such as Apollo Federation and GraphQL Tools are pivotal in establishing a unified schema that can seamlessly integrate multiple microservices. Apollo Federation, for instance, provides a set of tools and conventions for building a federated schema that can be composed of various services. It supports the creation of a central gateway that aggregates schemas from different services and exposes a unified API to clients.

This allows for a more modular approach to building GraphQL APIs, where each microservice can maintain its own schema and resolvers, yet contribute to a cohesive global schema.

GraphQL Tools is another essential library in this ecosystem, offering utilities for building and merging GraphQL schemas. It provides the capability to stitch schemas together, a technique that can be employed when integrating existing GraphQL services into a federated setup. Schema stitching allows for the combination of multiple GraphQL schemas into a single schema, providing a way to integrate services that are not originally designed for federation.

In addition to core libraries, various tooling and frameworks play a significant role in enhancing the functionality of a federated GraphQL setup. For instance, the Apollo Server integrates seamlessly with Apollo Federation, offering a comprehensive server-side implementation that supports federated schemas. Apollo Server provides advanced features such as query batching, caching, and performance monitoring, which are critical for maintaining optimal performance in a federated environment.

For client-side integration, Apollo Client is a popular choice. It supports querying federated schemas and manages client-side cache, which can be particularly beneficial in a federated setup. Apollo Client's cache management capabilities help in reducing redundant requests and improving the overall responsiveness of applications by serving data from the cache when appropriate.

Moreover, incorporating monitoring and observability tools into the GraphQL Federation ecosystem is crucial for maintaining the health and performance of the system. Tools such as Apollo Studio provide insights into query performance, error rates, and other metrics, allowing for proactive management of the federated architecture.

Observability tools help in identifying performance bottlenecks, tracking query execution times, and analyzing the impact of changes across the federation. These insights are invaluable for optimizing queries and ensuring that the federated system operates smoothly.

Another important aspect of building a federated ecosystem is security. Implementing robust security practices involves using libraries and frameworks that support authentication and authorization in a federated context. For example, integrating authentication mechanisms such as OAuth or JWT (JSON Web Tokens) with Apollo Server allows for secure access control across the federated schema. Authorization strategies can be applied at various levels, including service-specific and global levels, ensuring that only authorized users can access certain parts of the schema.

When constructing a federated GraphQL ecosystem, it is also essential to consider the integration of development and deployment workflows. CI/CD (Continuous Integration/Continuous Deployment) pipelines play a pivotal role in managing the lifecycle of federated services. Tools like GitHub Actions, GitLab CI, or Jenkins can automate the testing and deployment of federated services, ensuring that updates are integrated smoothly and that any issues are detected early in the development process.

Finally, documentation and developer experience are key components of a successful federated ecosystem. Providing clear and comprehensive documentation for the federated schema, including details on how to extend and integrate services, helps in ensuring that developers can effectively contribute to and work with the federation. Tools such as GraphQL Playground or GraphiQL offer interactive environments for testing and exploring the federated schema, improving the overall developer experience.

In summary, building a comprehensive GraphQL Federation ecosystem involves leveraging a variety of tools, libraries, and frameworks that collectively enhance the functionality and manageability of federated architectures. By integrating core libraries such as Apollo Federation and GraphQL Tools, incorporating advanced features from tools like Apollo Server and Apollo Client, and focusing on monitoring, security, and development workflows, organizations can create a robust and scalable federated GraphQL environment. This approach not only streamlines development but also ensures optimal performance and maintainability across distributed services.

The integration of monitoring and observability tools within a GraphQL Federation ecosystem is essential for managing the complex interactions between multiple services. Advanced monitoring solutions, such as those provided by Apollo Studio, offer real-time insights into query performance, latency, and error rates. These tools facilitate proactive management by identifying performance bottlenecks and diagnosing issues before they impact users. They also enable detailed traceability of queries across services, which is crucial for debugging and optimizing federated architectures.

Furthermore, integrating distributed tracing tools like Jaeger or Zipkin can provide visibility into the end-to-end flow of requests within the federated system. Distributed tracing allows for the tracking of a single request as it traverses through various microservices, offering insights into the performance characteristics of each service and the overall system. This is particularly valuable in a federated environment where requests are often routed through multiple services, each contributing to the final response.

Testing frameworks are another critical component of a federated GraphQL ecosystem. Tools like Jest and Apollo's testing utilities can be employed to ensure the correctness and reliability of individual services and the overall federation.

Automated testing of federated schemas helps in validating that changes in one service do not inadvertently break functionality across the federation. For example, integration tests can simulate queries across the federated schema to verify that the aggregation of multiple services yields the expected results. Additionally, schema validation tools ensure that the federated schema adheres to the expected structure and constraints, preventing runtime errors and inconsistencies.

The use of continuous integration (CI) and continuous deployment (CD) pipelines is instrumental in maintaining the quality and stability of a federated GraphQL system. CI/CD pipelines automate the process of building, testing, and deploying changes to both individual services and the federated schema. By integrating automated testing and deployment steps into the CI/CD process, teams can achieve faster feedback cycles and reduce the risk of introducing defects into the production environment. This also facilitates seamless coordination between multiple teams working on different services within the federation.

In addition to core libraries and tools, various practices can enhance the overall effectiveness of a federated GraphQL ecosystem. For instance, adopting a modular approach to schema design promotes reusability and maintainability. Each service should be designed with a clear and concise schema that aligns with its specific domain, allowing for easier integration into the federated system. Modular schema design also supports the independent evolution of services, as changes to one service's schema can be managed without disrupting the entire federation.

Caching strategies are another important consideration for optimizing performance in a federated setup. Implementing caching mechanisms at both the client and server levels can significantly reduce latency and improve response times.

Server-side caching, such as response caching and data loader patterns, helps in minimizing the load on backend services by storing frequently accessed data. On the client side, caching query results and using normalized data stores can further enhance performance by reducing the need for repeated network requests.

Finally, ensuring consistency and synchronization across services is crucial for a reliable federated architecture. Techniques such as schema stitching and schema federation help in maintaining a coherent and unified schema across multiple services. Regularly reviewing and updating the federation strategy to accommodate changes in service requirements or technology advancements is also essential for sustaining an effective and adaptable GraphQL ecosystem.

By leveraging the appropriate tools, libraries, and best practices, you can build a robust GraphQL Federation ecosystem that supports scalable, efficient, and reliable federated architectures. This comprehensive approach ensures that your federated setup is well-equipped to handle the complexities of modern application development and integration, providing a seamless experience for both developers and users.

The evolution of a federated GraphQL ecosystem also involves ensuring that the system scales effectively as the number of services and the volume of data grow. As federated systems are inherently distributed, managing the scale of data retrieval and ensuring efficient communication between services become crucial. Techniques such as sharding, caching, and query optimization are pivotal in addressing these challenges.

Sharding involves partitioning the data across different services or databases to improve performance and manageability. In a federated GraphQL setup, this can mean designing each service to handle a specific subset of data or queries, which can then be combined to serve client requests.

This not only enhances performance by distributing the load but also allows for more specialized and optimized data handling within each shard. Careful consideration must be given to how data is partitioned to ensure that queries that span multiple shards do not lead to inefficiencies or excessive complexity.

Caching is another critical strategy in optimizing performance within a federated architecture. Implementing a robust caching layer can significantly reduce the latency of queries by storing and reusing previously fetched results. This is particularly important in federated setups where multiple services may be involved in resolving a single query. By caching responses at various levels—such as at the gateway, the service layer, or even on the client side—systems can avoid redundant processing and improve response times. Utilizing distributed cache systems like Redis or Memcached can further enhance this capability by providing a shared cache that is accessible across different services.

Query optimization is essential for handling complex queries efficiently in a federated environment. Techniques such as query batching and query optimization at the gateway can be employed to improve performance. Query batching involves combining multiple queries into a single request to reduce the number of network round-trips and streamline processing. Additionally, optimizing the query plan by analyzing and restructuring queries to minimize the number of service calls and data transformations can help in managing performance and resource utilization effectively.

As the federated GraphQL ecosystem grows, ensuring effective communication and collaboration between different teams becomes increasingly important. Implementing clear guidelines for schema design and service interactions can prevent integration issues and ensure that services work harmoniously within the federation. Regularly reviewing and updating the documentation, maintaining a well-defined schema governance process, and establishing protocols for handling changes to the schema or services are all essential practices in fostering a collaborative environment.

Moreover, the use of observability tools and practices plays a crucial role in maintaining the health of a federated GraphQL ecosystem. Setting up comprehensive logging, monitoring, and alerting systems helps in detecting and addressing issues proactively. Logs can provide valuable insights into the behavior of individual services, while monitoring tools can track key metrics such as response times, error rates, and system load. Alerts can be configured to notify teams of anomalies or performance degradation, enabling timely intervention and resolution.

Building a federated GraphQL ecosystem also involves evaluating and integrating third-party tools and services that enhance functionality and simplify management. Tools for schema stitching, such as Apollo Federation, provide out-of-the-box solutions for integrating and managing federated schemas. Similarly, leveraging frameworks and libraries that support GraphQL best practices can streamline development and improve the overall quality of the system.

Finally, ensuring that the ecosystem remains adaptable and future-proof is vital for long-term success. This involves continuously assessing emerging technologies, industry trends, and evolving best practices to keep the federated architecture aligned with current advancements. Embracing a culture of continuous improvement and staying abreast of new developments can help in maintaining a modern and efficient GraphQL federation setup.

In summary, building a comprehensive GraphQL Federation ecosystem requires a multifaceted approach that includes selecting and integrating the right tools, optimizing performance, and ensuring effective collaboration and observability. By addressing these aspects, organizations can create a robust and scalable federated GraphQL environment that supports complex queries, scales with growth, and delivers an optimal user experience.

CHAPTER 29: MANAGING CROSS-SERVICE TRANSACTIONS IN FEDERATED GRAPHQL

In a federated GraphQL environment, managing transactions that span multiple services introduces significant complexity due to the distributed nature of the system. Unlike monolithic systems where transactions can be handled in a single database or service context, federated GraphQL setups require coordinating transactions across various services, each potentially maintaining its own data store. This chapter delves into the challenges of managing cross-service transactions and explores techniques for ensuring consistency and handling distributed transactions effectively.

Transactions in distributed systems face the challenge of ensuring atomicity, consistency, isolation, and durability (ACID properties) across different services. Traditional database transactions achieve these properties within a single database context. However, in a federated environment, maintaining these guarantees across multiple services requires additional strategies. We will examine both traditional and modern approaches to address these challenges.

One common approach to managing distributed transactions is the two-phase commit (2PC) protocol. This method involves a coordinator service that manages the transaction across all participating services. In the first phase, the coordinator sends a prepare request to each service, which then performs the necessary checks and locks the resources required for the transaction. Each service responds with a vote to either commit or abort the transaction. In the second phase, the coordinator decides based on the votes and sends a commit or abort command to each service. While 2PC ensures consistency, it introduces a single point of failure and can suffer from performance bottlenecks due to its blocking nature and need for coordination.

Another approach is the use of compensating transactions, often employed in conjunction with the Saga pattern. Sagas decompose a distributed transaction into a series of smaller, isolated transactions that are executed in sequence. Each step in the saga performs its own work and can be rolled back by a compensating transaction if needed. This method allows for greater flexibility and resilience, as it avoids the need for a central coordinator and reduces the impact of failures. However, implementing sagas requires careful design to ensure that compensating actions correctly reverse the effects of previous steps and that the overall process remains consistent.

Event sourcing is a modern technique that can be effectively integrated into federated GraphQL architectures to manage cross-service transactions. In event sourcing, changes to the state of a system are captured as a sequence of events, rather than updating the state directly. Each service records its events, and the current state can be reconstructed by replaying these events. This approach allows services to react to events in an asynchronous manner and ensures that all changes are logged and can be audited. By leveraging event sourcing, services can achieve eventual consistency, where all services eventually converge to a consistent state, even in the presence of failures.

To handle distributed transactions efficiently, adopting an event-driven architecture can also be beneficial. In this approach, services communicate through events, which are published to a message broker. Services subscribe to relevant events and update their state based on the events they receive. This decouples services and allows them to operate independently while still maintaining consistency across the system. Event-driven systems can use patterns such as CQRS (Command Query Responsibility Segregation) to separate the read and write responsibilities, further enhancing performance and scalability.

Consistency models play a crucial role in managing cross-service transactions. While strong consistency ensures that all services have the same view of the data at all times, it can be challenging to achieve in distributed systems due to network partitions and service failures. Alternative models, such as eventual consistency, provide a more relaxed guarantee where services are allowed to diverge temporarily but are expected to converge to a consistent state over time. Choosing the appropriate consistency model depends on the specific requirements of the application and the trade-offs between performance and consistency.

The integration of distributed tracing tools is essential for monitoring and debugging cross-service transactions. These tools provide visibility into the flow of requests and the interactions between services, allowing developers to trace the lifecycle of a transaction across the system. By visualizing the distributed transactions, teams can identify bottlenecks, track performance issues, and diagnose failures more effectively. Tools such as Jaeger, Zipkin, and OpenTelemetry support distributed tracing and can be integrated into federated GraphQL environments to enhance observability and operational insights.

In summary, managing cross-service transactions in a federated GraphQL environment involves addressing the complexities of ensuring consistency and handling distributed transactions. Traditional approaches like the two-phase commit protocol provide a foundational method but may face limitations in scalability and performance. Modern techniques, including the Saga pattern, event sourcing, and event-driven architectures, offer more flexible and scalable solutions. Adopting the right consistency model and leveraging distributed tracing tools further contribute to effective transaction management. By understanding and implementing these strategies, organizations can achieve reliable and consistent transaction management in their federated GraphQL systems.

Event sourcing, when combined with a publish-subscribe model, can provide an effective means of managing distributed transactions. In this approach, each service maintains its own event log, which records all changes in the form of events. When a service needs to participate in a cross-service transaction, it publishes relevant events to a message broker. Other services then subscribe to these events and update their own state accordingly. This method ensures that all services eventually reach a consistent state, albeit in an asynchronous manner. The challenge here lies in managing eventual consistency and ensuring that all services handle events in the correct order and with idempotency to prevent duplicate processing.

A related technique is the use of CQRS (Command Query Responsibility Segregation) combined with event sourcing.

CQRS separates the data modification operations (commands) from the data retrieval operations (queries). In a federated setup, this can help manage complex transactions by decoupling the command processing from the query side, thereby allowing for more flexible transaction handling. Commands can be processed asynchronously, and queries can be optimized for read performance, enhancing the overall responsiveness and scalability of the system.

Implementing these patterns requires a robust infrastructure for managing and propagating events across services. This often involves deploying a message broker or event streaming platform, such as Apache Kafka or RabbitMQ. These systems provide reliable message delivery, persistence, and fault tolerance, which are essential for handling distributed transactions. They also offer tools for managing message ordering and ensuring that all events are processed exactly once, which is crucial for maintaining data consistency.

Another crucial aspect of managing cross-service transactions is ensuring that services can recover gracefully from failures. In distributed systems, partial failures are common, and services must be designed to handle such scenarios without compromising the overall system integrity. Techniques such as retry policies, circuit breakers, and fallback mechanisms can be employed to handle transient failures and prevent them from cascading across services. Additionally, implementing comprehensive monitoring and alerting systems can help detect issues early and provide insights into the state of transactions across the ecosystem.

It is also important to consider the impact of latency and network partitions on distributed transactions. Since services in a federated GraphQL setup may be spread across different geographical locations or network segments, network delays and partitions can affect the timeliness and reliability of transactions. Designing for resilience in such environments involves employing strategies like distributed caching, local caching, and optimistic concurrency control to mitigate the impact of latency and improve system responsiveness.

One of the key challenges in managing cross-service transactions is ensuring that all services agree on the outcome of a transaction. In scenarios where services must coordinate their actions, using distributed consensus algorithms such as Paxos or Raft can help achieve agreement on the state of the transaction. These algorithms enable a group of services to agree on a single value or decision despite potential failures or network partitions, thereby ensuring consistency across the system.

When integrating these techniques into a federated GraphQL environment, it is essential to align the transaction management strategies with the overall architectural goals of the system. This involves considering factors such as service autonomy, scalability, and fault tolerance. Balancing these factors with the need for consistency and coordination can be challenging, but it is crucial for building a resilient and performant federated architecture.

In conclusion, managing cross-service transactions in a federated GraphQL setup involves a combination of traditional and modern approaches. Techniques such as two-phase commit, sagas, event sourcing, and CQRS each offer different advantages and trade-offs. By carefully selecting and implementing these techniques, organizations can ensure that their federated GraphQL systems maintain consistency, resilience, and performance across distributed services.

In addressing the complexities of cross-service transactions, modern federated architectures often turn to advanced strategies such as the Saga pattern. The Saga pattern is a design pattern used to manage distributed transactions by breaking them down into a series of smaller, manageable transactions, or sagas, which can be executed independently. Each saga typically includes a sequence of steps where each step either completes successfully or triggers compensatory actions if it fails. This approach allows for better control and monitoring of distributed transactions, ensuring that consistency is maintained across services even in the face of partial failures.

The Saga pattern operates in two main variations: orchestration and choreography. In orchestration-based sagas, a central orchestrator coordinates the execution of the sagas, ensuring that each step is executed in the correct order and handling compensations as necessary. This central coordinator simplifies the implementation and monitoring of sagas but introduces a single point of failure. Conversely, choreography-based sagas rely on services themselves to communicate directly with each other to execute and manage the saga steps. This decentralized approach reduces the risk of a single point of failure but can lead to more complex inter-service communication.

Implementing the Saga pattern requires careful design to ensure that each service properly handles compensations and maintains data consistency. Services must be designed to perform rollback operations or compensatory transactions in response to failures. This often involves maintaining detailed logs of transactions and compensations to facilitate recovery and debugging. Additionally, coordination mechanisms, whether centralized or decentralized, must be robust to handle network partitions and other transient issues.

In federated GraphQL environments, where services are frequently developed and maintained independently, aligning these services with a common strategy for managing transactions can be challenging. One way to address this is by adopting a well-defined contract or API for transaction management that all services adhere to. This contract ensures consistency in how transactions are initiated, monitored, and compensated, providing a uniform approach to handling distributed transactions.

Furthermore, integrating transaction management tools and libraries that support the Saga pattern or similar strategies can streamline the development and maintenance process. These tools can offer built-in support for managing distributed transactions, providing features such as automated compensation handling, monitoring, and reporting. By leveraging such tools, teams can focus more on implementing business logic and less on the intricacies of transaction management.

Effective transaction management in federated environments also involves addressing data consistency and integrity issues. Ensuring that each service maintains accurate and up-to-date data is crucial for the success of distributed transactions. Techniques such as data replication, eventual consistency models, and strong consistency guarantees should be evaluated and applied as appropriate to meet the requirements of the system.

When designing federated GraphQL systems with cross-service transactions in mind, it is important to consider the performance implications of the chosen strategies. Distributed transactions often introduce additional latency and overhead due to the need for coordination and communication between services. Performance optimization techniques, such as caching, load balancing, and efficient query execution, can help mitigate these impacts and ensure that the system remains responsive and scalable.

Ultimately, managing cross-service transactions in federated GraphQL environments requires a comprehensive approach that balances consistency, resilience, and performance. By leveraging advanced transaction management patterns like the Saga pattern, integrating robust tools and libraries, and addressing data consistency and performance considerations, teams can build effective and reliable federated systems capable of handling complex transactions across distributed services.

CHAPTER 30: INTEGRATING FEDERATED GRAPHQL WITH LEGACY SYSTEMS

Integrating federated GraphQL with legacy systems presents a unique set of challenges and opportunities for organizations looking to modernize their technology stack while preserving valuable existing investments. Legacy systems, often characterized by their use of older technologies, may include relational databases, monolithic applications, and various other outdated software or hardware components. These systems can be critical to business operations, making it essential to develop effective strategies for integrating them with newer, federated GraphQL architectures.

The integration process begins with understanding the existing legacy systems, which often involves mapping out their architecture, data models, and service interfaces. Legacy systems may be based on outdated programming languages, data storage techniques, or communication protocols. In contrast, federated GraphQL operates on a modern stack, leveraging GraphQL schemas, resolvers, and the federation concept to unify disparate services into a cohesive API.

Bridging the gap between these two paradigms requires careful planning and consideration of several factors.

One of the primary challenges in integrating federated GraphQL with legacy systems is handling data access and transformation. Legacy systems typically use relational databases with complex schemas and SQL-based querying. In contrast, GraphQL operates on a more flexible data model where clients request exactly the data they need. To connect these two worlds, it is often necessary to create an intermediary layer that translates GraphQL queries into the appropriate database queries and vice versa. This intermediary layer can take the form of a data access layer or a set of custom resolvers that interface with legacy databases.

Data transformation is another critical aspect of integration. Legacy systems may store data in formats or structures that differ significantly from those used by modern applications. This discrepancy can necessitate the use of data mapping or transformation tools to convert data between the legacy format and the GraphQL schema. Middleware solutions or ETL (extract, transform, load) processes can be employed to automate these transformations, ensuring that data is consistently and accurately represented in the federated GraphQL layer.

To further facilitate integration, organizations may adopt a phased approach, starting with a limited scope and gradually expanding the federated GraphQL implementation. This approach allows for incremental testing and validation, reducing the risk of disruptions to existing systems. Initial integration efforts may focus on less critical or less complex components of the legacy system, providing a controlled environment to address technical challenges and refine the integration strategy.

Another important consideration is the interface between

federated GraphQL and legacy services. Legacy systems may expose their functionality through various APIs or service endpoints, such as SOAP-based web services or older REST APIs. Integrating these services with federated GraphQL requires creating adapters or wrappers that translate GraphQL requests into the appropriate format for these legacy APIs. This process may involve developing custom middleware or using existing integration frameworks that support multiple protocols.

Security and compliance are also key factors in the integration process. Legacy systems may have specific security requirements or compliance constraints that must be adhered to. Ensuring that federated GraphQL implementations comply with these requirements involves implementing robust security measures, such as authentication and authorization, and conducting thorough audits and testing. Secure communication channels, data encryption, and access controls must be enforced to protect sensitive data and maintain regulatory compliance.

Finally, it is essential to consider the impact of integration on operational processes and staff. Integrating federated GraphQL with legacy systems may necessitate changes in workflow, training, and support procedures. Engaging with stakeholders, including developers, operations teams, and end-users, ensures that the integration process is smooth and that the transition to the new system is well-managed. Providing adequate training and support helps to address any concerns and facilitates the adoption of the new technology.

In summary, integrating federated GraphQL with legacy systems involves a multifaceted approach that addresses data access, transformation, and system interfaces while maintaining security and compliance. By understanding the intricacies of legacy systems and carefully planning the integration strategy, organizations can effectively bridge the gap between modern GraphQL implementations and traditional architectures. This integration not only enhances the flexibility and functionality of existing systems but also positions organizations to take advantage of the benefits offered by federated GraphQL.

As organizations proceed with integrating federated GraphQL with legacy systems, they encounter additional complexities related to service interoperability and data consistency. Legacy systems often operate within closed ecosystems and may lack the flexibility or interfaces required for seamless integration with modern GraphQL services. Addressing these challenges requires a strategic approach to ensure that the federated architecture can interact effectively with the existing technology stack.

Service interoperability is a critical consideration in this integration process. Legacy systems may expose their functionalities through older APIs or proprietary protocols that are not directly compatible with GraphQL. To address this, organizations might implement API gateways or adapters that can bridge the communication gap between GraphQL services and legacy APIs. These adapters translate GraphQL queries and mutations into requests that the legacy systems can understand, and conversely, convert responses from the legacy systems into formats that can be consumed by the federated GraphQL layer.

For instance, if a legacy system exposes data through a RESTful API, an adapter could be developed to translate GraphQL queries into REST requests. This adapter would handle the necessary mappings and ensure that the data returned by the legacy system is properly formatted and integrated into the federated GraphQL schema. By creating such adapters, organizations can extend the functionality of their legacy systems without requiring substantial modifications to the existing codebase.

Another aspect of integration involves managing data consistency and ensuring that changes in the legacy system are accurately reflected in the federated GraphQL layer. Legacy systems may have their own data consistency mechanisms, which could differ from those used by modern GraphQL services. Synchronization challenges arise when the data is updated in one system but not immediately reflected across the federated GraphQL ecosystem. To mitigate this issue, organizations may employ strategies such as periodic data synchronization, event-driven updates, or caching mechanisms.

Periodic data synchronization involves regularly updating the federated GraphQL layer with data from the legacy systems, ensuring that the data remains current and consistent. This approach can be implemented through scheduled jobs or batch processes that pull data from the legacy systems at predefined intervals. However, this method may introduce latency, and organizations need to balance the frequency of updates with the performance impact on both the legacy and federated systems.

Event-driven updates offer a more real-time solution for data consistency. By leveraging event streaming platforms or message queues, organizations can publish events whenever changes occur in the legacy systems. The federated GraphQL layer can then subscribe to these events and update its data accordingly. This approach allows for more immediate synchronization but requires robust event handling and processing infrastructure to ensure reliability and scalability.

Caching is another technique used to improve performance and maintain data consistency. Caching solutions can be employed to store frequently accessed data from the legacy systems, reducing the need for repeated queries and improving response times. Cache invalidation strategies must be carefully designed to ensure that cached data remains accurate and is refreshed when necessary.

Throughout the integration process, it is crucial to maintain a focus on testing and validation. Given the complexity of integrating federated GraphQL with legacy systems, thorough testing is essential to ensure that the integration is robust and does not introduce errors or inconsistencies. Testing should cover various aspects, including data accuracy, system performance, and error handling. Automated testing frameworks and monitoring tools can assist in identifying issues early and ensuring that the integration meets the desired quality standards.

Moreover, effective documentation and communication are vital for successful integration. Detailed documentation of the integration architecture, data mappings, and transformation processes helps ensure that all stakeholders have a clear understanding of the integration approach. Regular communication between teams responsible for the federated GraphQL implementation and those managing the legacy systems can facilitate collaboration and address any issues that arise during the integration process.

In summary, integrating federated GraphQL with legacy systems involves addressing challenges related to service interoperability, data consistency, and performance. By employing strategies such as developing adapters, managing data synchronization, leveraging event-driven updates, and implementing caching solutions, organizations can successfully bridge the gap between modern GraphQL implementations and traditional system architectures. Careful planning, testing, and documentation are essential for ensuring a smooth and effective integration, allowing organizations to enhance their technology stack while preserving the value of their legacy investments.

In addition to API gateways and data consistency challenges, organizations must also consider the implications of integrating security measures and managing transactions across federated GraphQL and legacy systems. Security becomes paramount when federated services interact with legacy systems, as the legacy systems might have different or less robust security practices compared to modern GraphQL implementations. Ensuring secure communication between these disparate systems involves several layers of protection, including authentication, authorization, and data encryption.

When integrating federated GraphQL with legacy systems, a common approach is to implement a unified authentication and authorization layer. This layer manages security policies and ensures that all services adhere to the same security standards. For example, organizations might deploy an OAuth-based authentication system or integrate Single Sign-On (SSO) solutions that provide secure access control across both modern GraphQL services and legacy systems. Implementing such solutions requires configuring identity providers to work with legacy systems and ensuring that all authentication tokens and credentials are securely managed and validated.

Encryption plays a critical role in safeguarding data as it traverses between federated GraphQL services and legacy systems. Data should be encrypted both in transit and at rest to protect against unauthorized access and data breaches. For in-transit encryption, organizations can use TLS (Transport Layer Security) to secure the communication channels between services. For data at rest, ensuring that legacy systems employ strong encryption standards and securely manage encryption keys is essential. Organizations might also need to retrofit older systems with encryption capabilities or use data masking techniques to maintain security.

Transaction management in a federated environment involving legacy systems introduces additional complexities. Unlike traditional monolithic applications where transactions are managed within a single system, federated systems often involve multiple services that may need to maintain transactional consistency across different boundaries. Addressing this challenge involves implementing patterns and strategies that can handle distributed transactions effectively.

One approach to managing cross-service transactions is the use of the Saga pattern. The Saga pattern breaks a distributed transaction into a series of smaller, isolated transactions that are managed independently. Each of these smaller transactions is executed in a specific order, and compensating actions are defined to handle failures or rollback if necessary. This pattern helps to maintain consistency across multiple services while allowing for better fault tolerance and recovery mechanisms.

Another approach is to use distributed transaction coordination techniques such as the Two-Phase Commit (2PC) protocol. In this protocol, a coordinator service oversees the commit process across multiple services. The coordinator first issues a prepare request to all participating services, asking them to prepare for a commit. Once all services respond affirmatively, the coordinator then sends a commit request to finalize the transaction. While 2PC provides strong consistency guarantees, it can introduce latency and complexity, especially in systems with high throughput requirements.

Additionally, leveraging eventual consistency models can be an effective strategy in scenarios where strict transactional consistency is not feasible or necessary. Eventual consistency allows services to reach a consistent state over time, even if immediate consistency is not guaranteed. This model can be implemented using distributed data stores that support replication and synchronization mechanisms, or by incorporating event sourcing and message queuing systems that capture and propagate changes across services.

Integrating federated GraphQL with legacy systems also requires careful consideration of performance implications. Legacy systems may not be optimized for the same performance characteristics as modern GraphQL implementations. Therefore, organizations must assess and optimize the performance of interactions between federated services and legacy systems. Techniques such as request batching, query optimization, and caching can help mitigate performance issues and improve the overall efficiency of the integrated system.

By applying these strategies, organizations can bridge the gap between modern GraphQL implementations and traditional legacy systems, creating a cohesive and effective federated architecture. Ensuring that all components of the ecosystem work together seamlessly involves addressing security concerns, managing transactions effectively, and optimizing performance. This holistic approach enables organizations to leverage the benefits of GraphQL Federation while maintaining compatibility with their existing technology stack.

CHAPTER 31: FEDERATION STRATEGIES FOR MULTI-REGION DEPLOYMENTS

Deploying federated GraphQL across multiple regions presents a complex set of challenges and opportunities. As organizations expand their operations globally, the need to ensure that applications perform optimally and remain reliable across diverse geographic locations becomes increasingly crucial. This chapter explores various strategies to address the unique difficulties of multi-region deployments, focusing on data replication, latency optimization, and cross-region communication.

In a multi-region deployment, one of the primary considerations is data replication. To provide a seamless experience for users regardless of their location, it is essential to ensure that data is available and consistent across all regions. Various replication strategies can be employed depending on the specific needs of the application and the underlying architecture of the federated GraphQL system.

For instance, synchronous replication involves updating all copies of the data simultaneously. This approach ensures strong consistency, meaning that all regions will have the same data at any given time. However, synchronous replication can introduce latency and impact performance, particularly in scenarios where regions are geographically distant. In contrast, asynchronous replication involves updating copies of the data at different times, which can reduce latency but may lead to eventual consistency issues. Asynchronous replication is often used in scenarios where strong consistency is less critical, and performance is a higher priority.

Another crucial aspect of managing a multi-region deployment is latency optimization. Latency, or the time it takes for a request to travel from the client to the server and back, can significantly impact user experience. In a federated GraphQL environment, optimizing latency involves ensuring that data fetching and query execution are as efficient as possible across different regions. Techniques such as content delivery networks (CDNs) and edge caching can help reduce latency by bringing data closer to users. CDNs distribute content across multiple servers located in various geographic locations, while edge caching stores frequently accessed data at locations closer to end-users.

In addition to data replication and latency optimization, cross-region communication is another critical consideration. Federated GraphQL setups typically involve multiple services and data sources that need to interact with each other across different regions. Ensuring reliable and efficient communication between these components is essential for maintaining overall system performance and availability. Techniques such as service meshes can help manage cross-region communication by providing features like load balancing, service discovery, and fault tolerance. Service meshes enable fine-grained control over how services communicate, allowing for better management of network traffic and improved reliability.

When deploying federated GraphQL in a multi-region setup, it is also important to consider the impact of network partitioning and failure scenarios. Network partitioning occurs when regions become temporarily isolated from each other due to network issues or outages. In such cases, it is essential to have strategies in place to handle these situations gracefully and ensure that the system remains functional. Techniques such as fallback mechanisms, where requests are redirected to alternative services or data sources during outages, can help maintain service availability. Additionally, designing the system to be resilient to network failures and implementing robust monitoring and alerting systems can help quickly identify and address issues that arise.

Overall, deploying federated GraphQL across multiple regions requires careful planning and consideration of various factors, including data replication, latency optimization, and cross-region communication. By employing appropriate strategies and leveraging modern technologies, organizations can ensure that their federated GraphQL systems deliver high performance and reliability to users around the world.

When tackling the challenges of multi-region deployments in a federated GraphQL environment, the approach to data consistency and availability must be meticulously designed. Given that data needs to be shared and synchronized across various regions, it is crucial to implement strategies that balance consistency, availability, and partition tolerance, often referred to as the CAP theorem.

A robust strategy for data replication in multi-region deployments involves carefully selecting the replication model based on the specific use case. Synchronous replication, while ensuring data consistency across regions, may not always be feasible due to its impact on performance. On the other hand, asynchronous replication, although less demanding on system performance, requires mechanisms to handle eventual consistency, such as conflict resolution protocols and consistency checks. These protocols ensure that updates propagate correctly and that any discrepancies between regions are resolved in a timely manner.

Latency optimization, another critical factor, necessitates an understanding of the geographical distribution of users and the physical location of servers. Effective latency reduction strategies include the use of caching mechanisms and CDN integration. Caching frequently accessed data closer to the user's location can significantly improve response times and reduce the load on the central servers. CDNs not only cache static assets but can also be configured to cache dynamic GraphQL query results, depending on the nature of the data and the application's requirements.

Moreover, data sharding and partitioning can be used to optimize performance by distributing the load across multiple servers. This technique involves dividing the data into smaller, more manageable chunks, which can then be stored and processed in different regions. Properly implemented, sharding can improve query performance and reduce latency by ensuring that data retrieval is performed as close to the user as possible. However, it also introduces complexity in managing data consistency and handling cross-shard queries, necessitating careful design and implementation of the sharding strategy.

Cross-region communication is another significant challenge that must be addressed to ensure smooth operation in a multi-region setup. Efficient communication between federated services across regions requires a well-defined architecture for inter-service communication. One effective approach is to leverage service meshes, which provide advanced capabilities for managing cross-region interactions. Service meshes facilitate load balancing, automatic failover, and observability, which are essential for maintaining high availability and performance in a distributed environment.

Additionally, implementing distributed tracing and monitoring tools is crucial for managing and diagnosing issues in a multi-region deployment. These tools provide visibility into the performance and behavior of the federated GraphQL system, enabling you to identify bottlenecks, monitor latency, and ensure that data is being replicated and synchronized correctly across regions. By integrating distributed tracing into your system, you can gain insights into how requests traverse through various services and regions, which is invaluable for troubleshooting and performance tuning.

In summary, deploying federated GraphQL across multiple regions requires a multifaceted approach that addresses data replication, latency optimization, and cross-region communication. By carefully selecting the replication strategy, employing caching and CDN techniques, and leveraging service meshes for efficient communication, organizations can enhance the performance and reliability of their federated GraphQL systems on a global scale. The integration of distributed tracing and monitoring further supports the management of these complex deployments, ensuring that issues can be identified and resolved promptly.

To ensure the reliability and consistency of a federated GraphQL system across multiple regions, implementing robust mechanisms for data consistency and fault tolerance is essential. The inherent challenges of maintaining a consistent state across geographically dispersed data sources necessitate advanced techniques and tools designed to handle distributed data effectively.

One important strategy for maintaining consistency is the use of distributed consensus protocols. Protocols such as Paxos or Raft can be employed to manage state across multiple regions by ensuring that all nodes in the system agree on the current state of the data, even in the face of failures or network partitions. These protocols help to prevent situations where different regions might have conflicting data states, thus ensuring that the system remains reliable and consistent.

In addition to consensus protocols, implementing a strategy for conflict resolution is critical. In scenarios where eventual consistency is acceptable, it is important to have well-defined rules and mechanisms for resolving conflicts that arise when data changes are propagated between regions. This could involve versioning strategies, last-write-wins policies, or application-specific conflict resolution logic. The choice of strategy should align with the application's requirements for consistency and availability, as well as the nature of the data being handled.

Fault tolerance and resilience also play a crucial role in multi-region deployments. Designing for failure involves anticipating potential points of failure and implementing redundancy to ensure system continuity. This can include deploying multiple instances of services across regions, setting up failover mechanisms, and ensuring that backups are consistently updated and easily accessible. Additionally, using techniques such as automated failover and disaster recovery plans can help mitigate the impact of regional outages or disruptions.

Monitoring and observability are indispensable for managing complex, multi-region deployments. Implementing distributed tracing and logging allows for real-time visibility into the system's performance and health. By correlating logs and traces across different regions, you can identify and troubleshoot issues more effectively. Tools such as Jaeger or Zipkin can be integrated to provide end-to-end tracing of requests as they traverse multiple regions, helping to pinpoint performance bottlenecks or failures.

Another key aspect of managing multi-region deployments is ensuring that all regions are synchronized in terms of configuration and deployment. Configuration management tools, such as Kubernetes operators or infrastructure-as-code frameworks, can be employed to maintain consistency across different environments. These tools automate the deployment process, reduce the likelihood of configuration drift, and ensure that all regions are aligned with the latest updates and patches.

Furthermore, when dealing with cross-region communication, optimizing network routes and reducing latency is vital. Techniques such as geo-routing and content delivery networks (CDNs) can be utilized to direct user traffic to the nearest available region, thereby improving response times and reducing the load on distant servers. Additionally, employing efficient data serialization formats and minimizing the size of data transmitted between regions can further enhance performance.

The integration of federated GraphQL with multi-region strategies also involves addressing the challenges of cross-region data access. When services in one region need to query data from another region, it is important to design the system in a way that minimizes the performance impact of these inter-region queries. This might involve optimizing the GraphQL schema to reduce the need for cross-region calls or caching data at the regional level to avoid frequent remote lookups.

Lastly, continuous testing and validation are essential to ensure that the system performs as expected under various conditions. Implementing automated tests that simulate multi-region scenarios can help identify potential issues and ensure that the system remains resilient in the face of network partitions, regional failures, or high load conditions.

In summary, managing federated GraphQL deployments across multiple regions involves a multifaceted approach that includes ensuring data consistency through consensus protocols, resolving conflicts, and designing for fault tolerance. Optimizing network communication, maintaining configuration consistency, and leveraging observability tools are critical for managing performance and reliability. By employing these strategies, organizations can achieve a robust and efficient multi-region federated GraphQL architecture that delivers a seamless experience to users globally.

CHAPTER 32: FEDERATED GRAPHQL AND SERVICE MESHES

Integrating federated GraphQL with service meshes represents a strategic advancement in the management and operation of microservices architectures. Service meshes provide a robust framework for managing communication between microservices, offering enhanced features for observability, security, and traffic management. This chapter explores how to leverage service meshes in conjunction with federated GraphQL to optimize and secure distributed systems.

Service meshes act as an infrastructure layer that controls the communication between microservices, typically through a sidecar proxy model. This architecture allows service meshes to manage inter-service communications independently of the application logic, offering benefits such as traffic control, load balancing, and observability. When integrated with federated GraphQL, service meshes can provide significant enhancements to the management of queries and mutations across distributed services.

One of the primary advantages of using a service mesh with federated GraphQL is improved observability. Service meshes often come equipped with built-in tools for tracing, metrics collection, and logging, which are crucial for monitoring and debugging complex federated systems. By deploying a service mesh, you gain visibility into the interactions between microservices, which can help identify bottlenecks, troubleshoot issues, and understand the performance characteristics of your federated GraphQL setup. For example, service meshes such as Istio or Linkerd offer distributed tracing capabilities that allow you to trace GraphQL queries as they traverse different microservices, providing insights into the overall system performance and pinpointing areas for optimization.

In addition to observability, service meshes enhance the security of federated GraphQL deployments through robust authentication and authorization mechanisms. Service meshes enable mutual TLS (mTLS) for encrypting communication between services, ensuring that data is securely transmitted across the network. They also support fine-grained access control policies, allowing you to enforce security rules for interactions between services. This can be particularly useful in federated environments where multiple services from different domains need to interact securely. By integrating service mesh security features with federated GraphQL, you can establish a strong security posture that protects your data and mitigates risks associated with inter-service communication.

Traffic management is another critical aspect where service meshes add value to federated GraphQL architectures. Service meshes offer advanced routing capabilities, including traffic splitting, retries, and circuit breaking. These features can be used to manage the distribution of GraphQL queries across different microservices, handle failures gracefully, and optimize the routing of requests based on various criteria. For instance, traffic splitting can be used to perform canary deployments or blue-green deployments, enabling gradual rollouts of new features while minimizing disruption to users. Circuit breaking helps to prevent cascading failures by stopping traffic to services that are experiencing issues, thus enhancing the overall reliability of the federated GraphQL system.

The integration of a service mesh with federated GraphQL also simplifies the management of service-to-service communication by abstracting the complexity of networking. Service meshes provide a unified control plane for configuring and managing service interactions, which can streamline the deployment and operation of federated systems. This abstraction reduces the need for custom networking code and configuration, allowing developers to focus on building and optimizing their GraphQL schemas and resolvers. Additionally, the declarative nature of service mesh configurations aligns well with modern infrastructure-as-code practices, facilitating automated and consistent deployments across multiple environments.

When implementing a service mesh with federated GraphQL, it is important to consider the configuration and operational aspects of the integration. Service meshes require careful planning to ensure that they complement rather than complicate the existing architecture. Proper configuration of the sidecar proxies, including setting up correct routing rules and policies, is essential for achieving the desired outcomes. Additionally, monitoring and maintaining the service mesh itself requires attention to ensure that it operates efficiently and does not introduce overhead or latency.

In summary, integrating service meshes with federated GraphQL provides substantial benefits in terms of observability, security, and traffic management. Service meshes enhance the ability to monitor and debug distributed systems, strengthen security through mTLS and access control, and offer advanced traffic management features.

By leveraging these capabilities, organizations can build more resilient, secure, and efficient federated GraphQL environments. However, successful integration requires careful planning and configuration to align the service mesh capabilities with the needs of the federated architecture.

Integrating federated GraphQL with service meshes necessitates a nuanced understanding of both technologies and their interplay. The effectiveness of this integration hinges on the ability of service meshes to manage and optimize the communication and functionality of microservices within a federated GraphQL environment.

One of the key considerations when integrating service meshes with federated GraphQL is traffic management. Federated GraphQL setups often involve multiple services that must handle various types of queries and mutations. Service meshes enhance traffic management by offering sophisticated routing capabilities that can be used to control the flow of GraphQL requests. For instance, service meshes allow for fine-grained control over request routing, including features such as weighted load balancing and traffic splitting. This capability is particularly useful when deploying new versions of microservices or when performing gradual rollouts. By configuring traffic management rules, you can direct a percentage of GraphQL requests to a new service version while maintaining stability for the existing version, ensuring that changes do not disrupt the overall system.

In addition to routing, service meshes provide powerful features for managing retries and circuit breaking. When a service experiences temporary failures, the service mesh can automatically retry the request or redirect it to a healthy instance, minimizing the impact on end users. Circuit breaking mechanisms can also prevent cascading failures by detecting and halting requests to failing services before they cause widespread disruptions. These features are critical in a federated GraphQL environment, where failures in one microservice can potentially affect the entire system. By leveraging service mesh capabilities, you can enhance the resilience and reliability of your federated GraphQL setup.

Security is another area where service meshes provide significant benefits. In a federated GraphQL environment, security must be robust due to the numerous interactions between services that span different domains or organizational boundaries. Service meshes offer features like mutual TLS (mTLS), which encrypts the communication between services, thereby ensuring data integrity and confidentiality. Additionally, service meshes facilitate the implementation of fine-grained access control policies, enabling you to enforce rules that govern which services can communicate with each other and under what conditions. This can be crucial for adhering to compliance requirements and securing sensitive data as it moves between services.

Observability, a critical component of modern microservices architectures, is greatly enhanced by the use of service meshes. Service meshes provide detailed metrics, distributed tracing, and logging capabilities, which are invaluable for monitoring and troubleshooting federated GraphQL setups. Distributed tracing, for example, allows you to follow the path of a GraphQL request as it travels through different microservices, providing insights into performance bottlenecks and the overall health of the system. Logs and metrics collected by the service mesh can be analyzed to detect anomalies, identify performance issues, and gain a deeper understanding of how GraphQL queries are being processed across services.

Configuring a service mesh to work with federated GraphQL requires careful consideration of the service mesh's capabilities and how they align with the requirements of your federated architecture. Most service meshes are designed to work with HTTP-based services, making them well-suited for GraphQL, which typically operates over HTTP. However, the integration involves setting up the service mesh proxies (sidecars) alongside your GraphQL services and configuring them to handle GraphQL-specific routing, security, and observability needs.

When implementing service meshes in a federated GraphQL environment, it is essential to plan for the additional complexity introduced by this integration. Service meshes add an extra layer of infrastructure that must be managed and maintained. This includes configuring and monitoring the mesh itself, as well as ensuring that it does not introduce latency or other performance issues into your federated GraphQL setup. It is also important to test the integration thoroughly to verify that it meets your performance, security, and reliability requirements.

In summary, integrating federated GraphQL with service meshes offers significant benefits in terms of observability, security, and traffic management. By leveraging the advanced features provided by service meshes, you can enhance the performance, reliability, and security of your federated GraphQL architecture. However, this integration also requires careful planning and configuration to ensure that it aligns with the specific needs and challenges of your system. With the right approach, service meshes can greatly improve the management and operation of federated GraphQL environments, enabling more efficient and secure communication between microservices.

The integration of federated GraphQL with service meshes not only enhances observability and security but also plays a pivotal role in streamlining the overall management of microservices. Observability, in particular, is crucial in a federated setup, where tracing and debugging can become complex due to the distributed nature of services. Service meshes simplify this by providing comprehensive tracing and monitoring capabilities.

Service meshes deploy sidecar proxies alongside each microservice, capturing detailed telemetry data about service interactions. This includes metrics on latency, error rates, and request volumes, as well as trace data that helps track the journey of a request across multiple services. For federated GraphQL setups, where a single GraphQL request may touch several microservices, the ability to trace these requests end-to-end is invaluable. It allows developers to pinpoint bottlenecks, identify performance issues, and understand the interdependencies between different parts of the system. With advanced visualization tools and dashboards provided by service meshes, teams can gain deep insights into system behavior and health, making it easier to maintain and optimize the federated GraphQL infrastructure.

Furthermore, service meshes facilitate the creation of more sophisticated monitoring and alerting systems. By leveraging the metrics and tracing data collected, teams can set up alerts for specific conditions, such as increased error rates or latency spikes. These alerts enable proactive responses to potential issues before they impact end users, thus improving the overall reliability and performance of the federated GraphQL setup. Additionally, integration with logging systems allows for detailed analysis and troubleshooting, providing a complete view of service interactions and aiding in the resolution of complex issues.

Another significant benefit of integrating service meshes with federated GraphQL is the support for advanced deployment strategies. Service meshes enable the implementation of canary releases and blue-green deployments, which are essential for managing updates and changes in a controlled manner. Canary releases allow you to deploy a new version of a service to a small subset of users before rolling it out more broadly. This approach minimizes risk and provides an opportunity to test new features or changes in a real-world environment with minimal impact. Blue-green deployments, on the other hand, involve maintaining two separate environments (blue and green) and switching traffic between them. This strategy ensures that deployments are seamless and that any issues can be quickly rolled back.

Service meshes also assist in managing service discovery and load balancing. In a federated GraphQL environment, where services may be dynamically scaled or updated, service meshes automatically handle service discovery and routing. They ensure that requests are directed to the appropriate service instances, balancing the load effectively across multiple instances and avoiding overloading any single instance. This dynamic routing capability is particularly beneficial in federated setups where service locations and availability can change frequently.

While integrating service meshes with federated GraphQL offers many advantages, it also requires careful planning and configuration. Service meshes introduce additional layers of complexity to the architecture, and proper configuration is essential to avoid potential pitfalls. For instance, managing the sidecar proxies and ensuring they are properly aligned with the federated GraphQL services requires thorough testing and validation. Moreover, the overhead introduced by the service mesh in terms of latency and resource consumption should be monitored and optimized to ensure that the benefits outweigh the costs.

In summary, the integration of service meshes with federated GraphQL provides a robust framework for managing microservices. It enhances observability through detailed metrics and tracing, improves security with features like mutual TLS, and supports sophisticated traffic management and deployment strategies. By addressing the challenges and complexities associated with this integration, organizations can achieve a highly resilient and efficient federated GraphQL architecture that scales effectively and maintains high performance across diverse environments.

CHAPTER 33: AUTOMATING SCHEMA DOCUMENTATION AND DISCOVERY

In the evolving landscape of federated GraphQL architectures, the automation of schema documentation and discovery is a pivotal aspect that greatly enhances the usability and maintainability of the system. As federated GraphQL setups involve multiple microservices, each contributing its own schema to a unified graph, maintaining accurate and comprehensive documentation becomes increasingly complex. Automation tools and techniques address these challenges, ensuring that schema documentation remains up-to-date and accessible.

The primary objective of automating schema documentation is to keep the schema information current without requiring manual updates. In a federated GraphQL environment, where services are continuously evolving and new features are being integrated, manual documentation processes can quickly become outdated. Automated documentation tools leverage the schema definitions provided by the various services to generate documentation dynamically. This approach ensures that the documentation reflects the latest changes in the schema, providing developers and consumers with accurate and timely information.

One widely adopted method for automating schema documentation is the use of tools that integrate directly with the GraphQL schema. For instance, tools such as GraphiQL, Apollo Studio, and GraphQL Playground offer interactive interfaces that automatically display the current schema and its documentation. These tools parse the GraphQL schema files and generate a user-friendly representation of the types, queries, mutations, and their descriptions. By incorporating these tools into the development workflow, teams can ensure that the documentation is consistently synchronized with the schema.

In addition to interactive tools, schema documentation can be generated in static formats, such as HTML or Markdown, using automated scripts and integrations. Tools like Apollo Server and GraphQL Code Generator provide capabilities to extract and format schema documentation into various formats that can be hosted and accessed via documentation websites. These tools often include options for customizing the appearance and organization of the documentation, allowing teams to tailor it to their specific needs. Automation scripts can be scheduled to run periodically or triggered by changes in the schema, ensuring that the documentation remains current without manual intervention.

Another important aspect of schema documentation is discovery—the ability for developers and consumers to easily find and understand the schema components they need. Automation tools can aid in schema discovery by providing centralized repositories or portals where all the schema information is aggregated. For example, tools such as Apollo Graph Manager and Hasura allow for the aggregation of schema information from multiple federated services, providing a single point of access for exploring and querying the schema. These platforms often include search and filtering capabilities, making it easier for users to navigate large and complex schemas.

Schema discovery is further facilitated by implementing consistent naming conventions and documentation practices across services. Automated tools can enforce these practices by integrating with linting and validation systems that check for schema consistency and completeness. Ensuring that all services adhere to a common set of documentation standards helps in maintaining a coherent and user-friendly schema presentation. Additionally, automated discovery tools can provide visualizations and diagrams that illustrate the relationships between different schema components, offering a more intuitive understanding of the schema structure.

To support schema documentation and discovery, it is essential to establish a robust process for version control and change management. Automated documentation tools should be integrated into the CI/CD pipeline to ensure that updates to the schema trigger corresponding updates in the documentation. This integration helps in maintaining alignment between the schema and its documentation, reducing the risk of discrepancies that can arise from manual updates. Version control systems can track changes in the schema over time, providing historical context and enabling rollback if needed. This approach supports effective management of schema evolution and ensures that documentation remains accurate throughout the development lifecycle.

Finally, it is crucial to consider the accessibility of automated schema documentation. Documentation should be easily accessible to all relevant stakeholders, including developers, testers, and external consumers. By providing clear and intuitive documentation interfaces, teams can improve the overall developer experience and facilitate better utilization of the GraphQL API. Automated tools can enhance accessibility by generating documentation that is responsive and compatible with various devices and platforms. Furthermore, integrating documentation with developer portals and support channels can streamline access and encourage engagement with the schema.

In conclusion, automating schema documentation and discovery in a federated GraphQL environment involves leveraging tools and techniques that ensure up-to-date, comprehensive, and accessible documentation. By integrating interactive interfaces, static documentation generation, centralized discovery platforms, and consistent practices, teams can effectively manage the complexity of federated schemas. Automation not only improves the accuracy and usability of schema documentation but also supports efficient development workflows and enhances the overall experience for developers and consumers.

To further enhance the effectiveness of schema documentation and discovery in a federated GraphQL setup, it is crucial to implement strategies that address both the technical and organizational aspects of schema management. The automation of these processes not only improves efficiency but also ensures consistency and accuracy across various services.

One significant benefit of automating schema documentation is the reduction of manual errors. When documentation is generated automatically from the schema definitions, it minimizes the risk of discrepancies between the documented and actual schema. This is particularly important in a federated environment where multiple services contribute to the overall schema. Automated tools that parse schema files and generate documentation directly from these files ensure that any updates or changes are reflected immediately.

This real-time synchronization is critical for maintaining an accurate and reliable reference for developers and consumers alike.

Furthermore, the integration of schema documentation tools into the continuous integration (CI) and continuous deployment (CD) pipelines can significantly streamline the documentation process. By incorporating automated documentation generation into these pipelines, teams can ensure that the documentation is updated with each deployment or schema change. This approach also allows for the documentation to be tested alongside code changes, identifying any discrepancies or issues before they impact users. Automated testing of documentation can involve verifying that descriptions and examples are accurate and that deprecated fields or types are properly flagged.

Another key aspect of schema discovery is the ability to provide meaningful and context-rich documentation. Automated tools can enhance schema documentation by including detailed descriptions, examples, and usage guidelines. For instance, tools like GraphQL Voyager and Schema Definition Language (SDL) visualizers can create interactive diagrams of the schema, illustrating relationships between types and their fields. This visual representation can make it easier for developers to understand the structure and capabilities of the schema. Additionally, incorporating examples of common queries and mutations in the documentation can provide practical guidance on how to interact with the schema.

For large federated systems, centralizing schema documentation in a unified portal or repository can greatly facilitate discovery. Tools such as Apollo Graph Manager offer features for aggregating schema information from multiple services into a single interface. This centralization allows developers to search and explore the entire federated schema from one location, improving accessibility and reducing the time spent navigating through different services. Additionally, centralized documentation platforms can include features for versioning and historical tracking, enabling users to view changes over time and understand the evolution of the schema.

Effective schema discovery also involves implementing search capabilities within the documentation. Automated search functions can help users quickly locate specific types, fields, or operations within the schema. Advanced search features, such as filtering by type or query complexity, can further enhance the user experience by allowing users to find relevant information more efficiently. Integrating these search capabilities into documentation portals ensures that users can easily access the information they need without extensive manual searching.

In conclusion, automating schema documentation and discovery in a federated GraphQL environment involves a combination of technical tools and best practices. By leveraging automated documentation generation, integrating these tools into CI/CD pipelines, and providing rich, centralized, and searchable documentation, organizations can improve the accuracy, accessibility, and usability of their schema documentation. This approach not only supports developers in understanding and working with the schema but also enhances the overall efficiency and reliability of the federated GraphQL system.

In addition to the integration of schema documentation tools into CI/CD pipelines and the establishment of centralized documentation repositories, another important aspect of automating schema documentation and discovery is the use of schema management platforms. These platforms offer advanced features for schema versioning, change tracking, and validation, which are essential for maintaining consistency and accuracy across a federated GraphQL environment.

Schema management platforms, such as Apollo Studio or GraphQL Inspector, provide robust capabilities for tracking changes to the schema over time. By comparing different versions of the schema, these tools can highlight modifications, additions, and deprecations, helping teams understand the impact of schema changes on existing queries and integrations. This versioning capability is crucial in a federated setup where multiple services evolve independently. The ability to review historical changes and their effects on the schema ensures that developers can anticipate and address potential issues before they arise.

Furthermore, these platforms often include validation features that can automatically check the schema against predefined rules or best practices. Validation can help enforce consistency and prevent common issues, such as schema misalignment or broken references. By integrating schema validation into the development workflow, teams can catch and address problems early, reducing the likelihood of runtime errors and inconsistencies in the documentation.

Incorporating feedback mechanisms into the documentation process is another valuable strategy. Automated tools can include options for users to submit feedback or report issues directly from the documentation interface. This feedback loop allows for continuous improvement and refinement of the documentation, ensuring that it meets the needs of its users. By addressing feedback promptly and updating the documentation accordingly, teams can enhance the overall usability and effectiveness of the schema documentation.

Finally, it is important to consider the integration of documentation tools with other aspects of the development ecosystem. For example, integrating schema documentation with code editors and development environments can provide developers with real-time access to schema information and documentation while writing code. Plugins or extensions for popular editors like VSCode or IntelliJ IDEA can offer context-sensitive documentation, autocomplete suggestions, and inline examples, improving the development experience and reducing the time spent searching for information.

Automated documentation should also be designed to support various user roles and access levels. For instance, providing different levels of documentation detail for developers, API consumers, and business stakeholders ensures that each audience receives the relevant information they need. Developers may require in-depth technical details and examples, while business stakeholders might benefit from high-level summaries and use cases. Tailoring the documentation to these different needs enhances its utility and ensures that all users can effectively navigate and utilize the federated GraphQL schema.

Overall, automating schema documentation and discovery in a federated GraphQL environment involves a multifaceted approach that leverages advanced tools, integrates with development workflows, and addresses the needs of various users. By implementing comprehensive strategies for automation, teams can maintain accurate and accessible documentation, facilitate schema discovery, and ultimately support the successful operation and evolution of their federated GraphQL systems.

CHAPTER 34: BUILDING SCALABLE CACHING STRATEGIES FOR FEDERATED GRAPHQL

In the realm of federated GraphQL architectures, effective caching strategies are paramount for achieving high performance and scalability. As GraphQL queries traverse multiple services, the potential for performance bottlenecks increases, making the implementation of robust caching mechanisms essential. This chapter delves into scalable caching strategies tailored for federated GraphQL systems, addressing in-memory caching, distributed caching solutions, and cache invalidation techniques to optimize system responsiveness and overall efficiency.

Caching, fundamentally, aims to reduce the latency associated with data retrieval and minimize the load on backend services by storing frequently accessed data closer to where it is needed. In a federated GraphQL environment, this involves several layers of caching, each addressing different performance concerns and operational scales.

In-memory caching is one of the most straightforward approaches and involves storing data directly in the memory of the service handling the request. This strategy is particularly effective for data that is frequently requested and does not change often. By keeping such data in memory, services can quickly respond to requests without repeatedly querying the underlying databases or microservices. However, in-memory caching has its limitations, especially when dealing with large-scale or distributed systems where memory constraints and the need for data consistency across multiple nodes come into play.

To address these limitations, distributed caching solutions offer a more scalable approach. Distributed caches, such as Redis or Memcached, provide a shared cache that can be accessed by multiple services across different instances or regions. This setup not only enhances the cache's scalability but also its resilience, as the cache can be replicated and partitioned to handle high volumes of requests and ensure fault tolerance. In a federated GraphQL setup, employing a distributed cache allows different services to leverage a common caching layer, reducing redundant data fetching and improving the efficiency of cross-service interactions.

When implementing distributed caching, it is crucial to design the cache schema and eviction policies carefully. Effective cache schemas ensure that the data is organized in a manner that facilitates quick access and minimizes contention. Additionally, eviction policies, such as Least Recently Used (LRU) or Time-To-Live (TTL), help manage the cache size and ensure that outdated or infrequently accessed data does not occupy valuable cache space. These policies balance the need to keep relevant data readily available while preventing the cache from becoming a performance bottleneck due to excessive size or stale data.

Cache invalidation is another critical aspect of caching strategy. In a federated GraphQL environment, where multiple services manage their data, ensuring that the cache remains consistent with the underlying data sources is a complex task. Cache invalidation techniques are employed to address this challenge by determining when cached data should be refreshed or removed based on changes in the data.

There are several approaches to cache invalidation, including explicit invalidation, where services or components actively remove or update cached data when changes occur, and implicit invalidation, where the cache expires data based on predefined policies such as TTL. Each approach has its trade-offs and may be used in combination to meet the specific needs of the system. For example, explicit invalidation can be beneficial for scenarios where data changes are infrequent but critical, while implicit invalidation is suitable for high-throughput environments where data freshness requirements can be managed through automatic expiration.

Moreover, federated GraphQL systems can benefit from a hybrid caching strategy that combines both client-side and server-side caching. Client-side caching, implemented in the client applications or through browser caches, can reduce the number of requests made to the federated services and provide faster response times for end users. On the other hand, server-side caching ensures that the backend services are not overwhelmed by repetitive queries and can efficiently handle requests from multiple clients.

In designing a caching strategy for federated GraphQL, it is essential to consider the specific access patterns and data characteristics of the system. Understanding the nature of the queries, the frequency of data changes, and the impact of caching on different services will guide the selection and configuration of appropriate caching mechanisms.

Additionally, monitoring and analyzing cache performance and hit rates are crucial for tuning the caching strategy and addressing any emerging issues.

By implementing scalable caching strategies, federated GraphQL systems can achieve significant improvements in performance and responsiveness. These strategies help mitigate the challenges associated with handling large volumes of requests and distributed data sources, ultimately enhancing the overall user experience and operational efficiency of the system.

In federated GraphQL systems, effective caching strategies are crucial for optimizing performance and enhancing user experience. A well-designed caching layer not only improves responsiveness but also alleviates the load on backend services by reducing redundant data processing and network overhead. As such, exploring scalable caching strategies is key to maintaining an efficient federated GraphQL architecture.

One of the core challenges in federated GraphQL is managing the cache coherently across multiple services. Given the distributed nature of the system, ensuring that cached data remains accurate and consistent across different nodes and services requires careful planning and execution. This is where the implementation of caching mechanisms such as in-memory caching and distributed caching solutions plays a significant role.

In-memory caching, while straightforward, offers immediate benefits by storing frequently accessed data in the local memory of a service. This approach drastically reduces the time required to fetch data as it eliminates the need for repeated database queries or inter-service communication. However, in-memory caching alone may not suffice for large-scale applications due to limitations in scalability and potential memory constraints. The size of the cache is inherently limited by the available memory on each service instance, which can become a bottleneck as the volume of data grows.

To address these scalability issues, distributed caching solutions provide a more robust alternative. Distributed caches, such as Redis or Memcached, enable multiple services to access a shared cache, thereby extending the caching layer beyond the constraints of individual service instances. These solutions facilitate the storage of large volumes of data across a cluster of cache servers, which can be partitioned and replicated to handle high traffic and ensure fault tolerance. By integrating a distributed cache into a federated GraphQL system, services can leverage a unified caching layer that improves data retrieval efficiency and reduces duplication of effort.

Implementing a distributed caching strategy involves several key considerations. First, designing the cache schema is essential to ensure that data is stored in a way that supports efficient retrieval and minimizes contention. The cache schema should align with the structure of the data and the access patterns of the application, which helps in maintaining optimal performance. Additionally, configuring eviction policies is critical to managing the cache size and ensuring that it does not become a performance bottleneck. Common eviction policies include Least Recently Used (LRU) and Time-To-Live (TTL), which help in keeping the cache relevant and up-to-date by removing outdated or less frequently accessed data.

Cache invalidation is another critical aspect of maintaining an effective caching strategy. In a federated GraphQL environment, where data consistency across multiple services is paramount, cache invalidation ensures that changes in the underlying data sources are promptly reflected in the cache. This can be particularly challenging due to the decentralized nature of federated architectures. Various techniques can be employed for cache invalidation, including explicit invalidation, where services explicitly notify the cache of changes, and automatic invalidation, where the cache itself determines when data should be refreshed based on predefined rules or patterns.

Explicit invalidation involves a service notifying the cache to remove or update specific entries whenever a change occurs. This approach ensures that the cache remains consistent with the underlying data but requires that each service is responsible for managing its cache entries. On the other hand, automatic invalidation uses strategies such as TTL or cache versioning to manage data freshness. For example, TTL-based invalidation automatically removes cache entries after a specified period, while cache versioning involves maintaining different versions of cached data and updating them as necessary.

Incorporating these cache invalidation techniques into a federated GraphQL setup requires careful coordination among services to ensure data consistency. One approach is to use a centralized cache invalidation service that manages cache entries across the entire system, providing a unified mechanism for updating or invalidating cache data. Alternatively, employing distributed cache management frameworks can facilitate more granular control over cache entries and invalidation processes.

Overall, building scalable caching strategies for federated GraphQL systems involves addressing both the technical and operational challenges of data storage and retrieval. By leveraging in-memory caching for quick access to frequently used data and distributed caching solutions for handling large-scale data storage, organizations can significantly enhance the performance of their federated GraphQL setups. Moreover, implementing robust cache invalidation techniques ensures that the system remains responsive and accurate, even as the underlying data evolves.

Implementing effective cache invalidation techniques is crucial for maintaining the accuracy and relevance of cached data in a federated GraphQL system. Since federated systems involve multiple services and data sources, ensuring that the cache remains synchronized with the underlying data requires a well-thought-out invalidation strategy. Failure to manage cache invalidation correctly can lead to issues such as stale data being served to users, which can degrade the reliability and trustworthiness of the system.

One common approach to cache invalidation is the use of explicit invalidation strategies, where the application or service explicitly instructs the cache to remove or update specific entries. This approach can be effective when the data changes in a predictable manner or when specific operations are known to affect particular cached data. For instance, a service might issue cache invalidation commands whenever an update operation is performed on the data it manages. This ensures that subsequent requests for that data will retrieve the most current version from the underlying data source.

Another method involves employing cache coherence protocols, which are particularly useful in distributed systems where multiple instances of the cache are involved. These protocols ensure that all instances of the cache are updated consistently, preventing discrepancies and ensuring that all users receive the same data. Techniques such as cache invalidation messages and distributed transactions can help synchronize cache updates across different nodes, though they may introduce additional complexity and overhead.

Furthermore, adopting a more proactive approach to cache invalidation can enhance system performance and accuracy. This includes leveraging techniques such as cache warming and pre-fetching. Cache warming involves pre-loading the cache with data that is anticipated to be needed shortly, based on historical usage patterns or predictive algorithms. By preparing the cache in advance, the system can reduce the time it takes to respond to user requests and improve overall efficiency. Pre-fetching, on the other hand, involves fetching and caching data that is likely to be requested in the near future. This strategy is particularly useful for handling anticipated spikes in traffic or for optimizing user experiences based on expected interactions.

It is also important to consider the impact of caching on the overall system architecture. In federated GraphQL environments, where different services interact and share data, caching decisions made at one service level can affect other services. Hence, coordination between services is essential to prevent issues such as cache pollution or inconsistencies. Implementing a unified caching strategy that considers the interactions between services can help mitigate these challenges. This might involve standardizing cache keys, ensuring consistent cache configurations across services, and maintaining clear documentation of caching policies and their implications for the entire system.

Performance monitoring and fine-tuning are integral to maintaining an effective caching strategy. Regularly assessing cache hit ratios, response times, and eviction rates can provide valuable insights into how well the cache is performing and where adjustments may be needed. Tools and metrics that track cache performance help in identifying bottlenecks or inefficiencies, enabling administrators to make informed decisions about optimizing cache configurations and strategies.

In summary, building scalable caching strategies for federated GraphQL systems involves a multifaceted approach that includes implementing both in-memory and distributed caching solutions, developing effective cache invalidation techniques, and considering the impact of caching on system architecture. By adopting a combination of these strategies and continuously monitoring and fine-tuning cache performance, organizations can enhance the responsiveness and efficiency of their federated GraphQL implementations, ultimately providing a better experience for end-users and maintaining system reliability.

CHAPTER 35: FEDERATED GRAPHQL AND CLOUD NATIVE TECHNOLOGIES

In the evolving landscape of software architecture, cloud native technologies have emerged as pivotal enablers of modern, scalable, and resilient systems. When applied to federated GraphQL, these technologies can significantly streamline the deployment and management of complex, distributed systems. This chapter delves into how cloud native tools such as container orchestration, serverless computing, and managed services can enhance the implementation and operation of federated GraphQL solutions.

Container orchestration is a cornerstone of cloud native technology, providing a robust framework for managing the deployment, scaling, and operation of containerized applications. In the context of federated GraphQL, container orchestration platforms such as Kubernetes facilitate the management of multiple services across various nodes in a cluster. Kubernetes, with its capabilities for automated deployment, scaling, and load balancing, ensures that federated GraphQL services are efficiently distributed and scaled according to demand. This orchestration is critical for maintaining performance and reliability as the number of microservices or federated services grows.

Containers, which encapsulate applications and their dependencies into isolated environments, offer several advantages for federated GraphQL implementations. They provide consistency across different environments, from development to production, and simplify the process of scaling services up or down based on load. By packaging GraphQL services in containers, organizations can achieve a high degree of portability and flexibility, facilitating seamless integration with other cloud native technologies.

Serverless computing is another transformative cloud native technology that can enhance federated GraphQL architectures. Serverless platforms, such as AWS Lambda or Azure Functions, allow developers to deploy functions or microservices without managing the underlying server infrastructure. This abstraction simplifies the development and operational aspects of federated GraphQL, enabling developers to focus on writing business logic rather than handling infrastructure concerns. Serverless functions can be used to handle specific tasks within a federated architecture, such as executing GraphQL resolvers or processing complex queries. This approach not only reduces operational overhead but also provides the ability to scale functions dynamically based on demand.

In federated GraphQL systems, serverless computing can be particularly beneficial for handling variable workloads and managing bursts of traffic. For instance, serverless functions can be employed to offload processing from primary GraphQL services, allowing for more efficient handling of heavy or complex queries. By leveraging serverless computing, organizations can achieve cost efficiency, as they only pay for the compute resources consumed during the execution of their functions.

Managed services represent a further advancement in cloud native technologies, offering pre-configured, fully managed solutions that integrate seamlessly with federated GraphQL setups. Managed services for databases, messaging systems, and authentication can significantly reduce the complexity of integrating and managing these components. For example, managed database services such as Amazon RDS or Google Cloud SQL provide reliable, scalable, and fully managed database solutions that can serve as the data sources for federated GraphQL services. These services handle administrative tasks such as backups, patching, and scaling, allowing developers to focus on building and deploying their GraphQL services.

Similarly, managed authentication services like AWS Cognito or Auth0 offer ready-made solutions for implementing user authentication and authorization within federated GraphQL environments. These services provide built-in support for user management, security, and integration with various identity providers, streamlining the process of adding authentication capabilities to federated GraphQL systems.

Incorporating cloud native technologies into a federated GraphQL setup not only enhances the deployment and management of services but also contributes to a more agile and resilient architecture. By leveraging container orchestration, serverless computing, and managed services, organizations can achieve greater efficiency, scalability, and flexibility in their federated GraphQL deployments. These technologies facilitate the dynamic handling of workloads, reduce operational complexity, and provide robust solutions for managing distributed services, ultimately supporting the creation of scalable and performant GraphQL architectures in the cloud.

In addition to container orchestration and serverless

computing, managed services play a crucial role in enhancing the deployment and management of federated GraphQL systems. Managed services, provided by cloud platforms such as AWS, Google Cloud Platform, and Microsoft Azure, offer pre-configured and fully managed infrastructure components that simplify the complexities associated with deploying and maintaining a federated GraphQL setup.

One of the primary advantages of using managed services is the reduction in operational overhead. Services such as managed databases, API gateways, and monitoring tools handle routine maintenance tasks such as patching, backups, and scaling, allowing developers to focus more on application development rather than infrastructure management. For federated GraphQL implementations, managed services can streamline data management, enhance performance, and ensure high availability.

Managed databases are particularly relevant in a federated GraphQL context. Federated architectures often rely on multiple databases distributed across different services. Managed database services, such as Amazon RDS or Azure SQL Database, provide automated backups, scaling, and performance optimization, ensuring that the data layer supporting federated GraphQL remains robust and responsive. These services support various database engines, from relational databases to NoSQL solutions, accommodating diverse data requirements and integration needs.

Another critical component in a cloud native ecosystem is the use of managed API gateways. API gateways serve as a unified entry point for API requests, facilitating routing, authentication, and rate limiting. In federated GraphQL systems, managed API gateways can simplify the management of multiple GraphQL endpoints, ensuring that requests are efficiently routed to the appropriate services and that security policies are enforced. These gateways often provide built-in features such as caching, logging, and analytics, which enhance the overall performance and observability of the federated GraphQL setup.

Monitoring and observability are essential for maintaining the health and performance of federated GraphQL systems. Managed monitoring services, such as AWS CloudWatch or Google Cloud Monitoring, offer comprehensive tools for tracking the performance of both individual services and the overall federated architecture. These services provide real-time metrics, logs, and alerts, enabling teams to detect and address issues proactively. Effective monitoring is crucial for ensuring that all components of the federated GraphQL system are functioning optimally and for identifying potential bottlenecks or failures.

Additionally, cloud native technologies offer robust support for security and compliance in federated GraphQL systems. Managed security services provide features such as identity and access management (IAM), encryption, and threat detection, which are essential for protecting sensitive data and ensuring regulatory compliance. By leveraging these services, organizations can implement security best practices and safeguard their federated GraphQL deployments from potential vulnerabilities.

Integrating these cloud native technologies into a federated GraphQL architecture not only simplifies deployment and management but also enhances the scalability, reliability, and security of the system. Container orchestration provides the flexibility to manage complex service interactions and scale resources efficiently. Serverless computing offers a cost-effective way to handle variable workloads and process intensive queries. Managed services reduce the burden of infrastructure management, allowing teams to focus on developing and optimizing their federated GraphQL solutions.

As organizations continue to embrace cloud native approaches, the integration of these technologies into federated GraphQL deployments will become increasingly essential. By leveraging container orchestration, serverless computing, and managed services, teams can build more resilient, scalable, and efficient federated GraphQL systems that meet the demands of modern applications and global user bases.

Integrating federated GraphQL with cloud native technologies not only enhances scalability and performance but also brings sophisticated capabilities to handle complex deployment scenarios. Among these capabilities, multi-region deployments and disaster recovery strategies are critical aspects that benefit significantly from cloud native approaches.

When deploying federated GraphQL systems across multiple regions, cloud native technologies offer robust solutions to address latency, data consistency, and high availability. Multi-region deployments enable applications to serve users from geographically dispersed locations, reducing latency by directing traffic to the nearest data center. Cloud providers offer global infrastructure with data centers in various regions, allowing federated GraphQL systems to leverage these facilities for optimal performance.

For effective multi-region deployments, data replication strategies are essential. Cloud platforms provide managed database services that support synchronous or asynchronous replication across regions. Synchronous replication ensures that data is consistently updated across all regions in real-time, which is crucial for applications that require immediate consistency. Asynchronous replication, on the other hand, offers higher performance by allowing some lag between updates, which can be acceptable for less critical data. Choosing the appropriate replication strategy depends on the specific consistency and latency requirements of the federated GraphQL implementation.

Disaster recovery is another critical area where cloud native technologies excel. Cloud providers offer backup and disaster recovery services that can be integrated into federated GraphQL architectures. These services allow for automated backups, snapshot management, and quick recovery in the event of a failure. Implementing a disaster recovery plan involves defining Recovery Point Objectives (RPO) and Recovery Time Objectives (RTO) to ensure that data loss is minimized and that services are restored within acceptable timeframes. By leveraging cloud-native backup solutions and replication strategies, organizations can ensure business continuity and resilience for their federated GraphQL systems.

Security is paramount in federated GraphQL deployments, and cloud native technologies provide advanced security features to protect data and applications. Managed security services, such as cloud-native firewalls, intrusion detection systems, and identity and access management (IAM) tools, offer comprehensive security controls. These services help enforce policies for data access, monitor for suspicious activity, and safeguard against cyber threats. Implementing encryption for data at rest and in transit is also essential to protect sensitive information. Cloud providers typically offer built-in encryption options that can be easily configured for federated GraphQL environments.

Moreover, cloud native technologies support the automation of deployment and operations through Infrastructure as Code (IaC) and continuous integration/continuous deployment (CI/CD) pipelines. IaC tools, such as Terraform or AWS CloudFormation, allow teams to define and manage infrastructure using code, enabling consistent and repeatable deployments. CI/CD pipelines automate the process of building, testing, and deploying federated GraphQL services, facilitating faster release cycles and more reliable updates. By integrating these practices, organizations can streamline the management of their federated GraphQL systems and reduce the risk of errors associated with manual configurations.

In summary, leveraging cloud native technologies for federated GraphQL systems provides numerous benefits, including enhanced scalability, performance, and security. Container orchestration and serverless computing offer flexible deployment models and resource management, while managed services simplify operations and maintenance. Multi-region deployments and disaster recovery strategies ensure resilience and high availability, and security features protect against threats. By incorporating these cloud native solutions, organizations can build and manage robust federated GraphQL architectures that meet the demands of modern, global applications.

CHAPTER 36: DESIGNING USER INTERFACES FOR FEDERATED GRAPHQL

Designing user interfaces (UIs) that interact with federated GraphQL presents a unique set of challenges and opportunities. Federated GraphQL architectures, with their complex data sources and service composition, require thoughtful design to ensure that UIs not only function effectively but also provide an optimal user experience. This chapter delves into best practices for designing and implementing UIs that can seamlessly consume federated GraphQL services, focusing on patterns and considerations that enhance user interactions with federated data.

At the core of designing UIs for federated GraphQL is understanding how data is aggregated and presented to users. Federated GraphQL allows for a single query to span multiple services, which can result in intricate data structures. UIs must be designed to handle these complex responses while maintaining clarity and usability. One approach to managing this complexity is to implement abstraction layers that simplify data interactions. These layers can map federated data structures into more manageable forms, providing a unified interface for UI components.

Effective data fetching is crucial in federated GraphQL applications. UIs should leverage GraphQL's ability to fetch precisely the data required by each component, minimizing over-fetching and under-fetching. This can be achieved through strategic use of queries and fragments that align with UI needs. Employing a client-side GraphQL library such as Apollo Client or Relay can facilitate efficient data management and caching, optimizing performance and responsiveness. These libraries provide built-in tools for query composition and caching, which are essential for handling federated data effectively.

In designing UI components, it is important to consider how they will interact with the federated GraphQL schema. Components should be designed with the flexibility to handle varying data formats and structures. Modular UI design patterns, such as component-based architecture, enable the creation of reusable and adaptable components that can be easily integrated with different parts of the federated schema. This modular approach allows for better maintenance and scalability, as components can be updated independently without affecting the overall application.

Another key consideration is managing the performance implications of federated GraphQL queries. Given that federated systems may involve multiple network requests and data transformations, it is essential to optimize UI performance. Techniques such as lazy loading, where components are loaded only when needed, and pagination, which loads data in chunks, can significantly improve the user experience. Additionally, employing techniques like optimistic UI updates can enhance perceived performance by allowing the UI to reflect changes before the data is fully resolved.

Handling errors and managing user feedback is also a critical aspect of UI design in federated GraphQL environments. Since federated GraphQL involves multiple services, errors may arise from different sources. Providing clear and actionable error messages is important for user satisfaction. Implementing error boundaries and fallback mechanisms can help manage unexpected issues gracefully. Additionally, designing for retries and providing visual indicators of data loading or fetching can improve user confidence and experience.

User interface design for federated GraphQL should also take into account the need for real-time data updates. For applications requiring live data, such as dashboards or collaborative tools, integrating GraphQL subscriptions can provide real-time data feeds. Subscriptions allow UIs to receive updates automatically as data changes, enhancing interactivity and user engagement. Designing UIs to handle real-time updates involves considering aspects such as data synchronization, user notifications, and the impact on overall performance.

Accessibility is another important consideration in UI design. Ensuring that interfaces are accessible to all users, including those with disabilities, requires adherence to best practices in accessibility design. This includes providing proper semantic markup, ensuring keyboard navigability, and implementing screen reader support. By incorporating accessibility features, UIs can be more inclusive and provide a better experience for all users.

Finally, it is essential to continuously test and iterate on UI designs. User feedback, usability testing, and performance analysis should guide the iterative design process. Gathering insights from real users can help identify pain points and areas for improvement, leading to more effective and user-friendly interfaces.

In summary, designing user interfaces for federated GraphQL involves addressing the complexities of data aggregation and presentation while ensuring optimal performance and user experience. By employing best practices in data fetching, component design, performance optimization, error handling, real-time updates, and accessibility, developers can create UIs that effectively leverage the capabilities of federated GraphQL services. This thoughtful approach to UI design not only enhances user interactions but also ensures that federated GraphQL systems deliver a seamless and efficient experience.

When designing user interfaces (UIs) for applications using federated GraphQL, the complexity of handling data across multiple services must be managed thoughtfully. One of the critical aspects of UI design in this context is ensuring that the interface remains responsive and intuitive despite the underlying complexity of federated queries. To achieve this, various strategies and considerations are essential.

Data fetching and state management are integral to the UI's interaction with federated GraphQL. Given that federated GraphQL can aggregate data from multiple sources, the UI should be designed to handle the asynchronous nature of data fetching. This involves implementing efficient loading states and error handling mechanisms. Users should receive clear feedback during data fetching processes, such as loading spinners or progress indicators, and errors should be communicated in a user-friendly manner. Providing meaningful error messages and retry options can significantly enhance user experience by managing expectations and allowing users to recover from failures seamlessly.

Caching plays a pivotal role in optimizing the performance of UIs that interact with federated GraphQL. Proper caching strategies can reduce the need for redundant data fetching and improve the responsiveness of the interface. Client-side caching mechanisms, such as those offered by Apollo Client or Relay, are particularly effective in storing previously fetched data and serving it quickly when needed. By leveraging these caching solutions, UIs can display data more rapidly and provide a smoother experience for users. Additionally, understanding and configuring cache invalidation strategies is crucial to ensure that the data remains up-to-date and consistent across different parts of the application.

As user interfaces interact with federated GraphQL schemas, ensuring that the data presentation is coherent and aligned with user expectations is vital. The UI should be designed to handle various data structures and formats that federated queries may return. This often involves creating flexible and adaptable components that can render data in a variety of ways depending on its type and structure. By employing design patterns that accommodate different data scenarios, such as conditional rendering or data transformations, the UI can present information effectively regardless of its complexity.

Another important consideration is the management of UI components' lifecycle in relation to federated data. Components should be able to handle updates and changes in data gracefully. For instance, when data is updated or refreshed, the UI should reflect these changes promptly without requiring a full reload or causing unnecessary re-renders. Techniques such as optimistic UI updates, where the interface assumes a successful operation and updates immediately before confirming the result, can enhance perceived performance and user satisfaction.

Designing user interfaces for federated GraphQL also involves optimizing for accessibility and inclusivity. Ensuring that the interface is usable by all users, including those with disabilities, requires adherence to accessibility standards such as the Web Content Accessibility Guidelines (WCAG).

Implementing features like keyboard navigation, screen reader support, and sufficient color contrast can make the UI more accessible. This not only aligns with best practices but also ensures that the application is usable by a broader audience.

Moreover, incorporating user feedback into the design process can lead to better outcomes. User testing and feedback collection should be integral parts of the UI development cycle. By understanding how users interact with the application and identifying pain points or areas for improvement, designers can make informed decisions that enhance the overall user experience. Iterative design, where prototypes are tested and refined based on user input, can lead to more effective and user-centered interfaces.

In summary, designing user interfaces for federated GraphQL involves managing the complexities of data aggregation and presentation while ensuring a responsive and intuitive experience for users. Efficient data fetching, effective caching, adaptable component design, and adherence to accessibility standards are critical considerations. By leveraging these strategies, designers can create UIs that not only interact seamlessly with federated GraphQL services but also provide a high-quality user experience that meets the needs of diverse users.

When designing user interfaces for applications leveraging federated GraphQL, it is essential to account for the complexity inherent in querying and displaying data from multiple services. A nuanced approach to design ensures that the interface is not only functional but also user-friendly, providing a seamless experience despite the underlying architectural complexity.

One effective approach to managing complexity is to adopt a modular design pattern for UI components. This involves breaking down the interface into smaller, reusable components that interact with federated data sources. By isolating different parts of the UI, such as forms, tables, or charts, developers can ensure that each component is responsible for handling its data interactions independently. This modularity helps in managing state and rendering data efficiently, as each component can be optimized and tested in isolation.

Moreover, the integration of federated GraphQL can benefit from employing abstracted data management solutions. Libraries such as Apollo Client and Relay provide robust tools for managing complex data interactions and caching strategies. They offer built-in mechanisms for query management, caching, and state handling, allowing developers to focus more on the UI design rather than the intricacies of data fetching and state management. These tools also support advanced features like pagination and optimistic UI updates, which enhance the responsiveness of the interface.

The user interface should be designed to provide clear and intuitive feedback during data interactions. Given the asynchronous nature of federated queries, it is crucial to incorporate loading indicators and error messages effectively. Loading states should be represented by visual cues such as spinners or skeleton screens, which keep users informed about the ongoing data fetches. Error handling should be equally prominent, offering users meaningful messages and potential solutions or retry options. This feedback loop is essential for maintaining user trust and ensuring a smooth interaction experience.

Another key consideration in UI design for federated GraphQL is managing user expectations through data presentation. The data returned from federated queries can vary significantly in structure and format. To handle this variability, the UI components should be designed to adapt dynamically to different data schemas. This might involve implementing conditional rendering, where the UI changes based on the presence or absence of certain data fields, or using data normalization techniques to ensure consistent presentation. By designing components that can flexibly handle diverse data structures, developers can create a more resilient and user-friendly interface.

In addition to these strategies, it is beneficial to implement client-side optimizations to enhance performance. For example, using batching techniques can help in reducing the number of network requests by combining multiple queries into a single request. This not only improves the efficiency of data fetching but also reduces the load on the server. Similarly, implementing debounce or throttle mechanisms can help in managing high-frequency user interactions, such as typing in search fields, to avoid excessive data fetching and improve overall performance.

The lifecycle management of UI components is also a critical factor when dealing with federated data. Components should be capable of handling data updates and changes seamlessly. For instance, when a data source is updated, the UI should reflect these changes promptly without requiring a full-page reload or causing unnecessary re-renders. Techniques like incremental updates, where only the changed parts of the data are refreshed, can significantly enhance the user experience by providing a more fluid and responsive interface.

Furthermore, ensuring a consistent and coherent user experience across different parts of the application is vital. Given the federated nature of the data, different sections of the UI might interact with different services or data sources. It is crucial to maintain a uniform design and interaction pattern across these sections to avoid disjointed experiences. This consistency can be achieved through the use of design systems and component libraries that provide standardized styles and behaviors.

Lastly, performance monitoring and optimization should be an ongoing process. Tools like performance profiling and user feedback mechanisms can provide valuable insights into how the UI performs under different conditions and identify areas for improvement. Regularly reviewing and refining the design based on these insights helps in maintaining a high-quality user experience as the application evolves and scales.

In conclusion, designing user interfaces for federated GraphQL requires a balanced approach that addresses both the technical and user experience aspects. By leveraging modular design, advanced data management libraries, and effective feedback mechanisms, developers can create interfaces that are not only performant but also intuitive and user-friendly. Through careful consideration of data presentation, component lifecycle management, and performance optimization, the complexities of federated data can be managed effectively, resulting in a seamless and engaging user experience.

CHAPTER 37: IMPLEMENTING RATE LIMITING AND THROTTLING IN FEDERATED GRAPHQL

In a federated GraphQL environment, managing API usage efficiently is crucial to ensuring that services remain responsive and accessible to all users. With the distributed nature of federated GraphQL, where multiple services are combined into a single schema, implementing rate limiting and throttling mechanisms becomes a complex but necessary task. This chapter explores strategies for implementing these mechanisms to control traffic and prevent abuse across multiple federated services.

Rate limiting and throttling are distinct yet related concepts aimed at controlling the volume of requests that can be made to an API. Rate limiting refers to the process of restricting the number of API requests that a user or client can make within a specified time window. Throttling, on the other hand, controls the rate of request processing to ensure that services are not overwhelmed by high request volumes. Together, these mechanisms help maintain API performance, protect against abuse, and ensure equitable resource allocation.

In a federated GraphQL setup, where each service may have its own rate limiting requirements and constraints, implementing a unified approach to rate limiting and throttling involves several key considerations. First, it is essential to establish a central point of control or a unified strategy for rate limiting across all federated services. This approach ensures that limits are consistently enforced, regardless of the service handling the request. Centralized rate limiting can be achieved using middleware or API gateways that sit in front of the federated GraphQL services, managing and enforcing request limits before they reach the individual services.

One effective method for implementing rate limiting in a federated GraphQL environment is through the use of distributed rate limiting tools. These tools can track and enforce limits across multiple services, ensuring that the total request volume does not exceed predefined thresholds. Redis, for example, is commonly used as a distributed cache and rate limiting store, where counters for request limits can be managed centrally and shared across services. By leveraging such tools, developers can ensure that rate limiting is consistently applied across the entire federated schema.

Another important aspect of rate limiting in federated GraphQL is defining the granularity of the limits. Rate limits can be applied at various levels, including globally across all services, per service, or even per specific fields within a service. The choice of granularity depends on the requirements of the application and the expected load on each service. For example, a service handling high-demand queries may require stricter rate limits compared to less frequently accessed services. Implementing fine-grained rate limiting helps in optimizing performance and resource utilization.

Throttling mechanisms are equally important in a federated GraphQL environment. Unlike rate limiting, which focuses on the volume of requests, throttling aims to manage the rate at which requests are processed. This is particularly relevant in scenarios where services may experience spikes in traffic or where certain operations are resource-intensive. Throttling can be implemented at various levels, including API gateways or individual services, using techniques such as queuing or delaying request processing to ensure that the system remains stable under load.

A common strategy for throttling is to use token buckets or leaky bucket algorithms. These algorithms control the rate at which requests are processed by allowing a certain number of requests to pass through within a given time frame, with excess requests being queued or delayed. Implementing these algorithms helps to smooth out traffic spikes and prevent sudden surges from overwhelming the system.

In addition to rate limiting and throttling, monitoring and logging are critical components of managing API usage in a federated GraphQL environment. By monitoring request patterns and enforcing limits, developers can gain insights into the performance of their services and detect potential issues before they impact users. Logging tools can provide detailed information on request rates, throttling events, and rate limit breaches, enabling developers to make informed decisions about adjusting limits and improving system performance.

Overall, implementing effective rate limiting and throttling strategies in a federated GraphQL environment requires careful planning and consideration of the unique characteristics of each service and the overall system. By adopting a unified approach to rate limiting, leveraging distributed tools, and employing throttling mechanisms, developers can ensure that their federated GraphQL services remain responsive, fair, and resilient to high traffic volumes and potential abuse.

In a federated GraphQL architecture, implementing effective rate limiting and throttling strategies requires a nuanced approach, given the distributed nature of the system. One of the primary challenges is ensuring that rate limits are consistently applied across different services, each potentially with its own set of rules and load characteristics. To address this, it is beneficial to use a combination of centralized and decentralized strategies.

Centralized rate limiting solutions often involve the use of an API gateway or a middleware layer that acts as a single point of entry for all incoming requests. This gateway can enforce global rate limits and distribute requests to the appropriate federated services while ensuring that limits are adhered to. By doing so, it provides a unified approach to rate limiting, simplifying management and ensuring consistency across the entire system.

Implementing rate limiting through an API gateway offers several advantages. It allows for a single point of configuration for rate limits, reducing the complexity involved in managing limits across multiple services. Moreover, the API gateway can provide features such as request logging, monitoring, and analytics, which are valuable for understanding usage patterns and identifying potential issues. Tools like Kong, NGINX, and AWS API Gateway are commonly used for this purpose, each offering a range of capabilities to support rate limiting.

In addition to centralized rate limiting, implementing rate limiting at the service level can address specific needs and constraints of individual services. This approach allows each service to define its own rate limits based on its capacity and performance characteristics. For example, a service that performs computationally intensive operations might have stricter limits compared to a service that primarily handles lightweight queries. Service-level rate limiting can be implemented using various techniques, such as in-memory counters or distributed caches like Redis, which maintain state across multiple instances of a service.

Throttling, as a complementary strategy, focuses on managing the rate at which requests are processed. Unlike rate limiting, which sets a hard cap on the number of requests, throttling can dynamically adjust the processing rate based on the current load and capacity of the service. This dynamic adjustment helps prevent services from being overwhelmed during peak times and ensures a more responsive and reliable system.

Implementing throttling often involves setting up policies that adjust request processing rates based on real-time metrics such as CPU usage, memory consumption, or request queue lengths. These policies can be integrated into the service logic or managed by external systems that monitor service health and adjust throttle settings accordingly. For example, a service might reduce the processing rate for incoming requests if it detects that its CPU usage exceeds a certain threshold, thereby preventing performance degradation and ensuring that it remains responsive.

Both rate limiting and throttling benefit from detailed monitoring and logging to track their effectiveness and identify potential issues. By analyzing metrics such as request rates, response times, and error rates, developers can gain insights into how rate limits and throttling policies are impacting the system's performance. This information is crucial for fine-tuning rate limiting and throttling configurations to better align with actual usage patterns and service capacities.

Furthermore, implementing a feedback loop for adjusting rate limits and throttling policies based on real-time data can enhance the system's adaptability. For instance, if a service consistently hits its rate limit or experiences throttling-related issues, the system can automatically adjust the limits or processing rates to better match the service's capabilities and usage patterns. This adaptive approach helps maintain optimal performance and user experience across the federated GraphQL system.

As federated GraphQL systems scale and evolve, it is essential to continuously review and refine rate limiting and throttling strategies. New services might be added, existing services might undergo changes, and traffic patterns might shift, all of which can impact the effectiveness of current rate limiting and throttling configurations. Regular assessments and adjustments ensure that the system remains resilient and performs well under varying conditions.

In summary, implementing rate limiting and throttling in a federated GraphQL environment involves a combination of centralized and decentralized approaches. By leveraging API gateways for global rate limiting and service-level mechanisms for more granular control, organizations can effectively manage API usage and ensure fair access to resources. Throttling strategies further enhance system performance by dynamically adjusting request processing rates based on real-time metrics. Through detailed monitoring and adaptive adjustments, developers can maintain optimal performance and user experience across the federated GraphQL architecture.

Incorporating throttling mechanisms into a federated GraphQL environment requires careful planning and integration. One effective approach is to use a combination of reactive and proactive throttling techniques. Reactive throttling involves dynamically adjusting the rate of request processing based on real-time system metrics. For instance, if a service detects an increase in CPU usage or response times exceeding acceptable thresholds, it can temporarily reduce the request throughput. This ensures that the system remains stable under high load and prevents sudden spikes from degrading performance.

Proactive throttling, on the other hand, involves setting predefined rules and policies that manage request rates even before they reach a critical level. This approach can include setting quotas based on user roles or subscription tiers, ensuring that high-priority users receive more resources than others. By implementing both reactive and proactive throttling, you create a layered defense against potential performance issues and ensure that your system can handle varying levels of demand.

To effectively manage rate limiting and throttling across multiple federated services, it is crucial to maintain visibility and coordination among all components of the system. This can be achieved through centralized monitoring and alerting systems that track request rates, service health, and other key metrics. Tools like Prometheus, Grafana, and ELK Stack provide comprehensive monitoring and visualization capabilities, enabling you to detect patterns and anomalies in real-time.

Another important aspect of implementing rate limiting and throttling is ensuring that these mechanisms do not introduce undue latency or complexity into the system. While it is essential to control traffic and prevent abuse, it is equally important to maintain a smooth and responsive user experience. Balancing these objectives requires careful tuning of rate limits and throttling policies, as well as thorough testing under various load conditions.

In a federated GraphQL setup, integrating rate limiting and throttling mechanisms may also involve coordinating with multiple teams and services. It is important to establish clear communication channels and documentation to ensure that all stakeholders are aware of the implemented policies and their implications. This collaborative approach helps in aligning rate limiting and throttling strategies with the overall system architecture and performance goals.

Moreover, implementing these mechanisms may involve addressing potential edge cases and scenarios where rate limits and throttling policies could impact user experience or service functionality. For example, handling cases where users exceed their allotted rate limits gracefully is crucial. Providing informative error messages and offering mechanisms for users to request higher limits or adjustments can improve user satisfaction and reduce frustration.

Ultimately, the goal of implementing rate limiting and throttling in a federated GraphQL environment is to create a balanced system that optimally manages traffic, ensures fair access, and maintains high performance. By carefully designing and integrating these mechanisms, you can enhance the robustness and reliability of your federated GraphQL architecture, providing a better experience for both users and developers.

Through thoughtful implementation and ongoing monitoring, you can address challenges related to traffic management and system load, ensuring that your federated GraphQL services operate efficiently and effectively. As the demand for API services continues to grow, having a well-designed approach to rate limiting and throttling will be increasingly important for maintaining optimal performance and user satisfaction.

CHAPTER 38: FEDERATED GRAPHQL IN MICROSERVICES ARCHITECTURES

In the landscape of modern software engineering, microservices architectures have emerged as a prominent design pattern due to their flexibility and scalability. Federated GraphQL plays a critical role in unifying data access across these distributed systems, offering a cohesive interface for querying and mutating data that spans multiple microservices. This chapter delves into the implementation of federated GraphQL within microservices architectures, providing a comprehensive overview of patterns and practices essential for successful integration.

Federated GraphQL offers a paradigm where a single GraphQL schema is composed from multiple microservices, each responsible for a distinct part of the overall schema. This approach contrasts with a monolithic schema where all data is managed within a single service. In a microservices environment, each service owns and exposes a portion of the GraphQL schema, which is then federated to create a unified API. This model facilitates a more manageable and modular approach to data handling, aligning well with the microservices principles of separation of concerns and independent deployment.

The primary challenge in implementing federated GraphQL in microservices is managing interactions between services and ensuring that the unified schema accurately represents the distributed data sources. One of the foundational patterns for achieving this is schema stitching, where individual schemas from different services are combined into a single GraphQL schema. Schema stitching involves merging types, queries, and mutations from various services, ensuring that the unified schema provides a comprehensive view of the data.

Another crucial aspect of federated GraphQL in microservices architectures is service composition. Service composition refers to the process of integrating multiple microservices into a cohesive GraphQL schema. This is achieved through techniques such as schema federation, which allows each microservice to define its part of the schema and specify how it relates to other parts. By leveraging schema federation, organizations can build scalable and maintainable GraphQL APIs that accurately reflect the underlying microservices architecture.

Effective service interaction and data flow management are central to the success of federated GraphQL implementations. In a federated setup, each microservice must be able to handle requests for its portion of the schema and resolve them efficiently. This requires a well-defined contract between services, ensuring that data can be queried and mutated across service boundaries without introducing inconsistencies or performance bottlenecks. Service interactions are typically managed through GraphQL resolvers, which are responsible for fetching and returning data for specific fields in the schema.

When integrating federated GraphQL with microservices, it is also essential to address issues related to data consistency and synchronization. Since each microservice may have its own data store and logic, ensuring that data remains consistent across services can be challenging. Techniques such as event sourcing and CQRS (Command Query Responsibility Segregation) can be employed to manage data consistency and synchronize changes across microservices. Event sourcing involves capturing state changes as a series of events, which can then be replayed to rebuild the state of the system. CQRS, on the other hand, separates read and write operations, allowing for optimized handling of queries and commands.

Another key consideration in a federated GraphQL setup is performance optimization. As the number of microservices and the complexity of the schema grow, the potential for performance issues increases. Techniques such as query batching and caching can be employed to enhance performance. Query batching involves combining multiple queries into a single request, reducing the number of round-trips between the client and the server. Caching, both at the service level and the API gateway level, can significantly improve response times by storing frequently accessed data and reducing the load on individual services.

Furthermore, managing authorization and security in a federated GraphQL environment requires careful planning. Each microservice may have its own security requirements and access controls, which need to be coordinated with the federated schema. Centralized authorization mechanisms, such as OAuth2 or JWT (JSON Web Tokens), can be used to ensure that users have appropriate access to the data they are requesting. Implementing fine-grained access controls and ensuring that security policies are consistently applied across services are essential for maintaining a secure federated GraphQL system.

In conclusion, implementing federated GraphQL in microservices architectures offers numerous benefits, including unified data access, modularity, and scalability. However, it also presents challenges related to service interactions, data consistency, performance, and security. By leveraging best practices such as schema stitching, service composition, query batching, and centralized authorization, organizations can build effective and resilient federated GraphQL systems that enhance their microservices architectures. As you advance in your implementation journey, remember that ongoing monitoring, testing, and iteration are key to ensuring that your federated GraphQL solution continues to meet the evolving needs of your application and its users.

In a federated GraphQL setup, managing service interactions and data flows across microservices becomes a critical aspect of ensuring a seamless and efficient integration. Each microservice in a federated architecture exposes its part of the schema and is responsible for resolving the data specific to its domain. This distribution of responsibilities introduces complexities in maintaining coherence and optimizing performance.

One of the core principles in federated GraphQL implementations is the use of resolvers. Resolvers are functions that handle the actual data retrieval for a given field in the schema. In a federated setup, resolvers are often implemented in each microservice to fetch and return data. When a query is made to the unified GraphQL API, the gateway service routes the request to the appropriate microservices based on the schema definitions. Each microservice's resolver processes the request and aggregates the data before returning it to the gateway. This process is crucial for achieving a unified view of data that spans multiple services.

Efficient resolver design is paramount in federated GraphQL

systems. Given that each microservice handles a segment of the schema, resolvers must be designed to minimize latency and avoid redundant data fetching. Techniques such as batching and caching are often employed to enhance performance. Batching involves aggregating multiple requests into a single query to reduce the number of network calls and improve efficiency. This is particularly useful in scenarios where a single field in the GraphQL query requires data from multiple microservices. Caching, on the other hand, helps store frequently accessed data temporarily, thereby reducing the need for repeated data retrieval from the underlying services.

Another significant consideration is the handling of errors and failures in a federated environment. Since the GraphQL schema is composed of multiple services, failures in one service can impact the overall response. To mitigate such issues, error handling strategies must be implemented at both the microservice and gateway levels. The gateway should be equipped to gracefully handle errors from downstream services, providing informative error messages to clients while maintaining the overall integrity of the response. Microservices themselves should implement robust error handling mechanisms to ensure that errors are logged, reported, and managed effectively.

Data consistency and integrity are additional challenges in a federated GraphQL architecture. Given that data is distributed across multiple services, maintaining consistency across these services can be complex. One approach to address this issue is through the use of data contracts and versioning. Data contracts define the expected data formats and interactions between services, ensuring that changes in one service do not inadvertently break others. Versioning allows services to evolve independently while providing a mechanism for clients to handle changes gracefully.

The federated GraphQL gateway plays a pivotal role in orchestrating requests and managing interactions between services. It acts as the central point of contact for clients, translating client queries into requests for individual microservices. The gateway is responsible for composing the final response from the various services and ensuring that the data is correctly aggregated and presented to the client. To handle the potentially complex interactions between services, the gateway must be designed to handle various scenarios, such as request timeouts, retries, and circuit breaking.

Incorporating monitoring and observability tools into the federated GraphQL architecture is also crucial for maintaining system health and performance. Monitoring tools provide visibility into the operations of the microservices and the gateway, allowing teams to track metrics such as response times, error rates, and throughput. Observability extends beyond monitoring to include tracing and logging, enabling teams to trace individual requests as they traverse through the various services and diagnose issues more effectively.

Integrating federated GraphQL with microservices architectures also necessitates considering security aspects. Each microservice must implement appropriate security measures to protect its data and ensure that only authorized requests are processed. Authentication and authorization mechanisms need to be consistently applied across the federated system. Additionally, securing communications between services and the gateway is essential to prevent unauthorized access and data breaches.

Ultimately, the implementation of federated GraphQL in microservices architectures requires a thoughtful approach to design and integration. By adhering to best practices for resolver implementation, error handling, data consistency, and monitoring, organizations can leverage the strengths of federated GraphQL to create a robust and scalable data access layer. As microservices continue to evolve and grow in complexity, federated GraphQL provides a powerful tool for unifying data access and optimizing the overall system architecture.

In the realm of federated GraphQL within microservices architectures, managing the interaction between services and ensuring effective data flow is pivotal to achieving a cohesive system. Each microservice in a federated GraphQL setup is responsible for a distinct subset of the schema, which it manages independently. However, this independence must be balanced with the need for seamless integration and data consistency across the system.

To optimize the interaction between services, it is important to focus on how queries are resolved across the federated schema. Federated GraphQL utilizes a gateway that orchestrates requests by delegating them to appropriate microservices based on the schema definitions. This gateway approach ensures that queries spanning multiple microservices are executed efficiently. When implementing federated GraphQL, the gateway must be designed to handle complex query resolutions that involve multiple services. It collects and aggregates the data retrieved from each service, consolidates it, and returns a unified response to the client. This process underscores the need for careful design and implementation of resolvers within each microservice.

One of the challenges in this architecture is ensuring that the resolvers are efficient and do not introduce unnecessary overhead. Since federated GraphQL can involve multiple data sources and microservices, resolving queries in an optimal manner is critical. Techniques such as batching and caching are essential for minimizing the performance impact of data retrieval. Batching, for instance, allows the aggregation of multiple requests into a single query to reduce the number of network calls and improve response times. This is particularly beneficial when a single query requires data from several microservices. Caching, on the other hand, involves storing frequently accessed data to avoid redundant fetch operations, thus improving overall system performance and reducing latency.

Error handling is another crucial aspect of federated GraphQL implementations. Given the distributed nature of the architecture, errors in one microservice can affect the entire response. Therefore, it is important to implement robust error handling mechanisms both at the microservice level and within the gateway. Microservices should be designed to manage errors internally and provide meaningful error messages to the gateway. The gateway, in turn, needs to aggregate these error messages and present a coherent response to the client. Implementing comprehensive logging and monitoring practices can help in identifying and troubleshooting issues effectively.

Data consistency and integrity are fundamental concerns in a federated environment. Since data is dispersed across multiple services, maintaining consistency requires careful planning. One approach is to establish clear data contracts and implement versioning strategies. Data contracts define the expected data formats and interfaces between services, ensuring that they can interact smoothly. Versioning allows services to evolve independently while maintaining compatibility with existing clients. By managing data contracts and versioning effectively, organizations can mitigate the risks of data inconsistency and ensure that changes in one service do not adversely affect others.

Additionally, managing service interactions and dependencies is key to maintaining a functional federated GraphQL setup. Microservices often rely on each other to fulfill client queries, making it important to establish well-defined communication patterns and service contracts. Service orchestration tools and patterns can help manage these interactions, ensuring that dependencies are resolved efficiently and that services can scale independently. Implementing practices such as circuit breakers and retries can enhance the resilience of the system, allowing it to handle service failures gracefully and maintain overall stability.

Security considerations also play a vital role in federated GraphQL architectures. With multiple microservices interacting to fulfill a single query, ensuring that security measures are consistently applied across all services is essential. Authentication and authorization mechanisms must be integrated into the gateway and individual services to enforce access controls and protect sensitive data. Implementing security practices such as encryption, token-based authentication, and fine-grained access controls can help safeguard the system against potential threats.

In conclusion, implementing federated GraphQL in microservices architectures involves addressing several key challenges, including efficient query resolution, error handling, data consistency, and security. By focusing on optimizing resolver performance, managing service interactions, and ensuring robust error handling, organizations can create a cohesive and efficient federated GraphQL system. Additionally, by implementing effective data contracts, versioning strategies, and security measures, they can maintain data integrity and safeguard their systems against potential vulnerabilities. As organizations continue to adopt microservices and federated GraphQL, these practices will be crucial in achieving a well-integrated and scalable architecture that meets the demands of modern applications.

CHAPTER 39: TESTING FEDERATED GRAPHQL IMPLEMENTATIONS

Ensuring the reliability of federated GraphQL systems is a complex but essential task. As federated GraphQL implementations become increasingly sophisticated, effective testing strategies become paramount. Testing these systems involves validating not only individual components but also the interactions between them. This chapter explores various testing strategies and tools necessary to maintain the integrity and performance of a federated GraphQL architecture.

To begin with, unit testing forms the foundation of a robust testing strategy. Unit tests focus on the smallest components of the system, such as individual resolvers or data sources, to ensure they function correctly in isolation. In the context of federated GraphQL, unit tests are used to verify that each microservice's resolver returns the expected results for given queries. This involves mocking dependencies and simulating different data scenarios to test the behavior of resolvers under various conditions. By isolating these components, developers can identify and address issues at an early stage, minimizing the risk of failures when these components interact in more complex scenarios.

Integration testing builds upon unit testing by examining the interactions between different components of the federated system. For federated GraphQL implementations, integration tests are crucial for verifying how well the microservices and the GraphQL gateway work together. These tests involve running scenarios where queries span multiple microservices, ensuring that the gateway correctly delegates the requests and aggregates responses. Integration tests also help to identify issues related to schema stitching, resolver interactions, and data consistency across services. Effective integration tests should cover a variety of query patterns and edge cases to ensure comprehensive validation of the federated architecture.

End-to-end testing represents a higher level of testing, encompassing the entire federated GraphQL system from the perspective of the client. These tests simulate real-world usage by sending queries and mutations through the gateway to observe how the system responds. End-to-end tests validate the end-to-end data flow, including query execution, response aggregation, and error handling. They are essential for ensuring that the federated system operates as expected under real-world conditions and can handle complex queries that involve multiple microservices. This type of testing is critical for verifying the overall system's reliability and performance before deployment.

Automated testing tools play a significant role in implementing these testing strategies effectively. For unit testing, frameworks such as Jest or Mocha can be used to write and execute tests for individual resolvers and data sources. These tools support mocking and stubbing, which are essential for isolating components and simulating different conditions. Integration testing can be facilitated by using tools like Apollo Server's integration testing utilities, which provide functionality for testing GraphQL queries against a mock server setup. This allows developers to test how the GraphQL gateway interacts with the underlying microservices.

End-to-end testing, on the other hand, often requires more comprehensive tools. Tools such as Cypress or Selenium can be used to automate interactions with the GraphQL API, simulating user behavior and capturing responses. These tools allow for the automation of test scenarios that involve real client requests and responses, providing a thorough validation of the system's behavior. Integrating end-to-end tests into the continuous integration/continuous deployment (CI/CD) pipeline ensures that any changes to the system are automatically tested and validated, reducing the likelihood of introducing regressions.

Another critical aspect of testing federated GraphQL systems is handling schema evolution. As the federated schema evolves over time, it is important to ensure that changes do not break existing functionality. Schema versioning and backward compatibility testing are essential to address this concern. Tools like Apollo's Schema Reporting can help track schema changes and their impact on existing queries. Additionally, implementing contract testing ensures that the interfaces between microservices remain consistent and that changes in one service do not negatively impact others.

In summary, a comprehensive testing strategy for federated GraphQL implementations involves unit tests, integration tests, and end-to-end tests, supported by appropriate tools and practices. By carefully designing and executing these tests, organizations can ensure the reliability and performance of their federated GraphQL systems. Automated testing tools, along with best practices for schema evolution and contract testing, further enhance the robustness of the testing strategy.

Automated testing tools play a significant role in implementing these testing strategies effectively. For unit testing, frameworks such as Jest or Mocha can be employed to write and execute tests for individual components, including resolvers and data sources. These tools provide mechanisms for mocking external dependencies and simulating various data scenarios, which is essential for isolating and testing specific functionalities. With these frameworks, developers can create automated tests that run quickly and frequently, providing rapid feedback during development and integration phases.

Integration testing tools, such as Postman or Apollo Server Testing, allow for the validation of interactions between microservices and the GraphQL gateway. These tools can be used to send test queries and mutations that span multiple services, ensuring that the gateway correctly delegates and aggregates data. Integration tests help uncover issues related to schema stitching, data consistency, and resolver coordination. In a federated GraphQL setup, it is crucial to ensure that the gateway handles query execution correctly and that responses from different services are combined accurately. Integration testing tools help verify that these interactions function as expected, providing insights into potential integration issues.

End-to-end testing tools, such as Cypress or Selenium, are used to simulate real-world scenarios and validate the overall system's functionality from a user's perspective. These tools can automate interactions with the GraphQL API, including sending queries and mutations, and validating the responses. End-to-end tests are essential for verifying that the federated GraphQL system operates as intended when deployed, ensuring that the entire system, including the gateway and all microservices, works together seamlessly. These tests also help identify performance bottlenecks and potential issues that may not be apparent in unit or integration tests. By simulating real user interactions, end-to-end testing provides a comprehensive view of how the system performs under actual usage conditions.

A crucial aspect of testing federated GraphQL systems is handling test data and environments. Given the distributed nature of federated architectures, managing test data across multiple microservices can be complex. Techniques such as using a shared mock server or leveraging in-memory databases can simplify the process. These approaches allow for consistent and controlled test environments, reducing the likelihood of test failures due to data discrepancies or service unavailability. Additionally, employing test data generators and fixtures can help create realistic scenarios and validate the system's behavior across a range of conditions.

Test automation also plays a pivotal role in maintaining the reliability of federated GraphQL systems. Continuous integration and continuous deployment (CI/CD) pipelines are often used to automate the execution of unit, integration, and end-to-end tests. By integrating automated tests into the CI/CD pipeline, teams can ensure that code changes are thoroughly validated before deployment, reducing the risk of introducing defects into production. This approach also facilitates rapid development cycles, as automated tests provide immediate feedback on code quality and system performance.

Monitoring and logging are also essential components of a comprehensive testing strategy. During the testing process, monitoring tools can provide real-time insights into system performance and behavior, helping to identify issues that may not be evident from test results alone. Logging mechanisms can capture detailed information about test execution, including error messages and stack traces, which are invaluable for diagnosing and resolving issues. By combining monitoring and logging with automated tests, teams can gain a deeper understanding of system behavior and improve the effectiveness of their testing efforts.

In summary, implementing a robust testing strategy for federated GraphQL systems involves a combination of unit tests, integration tests, and end-to-end tests, each addressing different aspects of the system's functionality and performance. Automated testing tools and CI/CD pipelines are critical for maintaining code quality and ensuring that the system operates reliably. Additionally, effective management of test data, coupled with monitoring and logging, enhances the ability to detect and resolve issues. By adopting these practices, organizations can build resilient federated GraphQL systems that meet the demands of modern applications and provide a seamless user experience.

Maintaining the quality and reliability of federated GraphQL systems extends beyond initial development and testing phases. Continuous integration (CI) and continuous deployment (CD) pipelines are essential for automating the testing process, ensuring that changes are validated before they reach production. Incorporating automated testing into CI/CD workflows allows teams to detect issues early, ensuring that new features or bug fixes do not introduce regressions or disrupt existing functionalities. By configuring CI/CD pipelines to run unit tests, integration tests, and end-to-end tests automatically on each commit or pull request, development teams can maintain high code quality and swiftly address potential issues.

Monitoring and logging also play a vital role in the ongoing assessment of a federated GraphQL system's performance and reliability. Implementing robust logging mechanisms helps capture detailed information about the execution of queries and mutations, which can be invaluable for diagnosing issues that arise in production. Monitoring tools such as Prometheus, Grafana, or New Relic can be used to track various performance metrics, including query execution times, error rates, and service latencies. These tools provide real-time insights into the system's health and performance, enabling teams to proactively address performance bottlenecks or failures.

In addition to automated testing and monitoring, establishing a comprehensive testing strategy involves incorporating feedback from real-world usage. User acceptance testing (UAT) and beta testing phases allow end-users to interact with the federated GraphQL system, providing valuable feedback on usability, functionality, and performance. Engaging users in testing helps identify issues that may not be apparent in controlled test environments, ensuring that the system meets users' needs and expectations.

Another important consideration in testing federated GraphQL systems is handling schema evolution and backward compatibility. As the system evolves, changes to the schema may affect existing queries and mutations. It is crucial to test schema changes thoroughly to ensure that they do not break existing clients or services. Techniques such as versioning, deprecation strategies, and schema evolution testing can help manage changes and maintain compatibility. Implementing strategies to test schema modifications in isolation and as part of the broader system ensures that updates do not inadvertently introduce breaking changes.

Finally, ensuring the security of federated GraphQL systems through testing is essential. Security testing tools and practices, such as static analysis, penetration testing, and vulnerability scanning, can help identify and address potential security issues. By including security tests as part of the regular testing regimen, teams can protect the system from common vulnerabilities and ensure that sensitive data is handled appropriately. Security testing should cover aspects such as authentication and authorization, input validation, and data encryption, among other critical security concerns.

In conclusion, testing federated GraphQL systems requires a multi-faceted approach that encompasses unit, integration, and end-to-end testing. Leveraging automated testing tools and incorporating CI/CD pipelines enhances the efficiency and effectiveness of the testing process. Additionally, monitoring, logging, and user feedback contribute to ongoing system assessment and refinement. Managing schema evolution and incorporating security testing further ensures that the federated GraphQL setup remains reliable, performant, and secure. By adopting a comprehensive testing strategy, development teams can build robust federated GraphQL systems that meet both functional and performance requirements.

CHAPTER 40: HANDLING DATA CONSISTENCY AND SYNCHRONIZATION

Ensuring data consistency and synchronization in federated GraphQL systems is pivotal for maintaining the integrity and reliability of distributed applications. In a federated environment, where multiple services contribute to a unified schema, managing data consistency presents unique challenges. This chapter delves into the techniques and strategies for addressing these challenges, focusing on maintaining consistency and effectively synchronizing data across different services.

At the core of managing data consistency in federated GraphQL systems is understanding the eventual consistency model. Unlike traditional systems that may strive for strong consistency, federated systems often adopt eventual consistency due to their distributed nature. This model allows updates to propagate across services asynchronously, ensuring that all parts of the system will eventually converge to a consistent state. However, this approach requires careful design to mitigate issues arising from temporary inconsistencies. Techniques such as conflict resolution strategies and consistency checks are crucial for maintaining overall data integrity.

One effective method for handling eventual consistency involves implementing conflict resolution mechanisms. When updates occur simultaneously across different services, conflicts may arise, leading to divergent data states. To address this, services can use various conflict resolution strategies, including last-write-wins, merge strategies, or custom resolution logic tailored to specific use cases. For example, in a scenario where two services concurrently update the same data, the last-write-wins strategy will ensure that the most recent update is preserved. Alternatively, merge strategies may involve combining updates from different sources to produce a unified result. The choice of conflict resolution strategy depends on the nature of the data and the application's consistency requirements.

Another technique for managing data consistency is leveraging distributed transaction patterns. While traditional transactions offer atomicity and consistency within a single database, distributed transactions extend these properties across multiple services. One approach is the two-phase commit protocol, which ensures that all involved services agree on the transaction outcome before committing changes. However, two-phase commit can introduce latency and complexity, making it less suitable for high-performance applications. Therefore, alternative patterns such as compensating transactions, which involve rolling back partial changes if a transaction fails, may be employed to maintain consistency in a more flexible manner.

Data synchronization strategies are equally important in federated systems. Synchronizing data across services involves ensuring that changes made in one service are accurately reflected in others. One approach is using change data capture (CDC) techniques, which track changes in data sources and propagate them to other services. CDC can be implemented using database triggers, log-based methods, or third-party tools that monitor data changes and publish them to a central event stream. This method allows services to stay updated with minimal latency, reducing the likelihood of stale or inconsistent data.

Event-driven architectures also play a significant role in data synchronization. By publishing events that describe changes in data, services can subscribe to these events and update their own state accordingly. This approach decouples services from direct data dependencies, allowing them to react to changes asynchronously. Event sourcing is a related pattern where changes are stored as a sequence of events rather than as a direct state. This enables services to reconstruct data state from events, facilitating both synchronization and auditability.

Implementing robust data consistency and synchronization requires careful attention to error handling and recovery mechanisms. In distributed systems, failures can occur during data propagation or synchronization, potentially leading to inconsistencies. Techniques such as retry logic, idempotency, and fault tolerance mechanisms help manage these challenges. Retry logic involves reattempting failed operations, while idempotency ensures that repeated operations produce the same result, preventing unintended side effects. Fault tolerance mechanisms, such as circuit breakers or fallback strategies, provide resilience against failures, maintaining system reliability even in the face of partial outages.

Monitoring and observability are essential for managing data consistency and synchronization effectively. By implementing comprehensive monitoring solutions, such as distributed tracing and logging, teams can gain insights into the flow of data and detect anomalies or inconsistencies. Distributed tracing tools, such as Zipkin or Jaeger, enable the tracking of requests as they traverse multiple services, providing visibility into data propagation and potential bottlenecks. Logging practices, including structured logging and centralized log aggregation, offer detailed information about data changes and synchronization events, aiding in troubleshooting and analysis.

In conclusion, handling data consistency and synchronization in federated GraphQL systems requires a combination of eventual consistency models, conflict resolution strategies, distributed transaction patterns, and synchronization techniques. By implementing these approaches and incorporating robust monitoring and error handling practices, organizations can ensure data integrity and reliability in their distributed applications. As federated systems continue to evolve, ongoing refinement of these strategies will be essential for maintaining consistency and delivering seamless user experiences.

To further explore synchronization strategies, it is essential to examine how change data capture (CDC) techniques can be employed to keep data consistent across federated services. CDC is a process that monitors and captures changes to data in real-time, allowing these changes to be propagated to other systems. By implementing CDC, services can react to modifications promptly, ensuring that all components of a federated GraphQL system are kept up-to-date with the most recent data. This method is particularly beneficial in environments where data updates occur frequently and need to be reflected immediately across multiple services.

In practice, CDC can be implemented using various technologies and tools, such as database triggers or specialized middleware that monitors data changes. For instance, some database management systems offer built-in CDC features that generate change logs for every modification made to the data. These logs can then be consumed by other services to synchronize their own data stores. Middleware solutions can also provide more advanced features, including transformation and enrichment of captured changes before they are applied to other systems.

Another key approach to managing data consistency is the use of synchronization services or brokers. These intermediaries facilitate data exchange between services, ensuring that all updates are propagated correctly. Synchronization brokers often handle the complexities of data transformation and conflict resolution, allowing services to focus on their core functionality. For example, a synchronization broker can ensure that a change in one service's data is accurately reflected in others, even if those services have different data schemas or structures.

In addition to brokers and CDC, adopting an event-driven architecture can enhance data synchronization efforts. Event-driven systems are based on the principle of emitting events whenever changes occur. Services subscribe to these events and update their own data stores accordingly. This pattern supports high levels of decoupling between services, allowing them to remain responsive to changes without direct dependencies. Events can be propagated through message queues or streaming platforms, providing real-time updates and facilitating efficient data synchronization across the federated system.

When implementing event-driven architectures, it is important to consider the reliability and ordering of events. Event delivery must be guaranteed, and events must be processed in the correct sequence to maintain data integrity. Techniques such as idempotency (ensuring that processing the same event multiple times does not alter the result) and sequence numbers (to track the order of events) can help address these challenges. Additionally, employing distributed tracing and logging can aid in monitoring the flow of events and diagnosing issues that may arise during synchronization.

Another consideration in managing data consistency is the role of data schema evolution. In a federated GraphQL system, changes to data schemas across services can affect data consistency and synchronization. It is crucial to implement strategies for schema versioning and migration to ensure that updates to schemas do not disrupt data integrity. Techniques such as schema stitching, which allows for incremental changes to be made to the schema while maintaining backward compatibility, can facilitate smooth transitions and avoid breaking changes.

Versioning strategies may include creating new schema versions while maintaining support for previous versions, allowing services to gradually transition to updated schemas. Automated migration tools can assist in managing these transitions by applying necessary updates to data stores and ensuring that new schema versions are correctly integrated across all services.

Finally, maintaining data consistency and synchronization in a federated GraphQL environment requires ongoing monitoring and validation. Regular consistency checks and reconciliation processes can help identify and address discrepancies between services. Automated testing frameworks that simulate real-world scenarios and validate data consistency across the system are essential for detecting issues early and ensuring that synchronization strategies remain effective.

By employing these techniques and strategies, organizations can effectively manage data consistency and synchronization in federated GraphQL systems. The combination of eventual consistency models, synchronization services, event-driven architectures, schema evolution management, and ongoing monitoring creates a robust framework for maintaining data integrity in distributed environments. As federated GraphQL continues to evolve, staying abreast of new tools and best practices will be critical for addressing emerging challenges and optimizing system performance.

To effectively manage data integrity in a distributed federated GraphQL system, it is crucial to address the challenges associated with eventual consistency. Unlike strong consistency models, which guarantee that all nodes in a system reflect the most recent data state immediately, eventual consistency allows for temporary discrepancies. These discrepancies are resolved over time as updates propagate through the system. This model is particularly well-suited for distributed systems where immediate consistency is impractical due to latency or network partitioning.

Eventual consistency relies on several principles to ensure that data converges to a consistent state eventually. One such principle is the use of conflict resolution mechanisms. Conflicts can arise when different services make concurrent updates to the same data. To handle these conflicts, systems must implement strategies to determine which update should prevail. Techniques include last-write-wins, where the most recent update takes precedence, or custom conflict resolution algorithms that consider the context of changes. Additionally, merging strategies can combine multiple updates into a coherent state, depending on the nature of the data and the business requirements.

Another principle is the use of consistency guarantees and SLAs (Service Level Agreements) to define acceptable levels of consistency and the timeframes within which consistency should be achieved. By establishing these guarantees, organizations can balance the trade-offs between performance and consistency. For example, a system might guarantee that data will be consistent within a certain window of time, allowing for temporary inconsistencies while ensuring that the system will eventually stabilize.

To further enhance data consistency, it is beneficial to implement consistency monitoring and alerting mechanisms. These tools can track the state of data across different services, identifying discrepancies and notifying administrators when consistency issues arise. Monitoring tools can be configured to detect patterns that indicate potential problems, such as significant delays in data propagation or frequent conflicts. By providing visibility into data consistency, these tools enable proactive management and resolution of issues before they impact the end users.

In addition to monitoring, applying strategies for data reconciliation is essential for maintaining overall system integrity. Data reconciliation involves comparing and synchronizing data across different services to ensure consistency. This can be achieved through periodic reconciliation processes that check for discrepancies and apply necessary updates. Reconciliation can be performed on a scheduled basis or triggered by specific events, such as significant changes in data volume or updates.

Furthermore, it is important to consider the impact of data partitioning and sharding on consistency. In a federated GraphQL environment, data may be partitioned across multiple services to improve scalability and performance. While partitioning can enhance efficiency, it can also introduce challenges related to data consistency and synchronization. Effective partitioning strategies must ensure that data is distributed in a way that minimizes the likelihood of conflicts and maximizes the efficiency of synchronization processes. Techniques such as consistent hashing can help distribute data evenly and reduce the impact of partitioning on consistency.

To address these complexities, federated GraphQL systems

often employ a combination of architectural patterns and technologies. For instance, the use of distributed caches and databases can help manage data consistency by providing mechanisms for synchronization and conflict resolution. These systems can store intermediate states and handle data replication across services, reducing the need for real-time updates and mitigating the effects of eventual consistency.

Finally, it is important to recognize that achieving perfect consistency in a distributed system is often impractical. Therefore, focusing on strategies that balance consistency, performance, and user experience is key. By implementing effective synchronization techniques, employing robust monitoring tools, and applying best practices for conflict resolution and data reconciliation, organizations can manage data consistency in federated GraphQL systems and ensure that their distributed environments remain reliable and efficient.

CHAPTER 41: FUTURE TRENDS IN GRAPHQL FEDERATION

The field of GraphQL Federation is rapidly advancing, with new trends and technologies continuously shaping its evolution. As organizations increasingly adopt federated GraphQL to streamline data access and management across microservices, several emerging trends are poised to redefine the landscape. This chapter explores these anticipated advancements, providing insights into how they will influence the future of federated GraphQL.

One significant trend is the growing adoption of GraphQL as a standard for API development across various domains. As the ecosystem matures, we can expect to see more organizations integrating GraphQL into their existing architectures, not just as an API layer but as a central component in their data management strategy. This broader adoption will drive the development of more robust and feature-rich GraphQL tools and frameworks, further enhancing the capabilities of federated GraphQL setups.

The rise of GraphQL tools and platforms designed specifically for federated architectures is another notable trend. These tools aim to simplify the management of federated schemas, automate common tasks, and provide deeper insights into data flows and dependencies. Innovations in this area include enhanced schema stitching capabilities, more sophisticated query optimization techniques, and improved support for complex federation use cases. Tools that offer better visualization and management of federated schemas will become increasingly important as organizations scale their GraphQL implementations.

In addition to tool advancements, we anticipate significant progress in the area of performance optimization for federated GraphQL systems. As federated architectures become more complex, performance challenges related to query execution, data fetching, and response aggregation will become more pronounced. Future developments will likely focus on addressing these challenges by improving query planning algorithms, implementing more efficient data fetching strategies, and leveraging cutting-edge technologies such as in-memory databases and distributed caching solutions. These advancements will be crucial for maintaining the high performance and responsiveness of federated GraphQL services as they scale.

Another trend to watch is the increasing integration of machine learning and artificial intelligence with GraphQL Federation. As data volumes and complexity grow, machine learning algorithms can play a critical role in optimizing query performance, detecting anomalies, and predicting data access patterns. By incorporating AI-driven insights into federated GraphQL systems, organizations can enhance their ability to manage large-scale data interactions and improve overall system efficiency.

The evolution of standards and best practices for federated GraphQL is also expected to be a major trend. As the community gains more experience and knowledge, new best practices will emerge to address common challenges and improve implementation strategies. These best practices will encompass areas such as schema design, security, and error handling, providing valuable guidance for organizations seeking to implement federated GraphQL effectively.

Finally, the expansion of GraphQL Federation into new domains and industries will continue to drive innovation. As more sectors recognize the benefits of federated GraphQL, we can expect to see specialized solutions and use cases tailored to specific industry needs. For instance, healthcare, finance, and e-commerce sectors may develop domain-specific federation patterns and tools to address their unique requirements, further enriching the federated GraphQL ecosystem.

In summary, the future of GraphQL Federation is set to be marked by a combination of increased adoption, technological advancements, and evolving best practices. By staying informed about these trends and proactively adapting to emerging developments, organizations can ensure they remain at the forefront of the federated GraphQL landscape, leveraging the latest tools and techniques to enhance their data management capabilities and drive innovation.

As GraphQL Federation continues to evolve, another significant trend is the enhanced focus on security and compliance. With the growing adoption of federated GraphQL, concerns regarding data security and privacy are becoming increasingly prominent. Future advancements are expected to introduce more sophisticated mechanisms for securing federated data exchanges. This includes improved support for authentication and authorization frameworks, such as OAuth 2.0 and OpenID Connect, which will provide more granular control over data access across federated services. Additionally, enhanced encryption techniques and privacy-preserving technologies, like differential privacy, will be integrated to ensure that sensitive information is protected even as it traverses multiple services.

The integration of federated GraphQL with emerging cloud-native technologies is another area poised for development. As cloud computing continues to advance, the deployment and management of federated GraphQL systems will increasingly leverage cloud-native principles. This includes the adoption of containerization and orchestration tools like Kubernetes, which offer greater scalability and flexibility in managing GraphQL services. Furthermore, serverless architectures are expected to play a more prominent role, providing a means to handle variable workloads and reduce operational overhead by allowing federated GraphQL services to scale dynamically based on demand.

The trend towards improved observability and monitoring of federated GraphQL systems is also gaining traction. As federated architectures grow more complex, it becomes crucial to have comprehensive visibility into the interactions between services, query performance, and system health. Future developments will likely include advanced monitoring tools that offer real-time insights into the performance of federated queries, track dependencies between services, and detect potential issues before they impact users. Enhanced observability will enable organizations to proactively manage their federated GraphQL systems and maintain optimal performance.

Additionally, the community around GraphQL Federation is expected to continue growing, fostering collaboration and innovation. Open-source contributions and community-driven projects will play a key role in shaping the future of federated GraphQL. As more organizations and developers get involved, we can anticipate the emergence of new best practices, frameworks, and tools that will drive the evolution of federated GraphQL. This collaborative environment will facilitate knowledge sharing and accelerate the development of solutions to common challenges faced in federated architectures.

In summary, the future of GraphQL Federation will be

marked by continued advancements in security, integration with cloud-native technologies, improved observability, and a growing community of contributors. These trends will collectively drive the evolution of federated GraphQL, enabling organizations to build more robust, scalable, and efficient systems. Staying abreast of these developments will be crucial for leveraging the full potential of federated GraphQL and maintaining a competitive edge in the ever-evolving landscape of data management and API integration.

Another important trend on the horizon is the increasing emphasis on developer experience and tooling. As federated GraphQL systems become more intricate, the need for robust development tools will grow. Future advancements will likely include more sophisticated Integrated Development Environments (IDEs) and plugins that offer enhanced support for schema design, query optimization, and real-time error detection. These tools will aim to streamline the development process, reduce the learning curve associated with federated GraphQL, and improve overall productivity. Additionally, we can expect advancements in automated code generation and scaffolding tools, which will simplify the process of setting up and maintaining federated services.

The evolution of federated GraphQL will also see a greater emphasis on interoperability and standardization. As the technology matures, there will be a push towards establishing industry-wide standards and best practices that ensure compatibility across different federated systems. This will involve efforts to standardize conventions for schema design, query handling, and error reporting, which will facilitate smoother integration and interaction between diverse services. Standardization will also support the development of cross-platform tools and libraries that can seamlessly work with various implementations of federated GraphQL.

Furthermore, the growing focus on performance optimization

will drive future developments in federated GraphQL. As federated systems scale, performance issues such as query latency and service response times will become more pronounced. Anticipated advancements will include enhanced query optimization techniques, better caching strategies, and more efficient data fetching mechanisms. Tools that provide detailed performance analytics and actionable insights will become integral to managing large-scale federated GraphQL deployments. These tools will enable developers to identify bottlenecks, optimize query performance, and ensure a responsive user experience.

The role of artificial intelligence and machine learning in federated GraphQL is another area of emerging interest. AI and ML technologies can be leveraged to improve various aspects of federated systems, from automated schema generation and query optimization to predictive analytics and anomaly detection. For example, machine learning algorithms could analyze historical query patterns to suggest optimizations or automatically adjust caching strategies based on usage patterns. AI-driven tools will contribute to making federated GraphQL systems more intelligent and adaptive to changing demands.

Additionally, as the federated GraphQL ecosystem evolves, there will be a growing focus on sustainability and energy efficiency. With the increasing complexity and scale of federated systems, there will be a need to address their environmental impact. Future developments may include energy-efficient computing practices, optimized data center operations, and technologies that reduce the carbon footprint of federated GraphQL deployments. Emphasizing sustainability will align with broader industry trends towards greener computing and responsible technology use.

In conclusion, the future of GraphQL Federation will be characterized by advancements in developer tools, standardization, performance optimization, the integration of AI and ML, and a focus on sustainability. As these trends unfold, they will shape the evolution of federated GraphQL, driving innovation and enhancing the capabilities of federated systems. Staying informed about these developments will be crucial for organizations and developers looking to leverage federated GraphQL effectively and remain competitive in a rapidly evolving technological landscape.

CHAPTER 42: BEST PRACTICES FOR FEDERATED GRAPHQL SECURITY

Security is a critical aspect of any federated GraphQL system, given the complex interactions between multiple services and the potential vulnerabilities that can arise from such integration. As federated GraphQL systems grow in both scale and complexity, the importance of implementing robust security practices cannot be overstated. This chapter delves into advanced security practices for federated GraphQL, focusing on threat modeling, secure coding practices, and compliance considerations to safeguard your federated implementation against various security risks.

To effectively secure a federated GraphQL system, it is essential to start with a comprehensive threat modeling process. Threat modeling involves identifying potential threats and vulnerabilities specific to your federated architecture. It begins with understanding the different components of your system, including the gateway, individual services, and the interactions between them. By mapping out how data flows through the system and identifying points where security breaches could occur, you can develop strategies to mitigate these risks.

One common threat in federated GraphQL systems is the risk of unauthorized access to sensitive data. Since federated GraphQL often involves multiple services, ensuring that each service enforces proper authentication and authorization checks is crucial. Implementing role-based access control (RBAC) and attribute-based access control (ABAC) can help manage permissions effectively. Role-based access control assigns permissions based on user roles, while attribute-based access control considers user attributes and contextual factors when granting access. Both approaches contribute to minimizing the risk of unauthorized data access.

Another important aspect of threat modeling is understanding the potential for injection attacks. GraphQL's flexible querying capabilities can sometimes be exploited if proper input validation is not in place. To prevent injection attacks, it is vital to implement rigorous input validation and sanitization procedures. Ensure that all inputs are checked for expected types and values, and employ parameterized queries to mitigate the risk of malicious data execution.

In addition to threat modeling, secure coding practices play a significant role in safeguarding federated GraphQL systems. Secure coding practices involve writing code in a way that minimizes vulnerabilities and potential attack vectors. For instance, implementing proper error handling mechanisms can prevent sensitive information from being exposed through error messages. It is essential to avoid exposing stack traces or detailed error information to end-users, as this can provide attackers with insights into your system's inner workings.

Another best practice is to employ encryption to protect data both in transit and at rest. Use HTTPS to secure communication between clients and the GraphQL gateway, and consider encrypting sensitive data stored in databases or other storage systems. Encryption ensures that even if data is intercepted or accessed without authorization, it remains unreadable to unauthorized parties.

Compliance considerations are also crucial for federated GraphQL security. Adhering to industry standards and regulations such as the General Data Protection Regulation (GDPR) and the Health Insurance Portability and Accountability Act (HIPAA) can help ensure that your federated GraphQL implementation meets legal and regulatory requirements. Compliance involves implementing data protection measures, such as data anonymization and access controls, to safeguard sensitive information.

Regular security assessments and audits are essential for maintaining the security of your federated GraphQL system. Conducting periodic security assessments helps identify vulnerabilities and weaknesses that may arise as the system evolves. Automated security testing tools can assist in identifying common vulnerabilities, such as cross-site scripting (XSS) and cross-site request forgery (CSRF). Additionally, engaging in manual code reviews and penetration testing can provide deeper insights into potential security issues.

Implementing a robust monitoring and logging strategy is another critical aspect of federated GraphQL security. Continuous monitoring helps detect and respond to security incidents in real time. By logging relevant security events, such as failed authentication attempts and access violations, you can analyze patterns and respond to potential threats promptly. Integration with security information and event management (SIEM) systems can further enhance your ability to monitor and manage security incidents.

In summary, securing a federated GraphQL system requires a multi-faceted approach that includes thorough threat modeling, adherence to secure coding practices, and compliance with relevant regulations. By understanding potential threats, implementing robust security measures, and continuously monitoring your system, you can protect your federated GraphQL implementation from security risks and ensure a secure and reliable data interaction environment. As federated GraphQL continues to evolve, staying informed about emerging security trends and best practices will be crucial for maintaining a strong security posture.

...employing data encryption both in transit and at rest. Encryption is a cornerstone of data security and ensures that sensitive information remains protected from unauthorized access. For federated GraphQL systems, encrypting data as it travels between the client and the server, as well as between different services within the federation, is essential. Transport Layer Security (TLS) should be used to encrypt data in transit, ensuring that data exchanged over the network is protected from eavesdropping and tampering.

Additionally, sensitive data stored within the system, such as authentication tokens or personal information, should be encrypted at rest. This practice helps safeguard data in the event of a data breach or unauthorized access to the storage infrastructure. By implementing strong encryption algorithms and managing encryption keys securely, you can reduce the risk of data exposure.

Compliance considerations are another crucial aspect of securing federated GraphQL systems. Organizations must adhere to various regulatory requirements and industry standards, such as the General Data Protection Regulation (GDPR), Health Insurance Portability and Accountability Act (HIPAA), or Payment Card Industry Data Security Standard (PCI DSS). Each of these regulations has specific requirements regarding data protection and privacy that must be incorporated into your security strategy.

To ensure compliance, regularly audit your federated GraphQL system against relevant standards and regulations. Implementing automated compliance checks and maintaining thorough documentation of your security practices can help demonstrate adherence to these requirements. Additionally, engaging with legal and compliance experts can provide valuable guidance on meeting specific regulatory obligations.

Another important aspect of security in federated GraphQL systems is monitoring and logging. Continuous monitoring of system activities allows you to detect and respond to potential security incidents in real-time. Implement comprehensive logging mechanisms to capture relevant events and activities within the system, including access attempts, query executions, and changes to data.

Effective logging and monitoring can help identify patterns indicative of malicious behavior or system vulnerabilities. Utilize automated alerting systems to notify administrators of suspicious activities, such as unusual query patterns or access attempts outside normal operational hours. Regularly review logs and audit trails to ensure that any anomalies are promptly addressed.

Finally, fostering a culture of security awareness within your development and operations teams is crucial. Security should be integrated into every stage of the development lifecycle, from design and implementation to deployment and maintenance. Conduct regular security training for your team members to keep them informed about the latest threats, vulnerabilities, and best practices.

By instilling a security-first mindset and encouraging proactive security measures, you can significantly enhance the overall security posture of your federated GraphQL system. Emphasize the importance of secure coding practices, data protection, and compliance adherence to ensure that your system remains resilient against evolving threats.

In summary, securing a federated GraphQL system involves a multifaceted approach that includes threat modeling, secure coding practices, data encryption, compliance considerations, monitoring and logging, and fostering a culture of security awareness. By implementing these advanced security practices, you can effectively protect your federated GraphQL system against potential risks and ensure the integrity and confidentiality of your data.

In addition to securing data at rest and in transit, another critical aspect of securing federated GraphQL systems is implementing robust access control mechanisms. Access control involves defining and enforcing permissions that dictate which users or systems can access specific resources or perform particular actions.

One effective approach to access control is the implementation of role-based access control (RBAC). RBAC assigns permissions to roles rather than individual users, making it easier to manage and enforce security policies across a federated system. In a federated GraphQL environment, roles can be defined at various levels, such as global, service-specific, or even at the field level within a schema. By associating roles with specific queries and mutations, you ensure that users only have access to the data and operations that are relevant to their role.

In addition to RBAC, consider implementing attribute-based access control (ABAC), which uses attributes (such as user roles, resource types, or request contexts) to make access decisions. ABAC provides more granular control compared to RBAC, allowing for complex access policies based on multiple attributes. For instance, you could define policies that restrict access based on the time of day, the user's location, or the sensitivity of the data being requested. ABAC can be particularly useful in a federated GraphQL system where data access requirements might vary significantly across different services.

Another vital security practice is to conduct regular security assessments and penetration testing. Security assessments involve evaluating your system's security posture through various methods, such as vulnerability scans and threat assessments. These assessments help identify potential weaknesses and vulnerabilities within your federated GraphQL implementation. Penetration testing, on the other hand, involves simulating real-world attacks to assess how well your system can withstand attempts to exploit its vulnerabilities. By regularly performing these tests, you can proactively address security gaps and enhance your overall security posture.

Furthermore, it is crucial to stay updated with the latest security trends and best practices. The security landscape is continually evolving, with new threats and vulnerabilities emerging regularly. Staying informed about the latest developments in security can help you adapt your security practices and ensure that your federated GraphQL system remains resilient against new and emerging threats. Engage with security communities, attend conferences, and participate in relevant training programs to stay current with industry standards and best practices.

Implementing a comprehensive incident response plan is also essential for managing security incidents effectively. An incident response plan outlines the procedures and steps to follow when a security breach or other incident occurs. This plan should include procedures for detecting, containing, and mitigating the impact of the incident, as well as communication protocols for notifying stakeholders and regulatory bodies if necessary. Regularly test and update your incident response plan to ensure that it remains effective and aligned with your security objectives.

Another important consideration is the secure management of authentication and authorization tokens. In federated GraphQL systems, tokens are often used to authenticate and authorize users across multiple services. Ensure that tokens are securely generated, stored, and transmitted. Use secure algorithms for token generation and implement token expiration and renewal mechanisms to reduce the risk of token theft or misuse. Additionally, consider using short-lived tokens and rotating them regularly to minimize the impact of any potential token compromise.

Integrating security into the development lifecycle is another best practice for ensuring the security of federated GraphQL systems. This approach, known as DevSecOps, emphasizes the inclusion of security practices throughout the software development lifecycle, from design and development to deployment and maintenance. By integrating security testing, code reviews, and vulnerability assessments into your development processes, you can identify and address security issues early, reducing the risk of vulnerabilities being introduced into your system.

In summary, securing a federated GraphQL system requires a multi-faceted approach that includes data encryption, access control, compliance considerations, monitoring and logging, and a culture of security awareness. By implementing advanced security practices and staying informed about the latest trends and developments, you can fortify your federated GraphQL implementation against potential security risks and ensure the protection of your data and systems.

CHAPTER 43: REAL-TIME ANALYTICS AND MONITORING FOR FEDERATED GRAPHQL

In the realm of federated GraphQL, where multiple services work in concert to provide a unified API, maintaining a robust and responsive system is paramount. Real-time analytics and monitoring play a crucial role in ensuring system health and optimizing performance. This chapter delves into the essential tools and techniques for achieving effective monitoring and analytics within a federated GraphQL environment, covering performance tracking, metric analysis, and real-time data processing.

To begin with, effective monitoring in a federated GraphQL system requires a comprehensive approach that includes both high-level overviews and granular insights. At the high level, monitoring tools should provide visibility into the overall health of the system, including the status of individual services, the efficiency of the gateway, and the performance of data fetching operations. Tools such as Prometheus, Grafana, and New Relic are popular choices for gathering and visualizing metrics across distributed systems. These tools can collect data from various sources, such as server logs, API response times, and resource usage, and present it in a unified dashboard.

At a more granular level, monitoring should focus on specific metrics relevant to GraphQL operations. This includes tracking query response times, error rates, and throughput. High response times can indicate performance bottlenecks, while elevated error rates may point to issues within individual services or the GraphQL gateway. By analyzing these metrics, teams can identify and address performance issues before they impact users. It is also essential to monitor the efficiency of the schema stitching and federation layers, ensuring that cross-service queries are executed optimally.

Another critical aspect of real-time monitoring is the ability to trace requests across the federated GraphQL system. Distributed tracing tools like Jaeger and Zipkin can help visualize the journey of a request as it traverses various services. These tools provide insights into how long each service takes to process a request, enabling teams to pinpoint latency issues and optimize the performance of individual services. Tracing can also reveal how well the federated GraphQL gateway is handling request distribution and service coordination.

Furthermore, real-time analytics involve not only monitoring current system performance but also predicting future trends and potential issues. Implementing alerting mechanisms based on predefined thresholds allows teams to respond proactively to anomalies. For instance, setting alerts for high latency or increased error rates can prompt immediate investigation and remediation. By leveraging machine learning and statistical analysis, it is possible to predict performance trends and detect deviations from normal behavior, facilitating more informed decision-making.

In addition to performance metrics, monitoring the health of data consistency and synchronization is crucial in a federated environment. Tools that provide insights into data replication, cache invalidation, and consistency models can help ensure that the system operates smoothly and that users receive accurate data. Monitoring the synchronization process between federated services can help identify issues related to data freshness and consistency, which are vital for maintaining a reliable system.

Integration with logging systems is also an integral part of real-time analytics. Centralized logging solutions, such as ELK (Elasticsearch, Logstash, Kibana) stack or Splunk, aggregate logs from various services and provide a searchable repository for troubleshooting and analysis. Logs can offer detailed information about specific queries, errors, and service interactions, complementing the metrics and traces collected by other monitoring tools. Correlating logs with performance metrics and traces can provide a comprehensive view of system health and facilitate more effective problem-solving.

Effective monitoring and real-time analytics are not only about collecting data but also about translating that data into actionable insights. Dashboards should be designed to highlight key performance indicators and anomalies, making it easier for teams to understand and act upon the data. Customizable dashboards allow for the visualization of metrics relevant to different stakeholders, from developers to operations teams, ensuring that everyone has access to the information needed to maintain system performance.

Moreover, the ability to perform historical analysis complements real-time monitoring by providing context for current performance. Analyzing historical data can reveal trends, identify recurring issues, and support capacity planning. By understanding how performance metrics have evolved over time, teams can make informed decisions about scaling and optimizing their federated GraphQL infrastructure.

In summary, real-time analytics and monitoring are fundamental to maintaining a healthy federated GraphQL system. By implementing comprehensive monitoring tools, tracking critical metrics, leveraging distributed tracing, and integrating with logging systems, teams can ensure optimal system performance and responsiveness. The insights gained from these practices enable proactive management of potential issues, support data consistency, and facilitate informed decision-making, ultimately contributing to a more robust and reliable federated GraphQL environment.

As organizations continue to leverage federated GraphQL for their API needs, the importance of implementing a robust monitoring and analytics strategy cannot be overstated. Effective real-time monitoring requires a nuanced approach, incorporating various techniques and tools to ensure that all aspects of the system are functioning optimally and any potential issues are promptly addressed.

One of the fundamental techniques in real-time monitoring is the collection and analysis of logs. Logs serve as a primary source of information about the system's operation, including details about queries, errors, and performance metrics. Modern logging solutions, such as ELK Stack (Elasticsearch, Logstash, Kibana) or the more recent OpenTelemetry, allow for detailed and scalable logging. These tools can aggregate logs from multiple sources, providing a centralized view of system activities. They also enable sophisticated search and filtering capabilities, which are crucial for diagnosing problems and understanding system behavior.

In addition to logs, real-time analytics involve analyzing metrics related to GraphQL operations. Metrics such as query execution time, response size, and resolver performance provide insights into how well the federated GraphQL system is performing. To effectively track these metrics, it is essential to instrument both the GraphQL gateway and individual services. Instrumentation involves adding code to measure specific performance indicators and send this data to monitoring tools. For example, integrating libraries such as Apollo Engine or GraphQL Metrics can help in collecting and visualizing performance data directly from GraphQL queries and mutations.

A critical aspect of monitoring federated GraphQL systems is the management of data synchronization and consistency. In a federated environment, where data is distributed across multiple services, ensuring that data remains consistent and up-to-date is crucial. Monitoring tools should track the synchronization processes and identify any discrepancies or delays in data propagation. Techniques such as anomaly detection and trend analysis can be applied to this data to proactively address potential synchronization issues before they affect the system's overall performance.

Moreover, real-time monitoring should be complemented by performance profiling to understand resource usage and detect inefficiencies. Profiling tools can help analyze CPU and memory usage, identify memory leaks, and monitor the impact of different queries on system resources. This analysis provides insights into how various queries affect the overall performance and helps in optimizing both the GraphQL schema and the underlying services.

The integration of monitoring and alerting systems is another vital component. Effective alerting ensures that issues are addressed before they escalate into significant problems. Alerts should be configured based on key performance indicators, such as high latency, increased error rates, or unusual patterns in query execution. When set up properly, alerting mechanisms can provide real-time notifications via email, SMS, or integration with incident management systems like PagerDuty or Opsgenie. This timely notification allows for rapid response and mitigation of issues, thus minimizing downtime and maintaining a high level of service quality.

In addition to traditional monitoring approaches, leveraging machine learning and artificial intelligence for predictive analytics is an emerging trend. These advanced techniques analyze historical data to forecast future performance trends and identify potential issues before they arise. By employing machine learning models, organizations can gain deeper insights into usage patterns, detect anomalies with higher accuracy, and optimize their federated GraphQL systems proactively.

Lastly, it is essential to consider the security implications of monitoring and analytics. Ensuring that sensitive data is protected while being analyzed and monitored is crucial. Implementing encryption for data in transit and at rest, as well as access controls and audit logs for monitoring systems, helps safeguard against unauthorized access and data breaches. Regular security reviews and compliance checks should be part of the monitoring strategy to ensure that all security best practices are adhered to.

By integrating these practices into a cohesive monitoring strategy, organizations can maintain the health and performance of their federated GraphQL systems effectively. Real-time analytics and monitoring not only help in maintaining system reliability but also enable continuous improvement by providing actionable insights into performance and operational efficiency.

Effective real-time monitoring and analytics for federated GraphQL systems not only require robust tooling but also a well-defined strategy for integrating these tools into your existing infrastructure. To achieve a comprehensive monitoring solution, consider adopting a multi-layered approach that encompasses both the infrastructure and application levels.

At the infrastructure level, monitoring tools must be configured to capture system-wide metrics that impact GraphQL performance. These include server load, network latency, and database performance. Tools like Prometheus and Grafana offer powerful capabilities for gathering and visualizing these metrics. Prometheus can be used to collect time-series data from various components of the system, while Grafana provides a flexible dashboard for visualizing and interpreting this data. Together, they enable teams to observe the health of the underlying infrastructure and identify issues that may affect the performance of federated GraphQL queries.

Application-level monitoring, on the other hand, focuses on the specific interactions and transactions within the federated GraphQL environment. This includes monitoring the GraphQL resolvers, query performance, and data-fetching mechanisms. Tools like Apollo Studio and GraphQL Voyager can help visualize query patterns and identify performance bottlenecks. Apollo Studio, for example, provides detailed insights into query execution times, error rates, and resolver performance, which are crucial for fine-tuning the federated schema and improving overall system efficiency.

An essential component of real-time monitoring is the implementation of automated alerts. Alerts are designed to notify teams of potential issues before they escalate into more significant problems. For effective alerting, it is important to set thresholds based on historical data and anticipated load. Tools such as Datadog and New Relic offer advanced alerting capabilities, allowing you to configure alerts based on specific conditions or anomalies detected in the metrics. For instance, if the response time of a particular GraphQL query exceeds a predefined threshold, an alert can be triggered to notify the relevant team members. This proactive approach enables timely intervention and resolution of issues, thereby maintaining system performance and reliability.

In addition to traditional metrics and alerts, incorporating user experience monitoring into your strategy is valuable. Real-time user experience monitoring tools can track how users interact with the federated GraphQL system, providing insights into any issues that affect end-users. Tools like Sentry and Raygun can capture frontend errors and performance issues, offering a holistic view of user experience and helping to identify any discrepancies between user expectations and system performance.

Another important aspect of real-time monitoring is ensuring data privacy and compliance with relevant regulations. In a federated GraphQL environment, where data is aggregated from various sources, it is crucial to implement monitoring practices that adhere to data protection standards. This involves configuring monitoring tools to avoid exposing sensitive information and ensuring that any data collected is handled in accordance with privacy regulations such as GDPR or CCPA. For example, when using logging or monitoring tools, sensitive data should be masked or anonymized to prevent unauthorized access.

Finally, the success of a real-time analytics and monitoring strategy depends on continuous evaluation and refinement. Regularly reviewing the effectiveness of your monitoring setup and adjusting it based on emerging needs and challenges is key to maintaining a healthy federated GraphQL environment. This involves analyzing historical data to identify trends, assessing the performance of alerts and metrics, and incorporating feedback from team members. By adopting a cycle of continuous improvement, you can ensure that your monitoring practices evolve in line with the growth and changes in your federated GraphQL system.

In conclusion, implementing effective real-time analytics and monitoring for federated GraphQL systems involves a comprehensive approach that integrates infrastructure and application-level monitoring, automated alerts, user experience tracking, and data privacy considerations. By employing these strategies and continuously refining your monitoring practices, you can ensure the health, performance, and reliability of your federated GraphQL environment, ultimately providing a seamless and efficient experience for users and stakeholders.

Building a community and ecosystem around federated GraphQL is crucial for driving adoption, innovation, and collaboration within the GraphQL landscape. A thriving community not only helps in refining your implementation but also contributes to the broader advancement of federated GraphQL practices. This chapter delves into effective strategies for fostering a dynamic community, engaging with open-source initiatives, and cultivating a supportive ecosystem.

To initiate the process of community building, it is important to establish a solid foundation through active engagement and contribution. One of the first steps is to participate in existing GraphQL forums, discussion groups, and conferences. Engaging with platforms like GitHub, Stack Overflow, and the GraphQL Slack community allows you to interact with other developers, share knowledge, and stay updated with the latest trends and best practices. This involvement helps build your credibility within the community and opens up opportunities for collaboration on various projects.

Organizing and participating in events such as meetups, webinars, and workshops can further enhance your presence and influence. These events provide a platform for sharing insights, discussing challenges, and showcasing successful implementations of federated GraphQL. By hosting or speaking at such events, you can contribute valuable knowledge to the community and also position yourself as a thought leader in the field. Additionally, contributing to conferences like GraphQL Summit or organizing local meetups can foster deeper connections with other professionals and enthusiasts.

Another vital aspect of community building is contributing to open-source projects. Open-source contributions are instrumental in driving innovation and providing practical solutions to common challenges. By contributing to popular GraphQL libraries, tools, or frameworks, you can collaborate with other developers and enhance the quality and capabilities of federated GraphQL implementations. This contribution not only benefits the community but also helps you gain recognition and establish a network of professional connections.

Creating and maintaining your own open-source projects or tools related to federated GraphQL can also be a significant contribution to the ecosystem. Developing libraries, plugins, or utilities that address specific needs or enhance the functionality of federated GraphQL can attract users and contributors who share similar interests. For example, creating a tool for visualizing federated schemas or a library for optimizing query performance could provide valuable resources to the community and stimulate further development.

To effectively build and sustain a community, it is crucial to provide ongoing support and resources. Establishing a comprehensive documentation site, writing blog posts, and producing tutorials can significantly aid users in understanding and utilizing federated GraphQL effectively. Documentation should cover best practices, common issues, and practical examples to assist both newcomers and experienced developers. Regularly updating these resources to reflect new developments and community feedback ensures that they remain relevant and useful.

Moreover, fostering an inclusive and supportive environment within the community is essential for its growth and sustainability. Encouraging collaboration, mentoring new developers, and recognizing contributions from others can create a positive and productive atmosphere. Providing platforms for feedback and discussion helps address concerns and improve the overall quality of the community's resources.

Building partnerships with other organizations and communities can also expand the reach and impact of your federated GraphQL initiatives. Collaborating with companies, educational institutions, and other technology communities can create opportunities for joint projects, knowledge sharing, and resource development. Such partnerships can enhance the visibility and credibility of your work and contribute to the overall advancement of federated GraphQL.

Finally, measuring the impact and success of your community-building efforts is important for continuous improvement. Collecting feedback, tracking engagement metrics, and assessing the effectiveness of your initiatives can provide insights into what is working well and what areas need improvement. This evaluation helps in refining your strategies and ensuring that your contributions are aligned with the needs and interests of the community.

In summary, building a community and ecosystem around federated GraphQL involves active engagement, open-source contributions, and the creation of valuable resources. By participating in discussions, organizing events, contributing to projects, and fostering an inclusive environment, you can significantly enhance your federated GraphQL implementation and contribute to the growth of the broader GraphQL ecosystem. As you establish yourself as a key player in this space, you will not only benefit from increased recognition but also help drive innovation and collaboration within the federated GraphQL community.

Creating a supportive and dynamic ecosystem around federated GraphQL also involves fostering collaboration and shared learning. Engaging in discussions and collaborations with other experts can lead to the development of best practices and innovative solutions. Consider initiating or joining working groups focused on specific aspects of federated GraphQL, such as performance optimization or security. These groups can serve as incubators for new ideas and can help in addressing common challenges faced by the community.

Encouraging feedback and facilitating discussions about your projects or contributions can help refine your work and ensure it meets the needs of the broader community. Creating forums or feedback channels where users can share their experiences and suggestions allows for continuous improvement and adaptation of your tools and practices. By actively listening to the community, you can address concerns, implement new features, and adapt to emerging needs.

Building a robust ecosystem also requires fostering relationships with other organizations and stakeholders involved in the GraphQL space. Establishing partnerships with companies that utilize GraphQL or contribute to its development can lead to collaborative efforts that benefit both parties. For example, partnering with companies that offer complementary tools or services can result in integrations that enhance the functionality and usability of federated GraphQL solutions. These partnerships can also lead to joint ventures, shared resources, and mutual promotion, further strengthening the ecosystem.

Education and training are critical components of community growth. Offering educational resources such as tutorials, courses, and webinars can help newcomers understand federated GraphQL and its benefits. These resources can range from beginner-level introductions to advanced technical deep dives, catering to a wide audience. By providing structured learning opportunities, you can help build a knowledgeable user base that is better equipped to implement and contribute to federated GraphQL solutions.

Moreover, creating comprehensive and accessible documentation is essential for the adoption and effective use of federated GraphQL tools and libraries. Well-organized documentation not only helps users understand how to utilize your tools but also provides guidance on best practices and common pitfalls. Investing time in maintaining up-to-date and clear documentation can significantly enhance the user experience and contribute to the overall success of your projects.

Networking and visibility are also important for community building. Engaging with influencers and thought leaders in the GraphQL space can amplify your presence and reach. Participating in interviews, writing guest posts for popular blogs, or contributing to industry publications can help spread awareness of your work and the benefits of federated GraphQL. Visibility in these channels can attract attention from potential collaborators, contributors, and users who can add value to your initiatives.

Finally, fostering an inclusive and welcoming environment is crucial for community health. Encouraging diverse perspectives and participation ensures that the community benefits from a wide range of ideas and experiences. Promoting a culture of respect and support helps in retaining contributors and building a positive reputation within the community. Implementing codes of conduct and providing mechanisms for resolving conflicts can help maintain a collaborative and productive atmosphere.

In summary, building a community and ecosystem around federated GraphQL involves a multifaceted approach that includes active participation, contribution to open-source projects, collaboration with stakeholders, and fostering a supportive and inclusive environment. By focusing on these strategies, you can help advance the federated GraphQL landscape, contribute to its growth, and ensure its continued success and relevance in the evolving world of data management and application development.

Active participation in conferences and meetups is another effective way to build and engage with the federated GraphQL community. By presenting your work at these events or participating in panel discussions, you can share your experiences, showcase your tools, and gain valuable feedback from peers and industry experts. These interactions not only help to establish your credibility but also provide opportunities to learn from others and stay informed about the latest trends and developments in GraphQL.

In addition to in-person events, contributing to online communities and forums can also be highly beneficial. Platforms like GitHub, Stack Overflow, and various social media channels offer spaces for discussion, problem-solving, and knowledge sharing. By being an active member of these communities, you can address questions, provide support, and share insights related to federated GraphQL. This presence helps build your reputation as a knowledgeable and helpful contributor, encouraging others to engage with your projects and initiatives.

Supporting open-source projects is a cornerstone of building a vibrant ecosystem. By contributing code, reporting issues, or reviewing pull requests, you help improve the tools and libraries that are crucial for federated GraphQL implementations. Open-source contributions not only benefit the projects you work on but also enhance the overall quality and reliability of the tools available to the community. Furthermore, these contributions often lead to collaborations with other developers, expanding your network and increasing your influence within the community.

Encouraging and facilitating contributions from others is equally important. Creating an inclusive environment where newcomers feel welcome and are encouraged to contribute can significantly enhance the growth and innovation within the ecosystem. Providing clear contribution guidelines, offering mentorship, and recognizing the efforts of contributors are effective ways to foster a collaborative and supportive community. Celebrating achievements and highlighting contributions can motivate others to participate and can help maintain a positive and dynamic atmosphere.

Building a strong ecosystem around federated GraphQL also involves creating and sharing valuable resources. Developing tools, libraries, and plugins that address common needs or challenges can attract interest and provide practical benefits to users. For example, creating a library that simplifies authentication or integrates with popular databases can address specific pain points and enhance the usability of federated GraphQL. Additionally, sharing case studies, best practices, and success stories can provide practical insights and inspire others to implement federated GraphQL in their own environments.

To ensure the long-term sustainability of your efforts, consider establishing governance models for your projects and initiatives. Governance frameworks help manage contributions, set priorities, and make decisions that align with the goals of the community and the ecosystem. Transparent and inclusive governance practices can help build trust and ensure that the projects remain focused on delivering value to users.

As the federated GraphQL ecosystem evolves, staying adaptable and responsive to changes is crucial. Emerging technologies, evolving best practices, and shifting community needs will influence the direction and focus of your efforts. Regularly assessing the impact of your contributions, seeking feedback, and staying engaged with industry developments will help you navigate these changes effectively and continue to contribute meaningfully to the community.

In summary, building a community and ecosystem around federated GraphQL involves a multifaceted approach that includes active participation, collaboration, and support for open-source initiatives. By engaging with the community, fostering contributions, and sharing valuable resources, you can help create a vibrant and thriving ecosystem. This collaborative effort not only enhances the effectiveness of federated GraphQL implementations but also contributes to the overall growth and advancement of the technology. Through these efforts, you will be well-positioned to play a significant role in the ongoing development and success of federated GraphQL.

www.ingramcontent.com/pod-product-compliance
Lightning Source LLC
Chambersburg PA
CBHW052139220526

45471CB00004B/1439